Worker Centered

T0315516

Worker Centered

*Allyship and Action in the Contemporary
Labor Movement*

BIKO KOENIG

OXFORD
UNIVERSITY PRESS

OXFORD
UNIVERSITY PRESS

Oxford University Press is a department of the University of Oxford.
It furthers the University's objective of excellence in research, scholarship,
and education by publishing worldwide. Oxford is a registered trade mark of
Oxford University Press in the UK and in certain other countries.

Published in the United States of America by Oxford University Press
198 Madison Avenue, New York, NY 10016, United States of America.

© Oxford University Press 2024

All rights reserved. No part of this publication may be reproduced, stored in
a retrieval system, transmitted, used for text and data mining, or used for training artificial
intelligence, in any form or by any means, without the
prior permission in writing of Oxford University Press, or as expressly permitted
by law, by license, or under terms agreed with the appropriate reprographics
rights organization. Inquiries concerning reproduction outside the scope of the
above should be sent to the Rights Department, Oxford University Press, at the
address above.

You must not circulate this work in any other form,
and you must impose this same condition on any acquirer.

CIP data is on file at the Library of Congress.

ISBN 9780197784907
ISBN 9780197784891 (hbk.)

DOI: 10.1093/oso/9780197784907.001.0001

Paperback printed by Integrated Books International, United States of America
Hardback printed by Bridgeport National Bindery, Inc., United States of America

MIX
Paper
FSC   FSC® C183721

For my goddaughter, Alice G. Tibbetts,

who is concerned that we all work too much.

Contents

Preface: On Movement Critique   viii
Acknowledgments   xii

1. Strategy, Power, and Worker Leadership   1
2. The History and Organizing Model of the Clara
   Lemlich Project   29
3. The FCC Campaign   53
4. "We're Getting Our Asses Kicked!"   71
5. Performing Worker Leadership   93
6. "It's Good to Be Back Out in the Streets."   114
7. The Meeting and the Aftermath   130

   Conclusion: A Courageous Experiment   150

Endnotes   170
Bibliography   172
Index   178

Preface

On Movement Critique

Political organizing on the Left often faces a chicken-and-egg predicament. Many of us believe that those who are most impacted by the inequities of modern society should be the ones identifying problems, developing solutions, and leading movements. And yet, examples of organic collective action, created and carried out solely by people experiencing these injustices, are few and far between. Collective action more often requires some form of organizing, where movements empower and persuade people to think differently about their conditions and their collective ability to make changes. Thus, alongside tactical questions of where to protest, how to put economic pressure on a target, or which media venues to emphasize, organizers develop and deploy interpretive narratives that enable people to see their locations in different ways. These narratives, known as "collective action frames" among social movement theorists, blend compelling stories about the world's injustices with arguments that foster a shared understanding of issues. When activists from outside of a community are moved to address the perceived injustices that other groups experience, the tension between the ethic of bottom-up leadership and the desire to change the status quo can be quite strong. This is especially noticeable when these actors expressly question the authenticity and efficacy of organizations they deem as not properly led by membership.

I explore this tension through an ethnographic account of the Clara Lemlich Project (CLP), a non-profit worker center with a strong reputation for worker leadership based in a history of successful campaigns to support fired and harassed workers.[1] Worker centers, organizations that are not formally unions but aim to help workers fight against poor and illegal treatment, have been a growing fixture in the labor movement for the past few decades. From my position within this organization, I explore the efforts of the CLP to evolve their strategic approach and spark a rank-and-file–led, direct-action union amid a low-wage and mainly immigrant workforce at the Fishtown Condiment Company (FCC). While the campaign was able to reach some important milestones, including convincing the company to meet for a series of meetings, it was ultimately unable to secure a union victory due to, among other things, low worker participation. And yet both staff and allies continually advanced a narrative that insisted that workers were leading the campaign, even at moments defined entirely by the power and activities of non-workers. The book is my attempt to understand what happened and its implications for contemporary social movement work.

In following the campaign at the FCC, I explore the complexities of member-led movement work. From my insider perspective as a member of the staff, I illustrate the challenges that we faced in our work—both internal tensions of strategy and analysis as well as external hurdles of an intransigent company and the strength of pro-employer narratives among workers. Though using an approach grounded in strategic thinking about power based in their political values of worker leadership, the CLP staff ultimately failed in their efforts at the FCC. The question is why.

The answer is not about a lack of commitment among staffers and allies, who were some of the fiercest organizers I have met doing movement work. And while I will show the importance of employer resistance to the FCC campaign, the answer is also not about a fervent counter-campaign on their part. This is not a story about mass firings, hordes of highly paid "union avoidance" consultants, or closing shop to stop a union drive. Throughout this volume I offer a much more ambiguous story, one characterized by an ambitious campaign strategy with limited capacity and a workforce with only, at best, muted enthusiasm for starting their own union. In this context I examine how the narrative of worker leadership continually defined how staff and allies made sense of the campaign and acted in its name. This story takes us inside this case of movement work to offer insights about allyship, power, and representation in the fight for a more just world.

While this research focuses on a case of a failed union campaign, it is neither a condemnation of the organization nor a denunciation of the individual actors involved in the story. Organizing oppressed communities is both a titanic and necessary task, and one where even the most highly resourced and skilled organizations routinely encounter setbacks and defeats. That the CLP would seek to innovate beyond their historic successes in their efforts to deepen the power of workers is a testament to the staff's political tenacity, and any critique that I or others might offer must be placed in conversation with the significant material gains they have achieved for workers in their campaigns. That they have done so in a social, political, and economic climate that leaves employers and opponents holding most of the power is a clear demonstration of the value of this kind of political work. And, as Janice Fine so eloquently put it in her early research on worker centers, "just because they have yet to succeed at broader labor market intervention does not mean that they never will" (Fine 2003, cited in Gray 2007, p. 217). Even within the critique I present, I remain committed to an assertive, worker-led labor movement. My hope is that the following analysis can further the goals of, and effective strategies toward, the centering of worker power and agency in movements and society. Worker organizations like the CLP remain crucial actors in achieving these ends.

And yet I cannot ignore the challenges that come with critical analyses of movement work. Some may find the act of exploring a failed campaign to be useless, politically dangerous, or even reactionary. Further, the findings I present in this book are in tension with some of the explanations provided by the staffers and allies that I interviewed, simply because no single narrative emerged as the "true" story of this campaign. Some sharply disagreed with my claims that worker leadership was mainly absent, and participation thin, indicating that there were meetings and other interactions with workers that I wasn't privy to. At the same time, others agreed with my assessment but were much more critical in their analysis of the organization than what I offer here. Some, in fact, felt I did not go far enough in my analysis, perhaps hoping that I would write an exposé of the campaign and what they saw as mismanagement. Others believed that it was simply inappropriate to comment on failed campaigns or offer criticisms of movement work, given the host of challenges that activists already face in their work. And some felt that the movement needs more critical reflections on organizing work, especially campaigns that fail to meet their goals. What I offer throughout is my attempt to square these complexities into an analysis that incorporates these warring impressions of what happened, why it mattered, and what it means for contemporary movement organizing.

I do not have a single answer to address the political concerns that some readers will hold about this project. I have, however, written this volume with an aim to maximize its analytical leverage while addressing concerns that critical engagements with movement work can only harm the movement. To this end, I have removed or obscured identifiers for all the actors and organizations involved. Further, the research collected for this project will be many years old when this book is published. In that time, all the organizations involved in the research have gone through major strategic changes, have experienced a full turnover in staff, or even closed shop. Further, the strategies and tactics have shifted dramatically for many worker centers, especially those interested in partnering with unions, who have adjusted their approaches in the wake of recent federal action that could challenge the non-profit status of some labor groups (Dirnbach 2019; Penn 2020). Thus, those who read this book with an aim to undercut the movement will find little purchase, but those interested in exploring the challenges of bottom-up organizing may find some provocative illustrations throughout.

When introducing me to a foundation program officer in the CLP offices, one of the staff members joked that my research would either "slam us for either being too radical, or not radical enough!" One of the primary discussions of this book is an exploration of how the ideological commitment to worker leadership and a radical union model likely impeded the organization's goals. But in the end, my intention in writing this book is to underline the importance of the radical vision of the CLP. As I state throughout, we need more creative organizations who are willing to experiment and strategize in search of a powerful worker-centric labor movement and the more just society it could help deliver. In this book I show why, as allies, we must *deepen* our involvement with organizations like the CLP. Not only do we possess our own power and resources, but thicker ties between allies, labor organizations, and workers would also encourage us to have a more nuanced approach to leadership development and its significance. Such collaborations would empower us to attach accountability to liberatory outcomes that produce leadership and member power rather than simplified notions of member agency in our collective struggle for liberation.

Acknowledgments

As with any book, numerous individuals have contributed to bringing this material to your hands or screen. I want to extend special gratitude to the dedicated and hardworking team at Oxford University Press. Without their efforts, and those of others like them, books of this nature would not be possible. As of May 2024, the Oxford University Press USA Union, represented by the NewsGuild-CWA and achieving 80% support in a union election back in Fall 2021, is currently engaged in contract negotiations with management. Hopefully, by the time this book is in print, the Guild will have secured a contract that includes fair wages and equitable treatment. But whatever the date is that this book has found its way to you, it is important to recognize and support these workers, who not only deserve our appreciation but also our solidarity. You can stay updated on the negotiations and find ways to contribute at https://twitter.com/oupusaguild.

This project had its roots in my time as a graduate student at the New School for Social Research, and words do not do justice to the support I received from the faculty. Without David Plotke's guidance, which continued long after I left the NSSR, I would still be writing the second chapter. I have greatly benefited from Deva Woodly's mentorship and insights into my research and social movements writ large. I have also been lucky enough to work with her as co-author on a related project, and this pedagogy-via-apprenticeship was a crucial step in my own development as a writer and thinker. Rachel Sherman consistently embodied Occam's Razor in dealing with my insecurities as a researcher. Timothy Pachirat is the intellectual mentor I never knew I needed. His passion and support for my work since my first semester of graduate school are responsible for much of my professional and intellectual growth. Victoria Hattam and Nevin Cohen offered helpful advice for the project design and initial fieldwork.

Tanya Schwartz and Elizabeth Bennett provided strong intellectual and emotional support since we first discussed our work at Qualitative Methods Summer Camp. My writing group at Franklin & Marshall College— Eve Bratman, Elizabeth DeSanto, Eric Hirsch, and Stephanie McNulty— provided excellent feedback during a crucial phase of writing.

Malgorzata Bakalarz, Mateusz Halawa, Rishabh Kuman, Shannon Mattern, Christina Moon, Julie Beth Napolin, Fabio Parasecoli, Rhea Rahman, Hugh Raffles, Philip Schauss, and Rachel Sherman all provided insights and feedback during our time together at the Graduate Institute for Design, Ethnography, and Social Thought. My two years as Visiting Instructor of Government helped to finish the initial draft. My time at the Institute for Advanced Studies in Princeton provided the opportunity to revise the manuscript, and I am especially thankful for the intellectual support I received from Julien Brachet, Wendy Brown, William Callison, Angela B. Cornell, Marielle Debos, Didier Fassin, Asli Iğsiz, Katherine Lemons, Kenneth M. Roberts, Elizabeth Saleh, Judith Scheele, Matthew Shafer, Yves Winter, Lirian, and Lewyn. A special shout-out to the sometimes scathing but exclusively productive team of anonymous reviewers to this manuscript. (Confidential to Reviewer #4 – I took your advice and swapped the introduction and conclusion. Let me know how it looks.)

Kate Diedrick, Eric Dirnbach, Abby Ferla, Abby Scher, and Cheyenna Weber all read through full drafts of the manuscript at different times in the writing and provided the kinds of insight I could never generate on my own. With a meticulous eye for passive voice and real care for the heart of the research, Jennifer Meyer helped get this book to the finish line. How does one thank these folks for this level of time, attention, and care? I know not. But thanks all the same!

A big old thanks to my editor, Angela Chnapko, at Oxford University Press, who handled many years of my revisions, questions, and fears as this book came together. Thanks to Andrea Smith and everyone else on the production side of the project at Oxford and Integra. And a big shout-out to Erik Ruin, whose art graces the cover of this book. You can find his work at www.ErikRuin.info and at www.justseeds.org (along with that of many other incredible artists).

I was also supported by many farms and farmers in the process of writing this book. I could not have asked for more beautiful spaces than the ski storage room of Porcupine Hill and the front porch of Foxtrot Herb Farm. I am grateful to all of the animal companions who kept me company during the years I worked on this project—Chauncy, Monkeycat, Finn, Gilly, Epee, Chaang, Rusty, Mango, Neko, Peaseblossom, Priciness Pickle, Moose, Stevie, Sophie, Maoz, Sandor Katz, Chloe, Ballou, Barnaby, Beanie, and most especially Zora the Cattledog and Cheesecat the Cat. Special thanks to Peavy

Memorial Library in Eastport, Maine, for allowing me to use their facility for two days without a library card.

I would like to recognize my extended family for their love and support through this multi-year project. Thanks to Abby, Kit, Cheyenna, Jenny, Eliot, Oliver, Clara, Alie, Emily, Lily, Eric, Emily, Bernie, Austin, Leila, Andy, Susan, Marc, John, Kazi, Leo, Maggie, Heather, Christina, Dylan, Jojo, Justin, Nell, Orla, Maude, Alice, Steven, Lee, Matteo, Brett, David, Alex, Tyson, Cam, Buddy, Cheev, Trott, and especially Eva for providing multiple spaces of community from which I could write this project. They know better than I do about the challenges this project posed in terms of writing, self-reflection, politics, and values.

Finally, the many workers, organizers, staffers, and activists I met throughout this research, some of whom read drafts of this work and all of whom were generous in their feedback, remain unnamed but made the entire endeavor possible. While some of my conclusions may be hard reading, this project stems from my deep respect of and commitment to the work of all those who struggle to make a better world for all of us.

1

Strategy, Power, and Worker Leadership

William, the executive director of the Clara Lemlich Project (CLP)—a small but well-established worker center in Philadelphia, erases some old notes from the whiteboard.[1] "Basically," he says, "it's a technical term." He takes the cap off of a marker and looks around the table where Miriam, Alejandro, Emma, and I are sitting—all of the CLP staff except James, our development lead. "A technical campaign term for where we are. He writes "W F I O" in large capital letters across the white board. "Pronounced wiffeeeooo," he says, drawing out the sounds for emphasis. "Anyone familiar with WFIO?" he asks with a big smile. "It's that moment in the campaign where you say, 'We're Fucked; It's Over.'" He laughs, writing the full phrase out on the board.[2]

He turns back, straightening up and getting serious. "WFIO means there's no good options, but you still have to find the option that's going to win, right? So, let's reflect on how we got here." As he continues, he outlines each thought on the whiteboard in his scrawling handwriting. "We went public..." he pauses to let his writing catch up to his speech ... "and then within a week the Leadership Committee crumbled in the face of union busting." He turns to us. "If we were a low-performing group, we could just blame the union busting, but since we're a high-performing group, we have to blame..."—he returns to his outline to drive the point home—"... the CLP!" He gives a laugh. "Obviously, the Leadership Committee, empirically speaking, wasn't ready to go public, or of course it wouldn't have crumbled the way it did." I lift my eyebrows in surprise at this last sentence, remembering how confident the staff was that the workers on the Committee—and the workers in general—were ready to launch their independent union campaign.

Five months ago, workers launched the public phase of the union-organizing campaign at the Fishtown Condiment Company (FCC) with an impressive show of public support. At a press conference held at the work-site, workers presented a demands letter asking for higher wages, affordable healthcare, and respectful treatment at work, delivered alongside a community petition with hundreds of ally signatures. This campaign marked an

Worker Centered. Biko Koenig, Oxford University Press. © Oxford University Press (2024).
DOI: 10.1093/oso/9780197784907.003.0001

intentional evolution in the work of the CLP, a deliberate shift away from a worker center model that staff felt was often limited to enforcing minimum legal standards. Historically, CLP campaigns involved fired workers fighting against illegal treatment, and success usually meant legal settlements for back pay and signed commitments that employers would follow the law moving forward. But these successes never translated to a standing membership base, as workers typically left the organization after a victory, and the promise of sparking a movement that could win above-minimum gains for workers seemed dim.

Drawing on the staff's uncompromising commitment to worker leadership and deep critiques of staff-driven advocacy organizations, their new vision was an ambitious attempt to, as one staff member put it, "fundamentally transform the food and labor movements" through the leadership and action of workers. Beginning with the campaign at FCC, CLP staff would train worker-members on how to organize their own unions at employers across the region. Independent from the CLP, these member-led unions would deploy a model defined by rank-and-file leadership and direct-action tactics to secure gains for workers above and beyond legal minimums. In addition to training workers in the fundamentals of union organizing, the CLP would support these campaigns from the outside by mobilizing allies, running media campaigns, offering legal advice, and implementing other tactics drawn from the classic worker center model. In this new "CLP 2.0," staff members imagined supporting a mass movement of militant worker-leaders organizing together in solidarity to raise standards across the region.

As I looked at "WFIO" scrawled across the whiteboard, this vision of radical labor transformation seemed to be slipping away. The wide media coverage of the press conference obscured the fact that, of the twenty workers who had agreed to attend, only six had actually done so. In the immediate aftermath, several workers had asked to take their names off the demands letter, and organizers struggled to get workers to return their calls. Now, five months after the launch, the handful of workers who the staff could still reach were decidedly negative about the future of the campaign, where workers like Marcos and Jose thought that aggressive tactics would, in the words of one organizer, "only alienate people since there is a rift between the organization and the workers." Given that, it was no surprise that our attempts to support the workers had been continually delayed as we struggled to get any workers to participate in campaign actions, and questions about the future of the campaign had come to dominate the office. Hence, WFIO.

After some reflection about the strategy of the campaign, William lays out the catch-22 in which we are caught. "A worker says, 'There's nothing happening, there's nothing here, there's nothing going on,' which is true, but for something to go on, the worker has to do something, because it's a worker-led campaign!" He takes a breath, lifting one hand as he presents the first side of his argument. "OK . . . so Marcos says that attacking the company is going to distance the campaign from the base, and there's no question that that's true, that's pretty well established through organizing experience that that's the case." He raises his other hand, as he pauses, raising his eyebrows. "Now the counterargument is that the base is already distanced from the campaign, and the last five months have been spent trying to *un-distance* the campaign from the base, right? And that hasn't been successful."

Emma nods along, and Alejandro agrees, venting his frustration that attempts to speak with workers have been fruitless. "They have only grown increasingly resistant, and this seems like a joke to them, it seems like. . . ." He pauses, looking at the ceiling as he searchers for the words, ". . . like we don't seem like a serious organization."

William nods. "I just don't think it's realistic—even though in our minds' eye it's attractive—to imagine Jose and Marcos and Miguel and David going out there and bringing their coworkers together. I don't think that's realistic." He shrugs with both hands, turning back to the whiteboard. "So, I think what victory looks like. . . ." He begins to sketch out an outline of his thoughts on the board. "Every worker has the right to oppose oppression in their life, you know? Everyone can resist wage slavery."

He stops to take a breath, speaking slowly as he writes out the next sentence. "So, the militant minority . . . of workers . . . will use . . . asymmetrical power . . . because of how the supply chain works . . . to open up . . . the organizing opportunity." Here, he turns back to us. "This is what has to set us apart. Because . . ."—he pauses here, his voice getting sharp as he taps the conference table—"the leaders . . . if we cut and run, the leaders will definitely get fired. I mean forget about it, they'll be fired in rapid succession. So . . ."—he straightens up—"does anyone disagree with this, or does anyone think there's a different pattern than this that could bring the campaign to victory?"

There is a long pause before Alejandro asks, "Well . . . what would the asymmetrical power look like?"

Quickly, counting with his fingers, William responds, his voice quiet but direct. "As much of a militant minority that we can muster to lead Phase II and Phase III of the campaign. Phase II being hitting the consequential, but not critical, relationships that the company depends on with the media and customers, and Phase III hitting the critical relationships that the company depends on, with wholesale buyers."

There is a long pause as the fierceness of his words hangs in the air. William has essentially laid down the gauntlet—regardless of low support, the fact that workers think an aggressive strategy would drive the base away, or that some think the campaign is "a joke," his call is for workers to increase the pressure in whatever way they can. The belief is that a show of strength will force the FCC to make a concession—any concession—which will then demonstrate to the workers that they have the power to hold the company accountable.

As he wraps up the meeting, William directs the organizers to schedule a meeting with those four workers we still count as members and get them to commit to some form of action, though William's recommendation is to hand out leaflets outside of one of the FCC's downtown retail customers. While he notes that the workers should lead this process—"That's the point of a democratic meeting"—he also dictates what they ought to do: "These people are going to fight against their boss, and fight like hell to bring their coworkers into the battle."

This final quote captures the fundamental tension at the heart of this project. While worker leadership was a central value for the organization, for staff, and for allies, our campaign at the FCC was defined as much by a lack of worker participation as it was by our need to continually discuss the campaign as worker-led. This book is my attempt to understand this world of grassroots movement work and, in drawing out the themes of allyship, power, and representation, to understand the significance of worker leadership in this story and its impact on our collective efforts to build a more just world.

The Case of the CLP—Allyship, Power, and Representation

The CLP campaign at the FCC offers a unique case study of social movement activity, one involving an innovative strategic model, resistance to the anti-confrontational influences of the nonprofit industrial complex, and actors with deeply committed ideological values. The organization's strategic evolution away from campaigns that primarily drew from workers who had been illegally treated and towards building standing unions addresses many of the arguments about the limitations of worker centers. Further, the model of unionization that the CLP hoped workers would use amounted to a wish list for progressive labor activists—direct action tactics, rank-and-file leadership, political education, and cross-cutting social movement unionism. The CLP also sought to organize a low-wage, mostly immigrant workforce that many believe needs to be at the forefront of the labor movement. An important tactic developed in their previous campaigns was the "supply-chain strategy," an approach that leveraged the relatively short geographic supply chains of food processing and distribution to launch "customer education campaigns" at the customers of their targets.[3] Historically, this tactic utilized a great deal of ally support, delivering on the promise of community–worker partnerships embedded in a strategy with real economic power to hold companies accountable to their workers. Finally, the ability of staffers to secure nonprofit funding to run confrontational campaigns based in a radical ideology of social change sets the organization apart from other grassroots organizations and even many worker centers.

In the end, the CLP was unable to help workers secure a union victory at the FCC. There are several reasons for this outcome, including the structural issues of a sector with low margins and high turnover, divisions within the workforce, and the general precarity that workers faced in society. And while the anti-union position of the company also played a role, any analysis of the campaign must include the reality of low levels of worker participation. In such a context, staff leadership and ally power emerged as crucial factors in sustaining the momentum of the campaign. Through a mix of public actions, media coverage, and moral pressure, the hope was to demonstrate to workers that the employer could be encouraged to make changes, which would "make space" for workers to organize and experience the efficacy of the campaign. And with low worker participation, this process included an important rhetorical component, where organizers attributed the gains secured by allies to the activity of workers in the hopes of convincing them of their own power. Almost a year after the public launch, allies did successfully engage the company to both meet with the campaign and publicly assure the workforce that their membership in the organization was allowed and protected. Nonetheless, these tactics did not lead to any significant increase in worker participation.

But the WFIO meeting recounted above captures the key conflict that I explore in this book, where a group of labor allies—activists and staffers who have devoted their lives to the importance of worker leadership—run a campaign that they continually frame as being led by workers though it is decidedly not. To be clear, this tension did not stem from some strategic portrayal of worker leadership to the media, funders, or opponents. Instead, a narrative of worker leadership continually defined how we as staff members discussed the campaign not only with outside actors but also with each other and with workers. This view of the world was emphasized on my first day, where Emma told me for the first of many times that "at the CLP workers lead and everything else follows." The outcome was a movement ecosystem where legitimacy required preexisting worker leadership, leading to a structural condition where movement actors had to perform worker leadership in order to secure the respect, resources, and reputation that we needed to try to spark that very leadership. Thus, in practice we held two seemingly contradictory positions, where worker leadership was both a goal to work toward and one that had already been achieved.

Rather than seeding worker-led unions, CLP ended up functioning much like a classic professionalized social movement organization, "started by 'entrepreneurs,' led by paid leaders, and funded largely by 'conscience' constituents driven by a commitment to movement goals rather than being directly affected themselves by the causes of social grievance" (Ashar and Fisk 2019, p. 145). This is not an inherent problem, and there is a rich history of such social movement organizations achieving important outcomes. But this is at odds with the CLP's own aims, and at times it left workers as "symbolic actors" whose primary role was to convey the human impact of the campaign to more important power holders (Jenkins 2002). In the end, the CLP enacted an advocacy model that contradicted our own political values, where important questions about governance, accountability, and authenticity—topics that should be important to proponents of worker leadership—were rendered moot through the very strength of our ideological convictions.

These principles permeated our work to the deepest degree. Even when staff members were hard pressed to find workers who would respond to their outreach, we discussed the campaign in terms of "what the workers wanted" and were often unable to consider the campaign as anything but worker-led. And while goals like good wages and respectful treatment were important, a key part of what we understood workers to want was translated through our strategic commitment to union militancy. This led us to assume that direct-action tactics and rank-and-file–led independent unions embodied what one staff member called the "authentic personality" of the workers. But in the space left by the absence of substantive worker participation, our dedication to both worker leadership and militant unionism filled this void with our beliefs about what workers *should* want. In carrying out our work, our beliefs envisioned a cadre of workers who were waiting for the proper organizing opportunity to assert their authentic personalities as militant union members. In such a context the political waters are murky, where we could commit to a militant minority strategy that embraced the very tactics that workers were suspicious of, all while discussing that decision as democratic and worker-led.

The focus of my argument is not about how we failed to live up to our values, nor is it a call to abandon efforts to center the voice of oppressed people in movement work. My aim instead is to critically assess the impact of such an intense, ideological commitment to worker leadership and how it can act at cross-purposes to the goal of building power. To make this assessment I think it's best to understand worker leadership at the CLP as not simply a slogan or a brand but as a discourse in the Foucauldian sense—a system of thought "composed of ideas, attitudes, courses of action, beliefs, and practices that systematically construct the subjects and the worlds of which they speak" (Lessa 2006, p. 285). A discourse is a way of making sense of the world and acting within it, a constitution of a certain kind of truth or the common sense that people use when they approach the world (Woodly 2015). And with this goes a good deal of power—they can either reinforce or challenge everyday knowledge about what is right or wrong and what should or should not be done about it. This makes discourse a key site of politics, albeit one less tangible than strike actions and street demonstrations. The discursive arena of politics is where people are persuaded to think about the world in ways that enables them to understand those actions as legitimate, necessary, and powerful. And in this story, the discourse of worker leadership functioned as the mortar that held all the pieces together.

Allyship and the Fear of Domination

The challenges of allyship and representation in movement work are not unique to the labor movement but characterize an ongoing predicament for justice-minded political actors on the Left. The past few decades have seen the rise of a strongly held political value, that the people most impacted by a circumstance should be the ones identifying problems and developing solutions. Within a "nothing about us, without us, is for us" framework, many feel that leadership should come from oppressed peoples themselves and not from top-down organizations or professionalized leadership. This principle stems from real concerns about groups that displace the agency of the marginalized people they aim to support, and especially so for organizations led by the privileged and with access to resources (Dempsey 2009). At the same time, the development of movements and organizations created and led solely by those experiencing the worst parts of our society is no easy task. This is, in part, because the social locations of people in relation to economic, political, and cultural structures do not often spark spontaneous political action—simply being a worker does not usually make one a unionist or anticapitalist. Such politicization is more often the intentional work of social movements, which, when successful, empower people to reframe their individual problems as shared with others in similar positions and to help develop viable strategies for addressing problems as a group. This work is sometimes lost in common narratives of social protest, where protest moments like the United Auto Workers strikes in the 1930s, the Montgomery Bus Boycott of the 1950s, or the more recent Black Lives Matter protests can appear from the outside to be spontaneous. When we go deeper into these histories we discover years, or even decades, of movements working to spur communities to action. Finally, for many on the Left, our analysis of the dire state of the world leads us to favor movements with transformative visions and confrontational tactics. But when we are moved to address the injustices that other, more marginalized groups experience, the tensions between the ethic of bottom-up leadership and the desire to change the status quo can be quite strong. The case of the CLP offers a way to reflect on these dynamics in our shared struggle for a more just world.

For those of us committed to liberatory struggle, what does the CLP campaign at FCC teach us? The story I tell in this book is a complicated narrative about allyship, power, and representation. And while there is an irony that an organization with such a strong commitment to worker leadership would unreflectively reproduce the top-down, staff-driven structure it aimed to transcend, we must take care with our critiques of the CLP in a movement landscape where many struggle—myself included—with our own privilege and positionality. My intention is not to denigrate the organization, allies, staff, or workers involved in the campaign. The CLP has been instrumental in the lives of many workers, and their campaigns have successfully fought against illegal practices and have brought worker voices into the public space. That an organization would have the courage to try something radically new in an attempt to empower workers to seriously contest capitalism at the workplace is an effort that must be not only examined but repeated. As I will stress throughout, we need more organizations like the CLP that are willing to use their limited resources on visionary experiments. In that spirit, a critical assessment of the organization's work is necessary if we are to cultivate additional innovations of worker-centric organization.

Consequently, an analysis of this case must reflect seriously on how the allies in this story—activists, staffers, donors, and all the non-workers supporting the campaign—were unable to consider the realities of our power and authority, and that this, when combined with our desire for worker leadership, had impacts on the outcome of the campaign. Given that many of us would like to see workers exert greater authority throughout society, we can treat this scenario as a critical case of commitment to worker leadership. In a movement landscape where many have called for centering workers as the leaders of the labor movement, it is hard to imagine a group of allies with a stronger belief in the necessity of worker leadership than those at the CLP.[4] Indeed, staff were mostly disapproving of other leftist labor organizations for not adhering to more radical worker-led ideologies and strategies.

The practice of allyship is the central theme of this project. Everyone who was involved in the project approached our participation from a place of real fear about an allyship that was performative and authoritative. We didn't want to support staff-driven, top-down organizations led by well-resourced nonprofit professionals or conservative union leaders that dominated the voices of workers. We wanted the workers to speak, to lead, to kick ass! Ultimately, we wanted workers who would lead *us* in a renewed labor movement that would transform society. We were on the hunt for an authentic version of worker leadership, where workers would organically take on the mantle of the militant unionist with our support but not our domination. This false choice between the leadership of workers or the domination of allies set up allyship as a passive, reactive, and politically feeble act, one that obscures the forms of power that allies do hold in their relationships with workers. In practice, our concerns about the nature of our allyship created a romanticized vision of worker leadership, as if the category of worker would somehow solve the challenges of power, authority, and representation that come with movement work. And in the end, our attachment to the purity of the vision simply did not help to build the power of the workers.

I argue that it is impossible to avoid the messiness and complexity that come with the positionality of movement work, of engaging with communities who have less privilege and power than us, and confronting the fact that we may want different things. This story underlines that workers are not radicals in waiting, simply biding their time for the right opportunity to take the lead so that we can step back. Instead, it emphasizes the transformative nature of movement work, where our aim is not to unveil some natural predisposition to collective action or justice but to fundamentally alter how someone sees the world and acts within it. It also means complicating the categories from which we approach these struggles, where campaign allies are also workers in other contexts, and where workers and allies alike can be parents, immigrants, or consumers. Everyone, regardless of our place in society, has a stake in a stronger and more fundamentally bottom-up labor movement.

Our fight does not happen only in the streets or on the shop floor, but also in the hearts and minds of people. But when groups like the CLP and its allies interact with oppressed communities, our dialogue does not happen in some neutral, power-free environment defined by "authentic" representation. It is instead a deeply political relationship, one that exists within the webs of power that shape our roles, affect our narratives, and influence the scope and style of our engagement. Organizing—convincing, reframing, cajoling—is a power-laden act that hinges on the skill and authority of the movement to challenge the status quo. To mentor a member of any movement in their journey from novice to leader involves the same dynamics. Rather than pretending that our power and leadership do not exist, we should ask how we can use our authority and privilege to not only assist but empower and transform those who are being oppressed. How can we help train, inspire, and develop the capacity of people to participate in the authorship of shared vision for liberation, and attach our accountability to that vision rather than a category of person? It begins with acknowledging our resources, skills, and leadership are not inherently an anathema to justice but can be essential ingredients in the struggle for liberation. To ignore this is to limit our strategic horizons, to retreat from the responsibility of our privilege, and to ask that the most marginalized take on the work to organize themselves, all in the name of an ideological purity, which, as this book illustrates, is not enough to win the world we want.

Strategy, Structure, and Authenticity

In this volume I provide an ethnographic account of the CLP from my perspective first as an intern and later as an unpaid staff member. In doing so, I hope to spur reflection on three topics important to contemporary movement work, which I discuss in the remainder of this chapter. The first reflects on the failure of the CLP to convince workers to start their own union at the FCC. Here I will consider some of the internal and external dilemmas that the organization faced, including the strategic plan, the economic context of the sector, and how workers thought about the campaign. I then turn to the structure of the organization, a nonprofit organization led and staffed by non-members and with few formal accountability mechanisms to the workers themselves. What I show is that this structure is at odds with the version of worker leadership espoused by the staff. And while these criticisms are important, my final argument is that our critiques of the CLP, whether about strategy, structure, or their internal contradictions, must reconcile a key tension—how can we hold a commitment to the leadership of marginalized people while simultaneously supporting efforts to organize those communities from our position as allies? To do so means recognizing that the most successful organizing work does not hinge on some authentic, pre-political identity determined by people's structural position. Rather, it is the outcome of intentional and transformative work that aims to get people to think differently about themselves.

Strategy and Power

Across this volume I explore the strategies used by the CLP to build and deploy power during the worker-led union campaign at the FCC. As a non-profit worker center, the CLP was known for using a worker-led model of organizing steeped in direct-action tactics. Using a mix of protests, media campaigns, litigation, and ally support, the CLP had recovered millions of dollars for workers and had never lost a campaign in its history when I began as an intern. Like many advocacy groups, the CLP exercised power in three ways: through the coalitional power of consumers, activists, workers, and other actors working in concert; through the moral power held by the public to hold employers accountable to ethical standards; and through the institutional power of the regulatory state to combat illegal behavior (Brookes 2013, Holgate 2021). And while none of these forms of power led to a unionized workforce or standing membership base, the CLP nonetheless delivered important gains for a low-income and often exploited workforce. Campaigns enforced wage standards, won back pay, compelled employers to follow safety requirements, provided restitution for illegal firings, and contested harassment and discrimination—essentially filling the enforcement gap left by an ineffective policy regime. As one organizer put it, "If employers just followed the law, I would be out of a job."

I arrived at the CLP at a time of strategic transition. Unsatisfied with enforcing legal standards, staffers aimed to use their experiences with workplace justice campaigns and the supply-chain model to train workers to run union drives that would deliver above-minimum compensation, better treatment, and increased agency. To put it differently, they aimed to combine the coalitional and moral power of the worker-center model with the structural power that is unique to workers and stems from their ability to withhold their labor from an employer (Holgate 2021). This approach fit into many of the best practices called for by labor scholars and practitioners in the past decade, and it was developed in consultation with strategists from successful campaigns around the country. Rather than solely relying on the persuasion of public elites by allies—a core strategy of the advocacy model—they aimed to equip workers with the skills and knowledge they needed to exercise their own power in the supply chain and on the shop floor. Staff and allies were still seen as playing important roles, as organizers built an integrative and comprehensive campaign strategy that would involve a variety of tactics, actors, and forms of power to support the workers in their union campaign (Bronfenbrenner and Hickey 2004; Milkman 2014).

This new orientation was itself the result of strategic research of the regional marketplace and was framed in intersectional terms regarding class, race, immigration status, and gender (Alberti, Holgate, and Tapia 2013). Like many worker centers, the CLP was organized as a nonprofit and received most of its funds from foundation grants. And while many have illustrated that the dynamics of the nonprofit industrial complex push organizations to abandon confrontational tactics in favor of neoliberal logics that blame the relatively powerless for their own straits, the CLP was able to put these funds to work in the service of collective worker power (INCITE! 2007; Frantz and Fernandes, 2016; Kohl-Arenas 2016). Underlying all this was a deep commitment to the centrality of workers, their power, and their leadership as the core of mass collective struggle. The CLP would measure victory in the ability of worker-led campaigns to successfully leverage power against employers and build standing unions. Within this approach, the experiment of the CLP 2.0 aimed to merge what they saw as the best parts of the worker center and labor union models.

But this commitment to worker leadership, and the narrative that it produced, is implicated in many of the strategic issues that we faced. When actors see the social world as one where the radical vision of direct-action unionization does not require the fundamental transformation of workers, strategies can be oversimplified and challenges obscured. Thus, any analysis about the campaign cannot only include considerations of strategies, tactics, or organizational structure. It must also consider how staff struggled, on a conceptual level, to recognize the power and leadership that we held in the campaign. As I discuss next, these strategic and interpretative trends are woven together in the story of how the FCC campaign unfolded.

First, the economic structure of the food industry within a broader context of low-wage precarity presented a relatively challenging organizing environment defined by high employee turnover, low profit margins, and a decidedly competitive marketplace. As we will see, this was true at the FCC, where the company eventually showed their books to the workers as evidence that it could not afford the higher wages and benefits demanded by the campaign. Further, the CLP's own research and campaign history illustrated the widespread problems of wage theft, harassment, and other illegal practices faced by workers. This context makes the sector difficult to organize as market conditions make low-wage employees easily replaceable and create large pools of labor, making it challenging to sustain higher wages or benefits. In a deep irony found in much low-wage work, the relationship between poor working conditions and high turnover makes it challenging for organizers to sustain momentum when workers may find it easier to move to a new job rather than fight for better treatment. And, as I discuss below, the relatively higher wages at companies like the FCC make it even more challenging to organize a workforce that feel their jobs are good within this broader sector.

Next, a lack of organizing capacity seemed to hamstring efforts to reach workers. A prime example is the Regional Distribution Strategy discussed in later chapters, where the CLP intended to start and launch three different campaigns in a twelve-month time frame, with the goal to start even more campaigns in the successive year. At the time the CLP employed only one full-time organizer, assisted by a half-time organizer and a volunteer. Clearly, the CLP would have preferred to hire more staff given a larger budget. But resource issues aside, this plan is only viable within a particular view of worker leadership. If one assumes that workers can readily be trained to start union Leadership Committees (LCs), run their own campaigns, and organize their own shops, then little staff support is necessary. In retrospect it seems clear that to find and train worker-leaders, the organization needed more staff. While it is impossible to know if additional organizers would have led to a substantially different outcome, it seems likely that the campaign would have had more opportunities to reach workers with more organizing capacity.

Further, strategic conversations about the campaign focused on how best to engage the company and hold it accountable. The goal was to simultaneously push the company to take actions it would prefer not to while illustrating the efficacy of the campaign to workers, and thus make space for them to join. But there was far less reflection about the strategy for persuading workers. The method that the staff used to organize workers involved reframing the concerns or frustrations that a worker might have into something that could be solved by working together to start their own union. While this approach followed best practices, it wasn't enough on its own to convince workers to join. When the campaign shifted toward the militant minority strategy, the goals of the staff were to illustrate to workers that they had power and that they wouldn't be fired when they used that power collectively. In both cases, what seemed missing to me was a deeper reflection on how to change the perspectives of workers and why the efforts of the organizers didn't seem to stick. Yes, the campaign could be effective, but did workers want the same things that the staff thought they wanted? Did they view the world in the same way?

Workers seemed to be a reluctant audience to the campaign, and one limitation of this research were the scant opportunities to participate with workers during the fieldwork. Outside of these limited interactions, I was able to secure only five worker interviews after I left the field, some who were involved in the campaign and others who were not, as it was challenging to find many workers who would speak with me. CLP staffers often discussed the lack of worker participation as coming from either a fear of losing one's job or the strength of the anti-union campaign impeding membership. Responses from workers I interviewed did discuss the problem of fear, but in very different terms from how the CLP typically framed it. Rather than the fear of management preventing otherwise radical desires to fight against the company, workers had concerns about losing jobs they felt were pretty good. More than one worker told me that their job at the FCC was the best job they had ever had when they first started. This is not to imply that these were highly paid jobs, with new hires making a few dollars more than minimum wage. When I asked one woman about workers being afraid to join the campaign, her response was more balanced than that of the staff, noting that many of her coworkers were making substantially more than they had at other jobs:

> The FCC is hiring people who have real problems finding any work at all. So being able to make a hundred dollars a day is pretty good no matter what if alternative is like forty or fifty dollars doing fast food.

Another worker framed it similarly:

> Many of them have worked here for ten, fifteen, even twenty years. . . . Because of the many years they have worked here, they've achieved wages that are more comfortable. So they don't want to join, that's my perception. Although they might not be the best wages, they don't want to take a risk of losing this job and not finding work for a while or finding work that pays less than this.

While a desire to retain jobs that paid higher wages was a key concern, other issues also played into low participation. National differences among the workforce got in the way of collective identities based on a shared work life. Drug and alcohol use was apparently a problem among some workers who didn't want to participate since their managers let them use on the job. All the workers I talked to also expressed concerns of getting mocked by co-workers for their participation, which happened to some of the original Leadership Committee members. Finally, many workers didn't seem to care or had other priorities: "I would talk to the guys on my shift every week, they would listen, and then go back to whatever they were talking about." Workers simply were not thinking about power and the workplace in the same ways that the CLP did.

The concerns that workers express about losing their jobs should be understood alongside a lack of trust and rapport with the CLP model. For those who participated in the campaign, there was frustration with the public launch and a concern it was not well organized alongside confusion or miscommunication about the goal of a worker-led union. Some workers expected, and desired, a traditional union campaign complete with staff leadership:

> I feel like some people who were involved at the beginning stepped back because they thought that it was going be faster. More of a "We're going vote to have a union and then it's going be that way. And then we're not going have to do anything anymore. We'll just be a union."

A common refrain was that workers felt the organizers should be handling the campaign directly and were surprised when they were not the ones delivering the demands letter to the company at the press conference. Another worker explained the lack of enthusiasm as stemming in part from their expectations around what unions are and should do:

> A lot of people believed that this was a union, and they thought that the union winning would lead to an office at the company to help the workers. A lot of people still don't trust the organization because [of the public launch] and they were expecting it to have a fancy office.

The value of the campaign and the particularities of the independent union model were ideologically important and self-evident to the staff and allies who supported this model in explicit opposition to traditional unions. But when organizers would discuss features such as collecting dues directly rather than taking them out of paychecks or a disdain for business agents, workers either didn't understand or didn't care about these details. Where the vision of the CLP called for a workforce with radical ideas of worker power, direct action, and solidarity, plans to move workers into that political mindset foundered on the consistent lack of interest from the workers.

In looking back at these aspects of the campaign, my takeaway is that our narratives of worker leadership structured how staff thought about organizing workers in ways that undercut our efforts. The staff appeared to think that seeding well-supported Leadership Committees at four different worksites over a year was a reasonable goal. Further, they expected that these worker-led groups would take on the responsibility for organizing the rest of the workforce and building their unions. If this assumption had borne fruit, it might have been possible to run multiple campaigns with a small staff. Staff members understood the value of these campaigns as self-evident, later explained to me as an "'if you build it, they will come' mentality." And even when the FCC campaign was at its lowest level of worker participation, some still worried about "staff initiative displacing worker initiative."

The outcome was a strategy that stressed giving workers the opportunity to join campaigns rather than focusing on how to persuade them to join. When workers didn't join, staff assumed the lack of participation was due to barriers rather than mindsets. As William put it, "The three top barriers [to workers joining the campaign] are one, futility. This employer, even if God rains down on the company, will never come to the table. Second is fear of retaliation, that if I step up, I'm going to be fired. Third is, concern about intra-coworker drama." The assumption was that if a campaign seemed effective and workers did not think they would be fired, then we should expect them to join. In convincing the company to attend a meeting to discuss the campaign, holding actions without anyone getting fired, and securing a public commitment that no workers would be punished for participation, we addressed the first two fears as well as any campaign could. But it led to no substantive changes in worker participation or interest. What's missing from this analysis is whether and why workers want to join a campaign in the first place, and if they do not, what their reasoning is and how to change their minds. If organizing is about re-framing how people see the world in order to inspire them to act differently, then it means that the organized are changed in the process. But at the CLP this process was complicated by the contours of a worker-leader narrative that both noted the need for leadership development and implied that workers did not need to change in order to lead.

Consequently, the notion of leadership was not well defined, and workers who the CLP identified as leaders tended to be those who simply showed up to meetings. If *all* workers are leaders, then critical reflections on what makes for effective leadership become difficult, and excitement about the campaign can be mistaken for the ability of a worker to organize their colleagues. And when only those whose prior enthusiasm for a campaign act as participants and leaders, then the ability to effectively organize those who do not already agree can be reduced (McAlevey 2016). This dynamic was amplified by low participation and limited resources, which meant that organizers were often left with no choice but to work with those workers who did answer calls or attend meetings. As I discuss in the concluding chapter, the challenge of approaching the leadership of workers with a nuanced appreciation for capabilities, inclinations, and capacities may be one of the most significant strategic gaps within the narrative of worker leadership.

But where workers expressed skepticism, allies were an attentive audience. They leveraged power in the name of campaigns and provided time and resources to help keep the office doors open. For practically all of the allies I spoke with, the point of this was to explicitly back worker-led organizing. While most workers recognized the importance of traditional labor unions, policy battles, and the "mere advocacy" of other groups, the promise of a "real" labor movement led by the workers themselves offered a higher call-ing for their support. In conversations and interviews I would ask why, out of all the labor organizations in the area, did they think the CLP deserved their support. For many, it came down to values and identity—it was the right thing to do, because workers *should* be leading. Assisting the CLP with money, time, and effort was an important act for allies as it publicly and internally articulated their values of participation and social justice.

Even so, the question of worker support at CLP would inevitably come up in conversations. Across the board, interviewees would admit that they knew, suspected, or had heard that membership numbers were low. Then why support the group anyway? One long-time labor activist summed up the responses I heard most often:

> What else are we supposed to do? Unions don't have the answers. Workers need to lead the movement for it to be successful, and groups like the CLP are holding that space until the workers are ready.

But what makes a worker "ready"? Mirroring the preceding discussion, there was little thought about what would need to happen for workers to join and lead the movement. Like staff, the process by which workers would organize was somewhat mystified behind assumptions about spontaneous worker leadership.

This illustrates both the potential and the limits of ally pressure. For orga-nizations with limited resources, the turn to ally power can be alluring because it often involves the mobilization of self-selecting actors who, com-pared to workers, are easier to engage. Finding ten labor activists in a city to hand out flyers at a store is a far different task from organizing ten work-ers out of one hundred to start their own union, stand up to their boss, and demand a better life. This case demonstrates how the ability of staff and allies to engage employers is not a substitute for worker power and may not, on its own, create the space needed for it to flourish. Such an approach requires either a preexisting and active interest by workers or a strategy that treats leadership development as its primary goal. But the insistence on worker leadership obscured the real power that the CLP had generated from an active and mobilized base of allies.

Accountability and Structure

Throughout my time at the CLP, we consistently presented both the organization and the FCC campaign as worker-led. This was not the case in any substantive way. The CLP was not formally structured as a member-led group at any level of its organization, from its board of directors, to staffing decisions, to its day-to-day operations. On the campaign end, staff members selected targets, designed strategy, and were the authors of the political vision of the organization. In the FCC campaign specifically, organizers had leadership roles typical of other worker-centric labor groups. In deciding which campaigns to run and what actions to plan, they provided political education, leadership development, and tactical know-how. Further, as the vision of a worker-led union never took root at the FCC, there was no substantial union infrastructure for workers to lead. Perhaps with a stronger campaign, workers would have had more opportunities to take on real leadership roles. And this is not to say that workers were entirely absent. But in practice, workers, even at their most assertive, generally did what staff told them to do, and the CLP made many decisions without their participation. One worker I spoke with explained it in this way:

> Whenever there was a meeting, someone from CLP would say something like, "We have this for you." They're basically just checking in. They're saying "We think it would be good to do X, Y, and Z." And usually I think that they were right, you know? There were a lot of things that were just kind of rubber stamped from the workers. And I understand wanting to have it be more worker-run, and I wanted it to be more worker-driven. But I didn't have the time to drive it as a worker and I knew that no one else was going to either so . . . I think it was as worker driven as it could be, you know? I think that the overall strategy was a hundred percent CLP.

This was an unsurprising relationship given that this was the first labor campaign for most of the workers. And while these circumstances did not align with our values, there was nothing nefarious about this structure. It mirrors what one might expect to find at many labor organizations, even ones that use worker-centric models. But this is an awkward finding when placed alongside the values held by staff and allies, and with implications for those who want to participate in and support bottom-up movement work. As such, we need to consider the internal structure of the organization and its relationship to the narrative of worker leadership. This aspect of the case touches on the dynamics of power that other movement scholars have discussed, where organizational and campaign structures can result in the centrality of staff, funders, and allies over that of members (Jenkins 2002, Gray 2007, Frantz and Fernandes 2016). But I also argue that the role of resources and the nonprofit structure, connected to the problems of authenticity and representation, undergird the challenges that leadership narratives can create for movement work.

Resources—the time and effort of volunteers and the money of donors and foundations—lead to important questions of power, representation, and accountability. If an organization raises significant funds on behalf of a group that has no real say over how they are used, how do we square this with the professed importance of that group's leadership? Of course, the CLP was able to garner support from foundations and donors while retaining a vision grounded in confrontational tactics, radical political ideology, and liberatory values. Such a vision is rare in the labor movement specifically and the nonprofit world more generally. The CLP was able to strategically navigate the nonprofit landscape by phrasing their mission in a deliberate manner, emphasizing the elite-friendly language of member-led campaigns against bad employers. In a world where it can be impossible to find the resources to back grassroots organizing, let alone more liberatory political agendas, this outcome is not insignificant. And, in fact, it may be necessary to keep liberatory organizations afloat "until the workers are ready."

But we also cannot escape the dynamics of how organizations like the CLP secure time, effort, and money from their networks of supporters. Simply put, narratives of worker leadership reproduced the type of power arrangements that the CLP aimed to contest, enabling it to collect and circulate the narratives of workers' lives and exchange them for resources then controlled by staff. In this way, our practices commodified the stories of worker oppression and leadership, which functioned as the symbolic currency for those interested in supporting worker-led campaigns. As both the articulator of appropriate worker identity and the functional voice of the workers, the CLP collected resources while also operating as a gatekeeper for the proper use of those resources. In doing so, we constructed the subjectivity of workers, defining what interests, practices, and narratives counted as authentic to the public. Recounting a conversation he had with a worker, a former staffer explained this dynamic in the following way a few months after I left the field:

> Do you know how the CLP makes their money? They pimp your experience, your work, and your suffering.... They pimp it out to foundations and individual donors. "This is the story about the work that we do. This is how we are unique. This is how we are distinct. This is what workers experience by being a part of this organization." Then they sell it to them.... They sell a story about the work that you do to other people, and they receive grants from it, they receive individual donations for it, because it is based on an idea—a mythology—that they tell the other people about what you do and how you participate in it. So *your* risks become *their* reward.

This critique, one clearly related to the staffer's own frustrations with the organization, characterizes many organizations that aim to represent communities without their full participation or control.

This dynamic is endemic in the world of nonprofit work. When professional advocacy groups speak for a community that is presented as in leadership, they project a conception of political action that is framed within a social imaginary of membership and participation. Narratives of member leadership explain organizations as merely the mouthpiece of communities, implying a relationship between organization and community that is seamless, apolitical, and free from internal power dynamics. Given that foundations and activists often prioritize bottom-up, grassroots, and community-initiated projects, the invocation of member leadership can offer ideological purity in contrast to top-down organizations that displace the agency of frontline communities (Dempsey 2009). Receptive audiences in these contexts not only supply nonprofits with resources, but they also confer political legitimacy by recognizing the work organizations do on behalf of relatively powerless groups of people (Strolovitch 2006).

But this relationship works both ways. As discussed above, people who support groups they believe are member-led have their own position as allies legitimated in the process. In a movement world where criticisms of advocacy organizations and bureaucratic unions are legion, supporting a bottom-up organization led directly by marginalized communities performs important identity work for the relatively privileged. It shows that we have a sharp political analysis, that we are not comfortable with the status quo of the nonprofit industrial complex, and that we've thrown our lot in with "real" organizations doing "real" work. The communicative labor that organizations like the CLP perform when they speak on behalf of the marginalized is thus a creative act in two ways (Dempsey 2009). First, the circulation of worker narratives actively produces a specific kind of worker for its audience, one constructed as authentic, politically engaged, and unencumbered by the bureaucratic weight of traditional unions and advocacy groups. And in spurring emotional reactions from the audience of allies—anger over the poor treatment of low-wage workers or enthusiasm about their campaign leadership—it constructs those allies as politically virtuous for their support of this organization over other options.[5]

This, at its core, is the central ambiguity of the CLP project. Their vision of radical rank-and-file–led unions was built in opposition to the conservatism of traditional unions and the inauthentic liberalism of staff-run advocacy organizations. But, in many ways, the practices of the FCC campaign mirrored the dynamics of staff leadership and representation that the organization was designed to combat. That most actors involved nonetheless saw their work as compatible with the vision is evidence of the strength that narrative, ideology, and discourse have in shaping how we understand the world. Of course, we cannot know how the staff would have responded with greater worker participation or a successful rank-and-file union campaign. But in the end, the CLP functioned as an organization that spoke *for* workers rather than an organization *of* workers, one that required the commodification of worker narratives to continue the work, one where we could only advance those causes that prefigured what workers should want, and one supported by allies whose participation was an important aspect of their own identities as allies. Taken as a whole, these dynamics are a poor fit with the strongly held values of worker leadership and agency held by staff and activists in the CLP network.

The Myth of Authenticity

By this point it may seem that the purpose of this book is to critique the CLP for not living up to its devotion to authentic worker leadership. This is not the case. My goal instead is to take aim at the problematic nature of that devotion. In the preceding section of this chapter I showed how the importance of worker leadership as an existential value impacted strategic choices and how it was not, surprisingly, reflected in the structure of the organization. But any critique that we offer should be careful to not simply reproduce an unreflective desire for authentic worker leadership as the overriding quality of worthwhile movement work. Instead, I want to encourage us to consider how the seemingly unforgivable practices of the organization—the commodification of worker narratives, the communicative labor of these narratives, and the insistence on how workers should think and act—are hard to avoid and may in fact serve liberatory ends.

There are two challenges with the desire that we hold for the authentic leadership of marginalized people, the first a practical one. One solution to the resource and representation dilemma is to just give workers the resources and let them take whatever actions they deem most necessary. While this might align with the goal of worker agency, it will be politically disappointing. Workers, like most people, are rarely radicals in waiting. Of course, we should celebrate when people do organize their own communities and demand change. But in many circumstances the contexts of people's lives are not enough to lead to political action. And when people do decide to get involved with a collective effort, we should recognize that they may need mentorship and support to realize their full power. Putting workers in charge of an organization without any leadership development or political education will most likely reproduce status-quo power arrangements.

Further, many of these challenges will still be at play when organizing occurs *within* a community. Even if the CLP had been worker-led, it would have had no choice but to continue to turn toward foundations and donors. Given the nature of the nonprofit industrial complex and the wider labor movement, it is hard to imagine alternative processes by which workers could generate the needed resources to begin organizing their colleagues. Absent a return to volunteerism or a worker-led dues structure—itself challenging with a low-wage workforce—it is difficult to imagine a funding model that would not rely on the commodification of worker narratives. A savvy worker-led organization would likely aim to commodify narratives in such a way as to bring in the most resources. And the same would be true for any worker-led union. The radical worker-leader who aims to persuade their unorganized coworkers will need these resources to engage in the messy work of identity construction. And this work will involve the same prescriptive and transformative narratives as the CLP—asserting what fellow workers should want as a way to broaden their horizons, stoke their collective identity, and spur them to take action.

These are not groundbreaking arguments, but they point to how the "authenticity" of workers discussed here is, in fact, future oriented. What we desire requires a transformation into a particular kind of subject. But at the same time, drawing on our concerns of authority, privilege, and top-down structures, we want workers to have this subjectivity without our direct influence. We don't want to tell them what to do or imply that their perspectives are wrong. The discomfort of the CLP project stems from this tension, where the authenticity we desire to support is something that must be built, constructed, and organized.

The second challenge stems from this understanding of and desire for the authentic leadership of frontline actors. In short, this desire is a mirage when it assumes that the "true" interests that people have are somehow in line with our own views. In reality, an individual's political orientation is contingent, dynamic, and malleable. As most of us know, we all have grievances in society and at our places of work that we *could* organize around but typically do not act on. And even when people do identify with a group or sympathize with a cause, the crystallization of individuals into a committed and mobilized group rarely happens spontaneously. Instead, it requires the work of organizers and movement actors, who weave together the raw material of grievances and social divisions with narratives that magnify those injustices, reframe them as common problems, and inspire people to take action. Movements do not simply remove barriers to participation in order to reveal authenticity—they persuade, agitate, and mobilize. This is routinely an uphill battle, as they must successfully challenge the dominant assumptions about who people are and what they deserve.

In a similar vein, collective interests are dynamic and emergent phenomena, as much the product of social movement activity as they are the spark for action. And when interests, collective identities, and solidarity are, in part, not just inputs but also *outcomes* of successful movement activity, then gauging the authenticity of an organization's attempt to represent the interests of an oppressed or marginalized group is a complex undertaking. Movement actors are not looking to sample the views of a community and then represent those views; they are looking to empower, persuade, and change those views. Had the CLP started *and ended* with the preexisting views of the workforce, they would have had to abandon their vision of direct-action unions in favor of individual gains, respect for the employer, and a disinterest in collective action or solidarity. This may have been more representative, but it would be far less political or transformative.

Rather than revealing authentic selves, movement work is therefore about contesting "popular meanings and common sense" (Smucker 2017, p. 222). In doing so, movements engage in "identity work" that aims to change how people "determine who they are, who they are not, and what political meaning they should attach to their identity" (Van Doorn, Prins, and Welschen 2013, p. 65). Social movement scholars refer to this as the politicization of collective identity, a dynamic, interpersonal, and multilevel process that rarely occurs without external influence and hinges on the successful persuasion of people by movements and organizers. Van Doorn, Prins, and Welschen argue that "whether a collective identity politicizes ultimately depends on whether group members come to share certain perceptions and interpretations of their own position as a group, its relation to other groups, and the broader social context" (2013, p. 60). In this way, movements strive to make collective identities more relevant, attach political meanings to them, and lay out convincing strategies for change. But however one describes it, the essence of the work is transformational.

The point here is not to say that staff leadership at the CLP was "displacing worker initiative," as some feared. It is simply not the case that the CLP could have engaged in a different process to more accurately represent or empower the "authentic" claims of workers when we define authenticity in terms of leftist political interests. The coupling of authenticity to a predetermined political orientation—a combination at the heart of CLP's worker-leader narrative—is a political tool whose value is its power to naturalize that orientation as legitimate. To miss this is to not only to fall prey to the strategic missteps described earlier, but also to invoke a neoliberal identity politics that assumes that one's individual identity is "evidence of some intrinsic ideological or strategic legitimacy" (Mitchell 2022). We assume that the structural power that workers have, given their relationship to the means of production, somehow makes all workers natural leaders and organically leftist at our own peril. The long history of failure of the labor movement to spark consistent and widespread mass mobilization is evidence of this.

This is the limitation of our critiques of staff-led models, the CLP included. We often want a linear story of social movement activity where a community has an organic, radical political awakening that leads them to take on the tactics, slogans, and analysis of what we feel are the best parts of the labor movement. As both leftists and outsiders to the workers' community, our suspicion of power and authority mean that we want the organizations we support to take direction from frontline communities. The notion that the relatively privileged might need to participate in efforts to *change* these groups, to get them to think and act differently, can be an anathema to values of bottom-up leadership and grassroots politics. But when we draw on false narratives of authenticity to conflate staff leadership with domination, we not only ignore the important roles that experience, training, and knowledge play in movement work but we reduce accountability by obscuring the centers of power that do exist.

Clearly, there are useful political reasons to invoke authenticity, primarily to claim legitimacy in the face of hegemonic neoliberal counter-narratives. But our analysis shouldn't reproduce this binary, given both the complexity of what effective social movement work looks like in practice and the evidence that an overreliance on the worker leadership narrative offered in this book isn't enough to win campaigns. We instead should prioritize approaches that are aimed at harnessing the skills, authority, and resources—the privilege—of those who have them aimed at developing workers and all people into liberatory political actors. As I discuss in the Conclusion, such a shift would likely require a more transparent appreciation for and application of the power and leadership of staff members, one that ultimately could provide greater mechanisms for worker leadership.

Exploring the Work of Worker Leadership

The following pages are the result of long-term ethnographic participant observation, which I later supplemented with interviews and analyses of internal records, press releases, and other organizational artifacts. The immersive style of the ethnographic method is comprised of not only what I observed in the field, but also how I experienced it, using my own reactions to the environment to understand the circulation of power and authority among the actors in this story. I entered the field with a perspective comparable to the allies who support the CLP and similar organizations, namely a belief in the presence of strong worker leadership and participation at the organization and a desire to see worker-led organizations invigorate the labor movement.

The inspiration for this project stemmed from my extensive involvement in the labor movement dating back to the early 2000s in a variety of ways, including as a union member, activist, researcher, and staff member. Over the years, I have participated with numerous organizations in these roles, often through campaigns intended to build strong partnerships between community and labor groups. Many of these initiatives aimed to bridge the gaps between worker centers, allies, and unions, with some of the most dynamic endeavors pushing the boundaries of conventional union frameworks. Interested in the innovations of worker center–union partnerships, I sought to assess what appeared to be a novel and successful model of worker leadership and its impacts on movement work in a variety of arenas.

Unsurprisingly, given the modest size of the organization, I performed many functions during my tenure, including coordinating interns and volunteers, developing strategic corporate research, managing a policy campaign, and handling internal operations. While my experience was primarily centered in the office, my work for the CLP took me to many different places—union halls, food warehouses, national strategy retreats around the country, endless conference calls, meetings with bosses, and street actions. While I started as a mainly silent listener in a wall-less office, by the end of my time I helped to make decisions and to craft strategy. I bear equal responsibility for the outcomes that I critique throughout.

As we will see, I also volunteered with the Philadelphia Labor Justice Alliance (PLJA), a grassroots ally organization, first as a member, later as the communications point person, and finally as the formal CLP representative. The PLJA became a crucial ally and partner of CLP during the FCC campaign and became a secondary site of major fieldwork (Simmons and Smith 2017). In a similar, though less regular, capacity, I acted as the CLP representative for other activist groups and local labor coalitions in Philadelphia and across the country; my experiences with these groups further contribute to my research, and my findings from these sites are reinforced by fieldwork and interviews with other labor organizations I came to know through the CLP.

At almost every point in my fieldwork, I was on my laptop actively taking notes. In most instances, I was the official notetaker for meetings. As such, the material in quotes is taken directly from my fieldnotes, official documents, or later interviews, with changes to remove identifying information or to increase the readability of spoken words. Most of this material was originally in English, save for meetings and interviews with workers, which were primarily in Spanish or, in mixed-language groups, through a translator.

This immersive component was necessary to explore the role of worker leadership in the world of the CLP. Any research design that relied on public narratives, in either interview or survey form, would have found slim purchase on which to explore the position of workers within this organization.[6] It is also important to highlight my own positionality within the organization—this research is not an objective "view from nowhere" but is a product of the temporality and spatiality of my presence in the field. I could not always be present in all campaign spaces and could only approach some parts of the story through the experiences and interpretations of other actors.

Examining the practices of the CLP from an insider perspective highlights the ambiguous nature of the worker-leader discourse. It illuminates how—absent widespread worker involvement—allies became crucial for the organization to build power in its campaigns. It demonstrates how the narrative, through its framing of historical and present campaigns as worker-led, creates a prefigurative space for workers to fill by providing stories of success and empowerment. Another world is not just possible, it is already happening! And, through long-term ethnographic immersion, it illustrates the tension between the lack of and desire for worker participation. Staffers, allies, and donors wanted to support worker-led projects, so that is what CLP offered to them and to itself.

2

The History and Organizing Model of the Clara Lemlich Project

What are the implications of the organization's historical narrative and institutional structure for the Clara Lemlich Project's (CLP) mission and its campaign at the Fishtown Condiment Company (FCC)? I begin with a discussion of the organization's history as explained to me on my first day by Emma, the staffer who would be my initial supervisor. While worker leadership is often portrayed as central to the CLP's successes, I will show the influence of allies, the structure of the low-wage economy, and the state of the labor movement in the development of organization's historical trajectory. While playing important roles, the substantive leadership of workers was far less central to the victories, growth, and overall function of the CLP than is suggested by public and insider discourse. Nonetheless, the organization developed a winning strategy that led to scores of successful campaigns against illegal labor practices at worksites across the region. This history also demonstrates the inherent tensions and challenges that nonprofit worker centers face in sustaining long-term membership growth and organizational effectiveness.

Further, in exploring the internal structures and workflows of the CLP, we will see how its nonprofit infrastructure and focus on metrics also became an effective smoke screen that distracted attention away from real problems of worker participation. The various meetings, deadlines, and measurements helped to present the image of a self-aware organization. The surprise was that even those structures that would seemingly force the issue of low worker participation to the surface were not enough to spark meaningful reflection or organizational change. As the next few chapters will demonstrate, the inability of staff members to reconcile low worker membership numbers with discussions of worker leadership and strategy was a key component to the struggles faced by the FCC campaign.

Worker Centered. Biko Koenig, Oxford University Press. © Oxford University Press (2024).
DOI: 10.1093/oso/9780197784907.003.0002

The Roots of the CLP

Sunlight explodes around me as the train makes its transition out of the tunnel. We gain altitude as the wheels screech into a turn, taking me on a journey past row homes and pizza shops, with the cluster of buildings that make up the downtown skyline looming in the background. I cannot fight the impulse to stand and look at the view of buildings and open sky, forehead bumping against the train car window. Today is my first day "in the field" at the CLP to start what I hope will be a worthwhile project. After a phone call with William, the CLP's executive director, and an in-person interview with three workers, I had received an email stating that I had been approved by the members and that the staff was ready to have me aboard. In my interview I mentioned a handful of relevant skills I'd be willing to offer in exchange for signing on as an intern to research the organization, adding that I would be happy to lick envelopes all day if that's what they needed. Laughing, William had said that he hoped they would find something more useful for me to do. On my first official day at the CLP as a research intern, I have some of the typical first-day jitters—will I fit in? What will the other staffers be like?—alongside my excitement about seeing the organization in action.

While northeast Philadelphia now has its share of new restaurants and apartment complexes, the same qualities that made the area attractive for industries a century ago remain constant, particularly in distribution where proximity to markets and infrastructure can make a difference to the bottom line. Since this is where many of the jobs are, this is also where the labor problems are. And since this is where the problems are, this is where the CLP has its office. As William described to me during our first conversation over the phone, to ensure worker leadership, the office must be close to the companies where members work and not an expensive office suite in a Center City high-rise. The train squeals to a halt and I am out the door, bounding out of the station and onto the street. Eventually, I see the corner building where the office stands, a solid four-story edifice with a corner store on the street level. Eyeing the inviting blue awning of the store, I go instead to the steel door set inside a brick archway, ringing the button marked "The CLP." At the sound of the buzzer, I first push, and then hip check the door open and step up the stairs into the off-white paint and fluorescent lighting of an office hallway. Together, the building and the hallway are utilitarian and straightforward in their design.

I cannot remember which of two office doors to use on this floor. Eventually a head pokes out from down the hall, inviting me inside. Emma welcomes me into the office with a smile and a handshake. Soft spoken, Emma is the Campaign Manager for the CLP. In this role, she leads strategic campaign planning and research, handles outreach to allies, manages interns, and runs most of the office management such as the budget and information technology. She is also the staffer who emailed me about starting my research after my initial interview. I will work mainly under Emma for the first half of my time at the CLP until she leaves the group nine months later, when I will take on many of her responsibilities. Today, she is giving me an orientation of how the group works, both its history and its future.

With a smile, Emma asks, "So how did you hear about us?" I share the handful of details I know, mainly from following them on the internet. According to their website, William and a group of workers founded the CLP to give immigrant workers a space to learn how to run their own workplace campaigns. I know they have never lost a campaign they've worked on. Together, these are the two reasons I hoped to join the organization and to study the cutting edge of the labor movement. I had also heard William speak at a labor event a few years past, where he discussed the value of worker leadership in worker center–union relationships. Across all of this, the dual refrain of worker leadership and a focus on worksite campaigns was consistent. I try to hold back my excitement, but I think it's clear to Emma that I think fairly highly of the CLP.

The Garrity Foods Campaign

Reading from a crumpled, heavily notated paper pulled from a three-ring binder, Emma walks me through the history of the organization. She explains that the CLP was born in the struggle of a labor dispute in the early 2000s at a company known as Garrity Foods. Workers, with support from labor activists and community allies, founded the CLP to help an ongoing campaign with legal, advocacy, and organizing support. The conditions at Garrity were dire—long hours without overtime pay, harassment, and discrimination against a mainly Caribbean and undocumented workforce; those workers who did complain were ignored or fired. In fact, during the initial public launch of the campaign, the owner illegally fired several workers for their participation. And while wage theft, harassment, and firing workers for speaking out are illegal, employers like Garrity Foods have an incentive to do so since the risks of enforcement are quite low. This was especially true for the undocumented and immigrant workforce at Garrity Foods.

After the company fired the workers, the campaign decided to combine a legal strategy with one focused on the customer base. As a first step, the workers filed a class action lawsuit against the company, holding a rally in front of a boutique downtown grocery store that was one of the company's most visible customers. This was an intentionally strategic decision. By informing people on the street that the store sold products "produced under illegal conditions," the goal was to push the store to stop selling Garrity Foods products until the dispute was resolved. The tactic worked—soon after the rally, the store dropped its contract with the company. Luckily, the ownership group controlled several other locations and agreed to completely drop Garrity Foods until the dispute was settled. Thus, the "supply-chain strategy" was born, where workers involved with the campaign leafleted at retail customers across the region multiple times a week for the several years as the number of buyers who agreed to the boycott steadily grew. I am genuinely surprised at the timeline, having not realized how long some of these fights could last. Garrity Foods, for their part, engaged in its own counter-campaign. In addition to illegal firings and on-site intimidation, there were countersuits, efforts to bribe workers to leave the campaign, and an attempt to bring in a company union with ties to organized crime.

The campaign continued to design high-profile and media-friendly tactics, leading to stories in the local and regional news as well as prominent blogs. But the boycott also had a wide reach, linking this public shaming in the media with the economic pain of losing multiple customers. By the end of the campaign, over forty locations had agreed to stop buying from Garrity Foods. Combined with support from other movement groups and politicians, the workers successfully convinced Garrity Foods to settle out of court for almost a half-million dollars, which included both unpaid wages and compensation for worksite intimidation. The company also signed an agreement to ensure that workers' rights were protected by following federal and state labor laws. This first victory helped to cement the CLP as an active participant in the labor movement, including attention from an early group of donors and foundations.

With the Garrity win, the CLP felt emboldened to fill the void they saw left by the mainstream labor movement to help low-wage and immigrant workers across the region. This focus placed their work in the center of our low-wage economy, where 44 percent of all workers earn low wages and 14 percent earn wages below the federal poverty line (Ross and Bateman 2019).[1] The characteristics of these jobs are worth noting. While whites constitute the largest demographic and thus hold the majority of low-wage jobs, immigrants, people of color, and women are disproportionately represented in this part of the economy (Capps et al. 2003; Entmacher et al. 2014; Martin 2015; Berube 2016). The qualities of low-wage jobs are significant in their challenges: high turnover; poor legal protection; higher instances of wage theft, harassment, and discrimination; and higher rates of injury (Cascio 2006; Garcia 2009; Leigh 2011; Cooper and Kroeger 2017; Frye 2017). And with a diminishing middle-wage segment, many low-wage workers have few opportunities for advancement (Ross and Bateman 2019). Many of these workers also have limited access to traditional forms of political representation, due either to their status as immigrants or the usual roadblocks that the non-wealthy face in securing a voice in the political arena (Bartels 2016).

Wages and income shares alone do not tell the whole story, as these numbers may imply full-time, year-round work. The structural changes to employment suggest that jobs that once offered long-term, stable positions will continue to shift toward contingent work arrangements. This rise of the "precariat" is linked to flexible employment practices typically framed as necessary to keep companies competitive (Standing 2014). Employment practices such as part-time employment, temporary work structures, independent contracting, short-term work contracts, non-compete agreements, franchising, third-party employer models, freelancing, and subcontracting all increase competition and profitability while shifting economic risk onto the backs of smaller firms and the workers themselves (Weil 2011). Current estimates indicate that these employment arrangements accounted for a shocking 94 percent of net employment growth between 2005 and 2015 (Katz and Krueger 2016). Though most of the workers involved in CLP campaigns held more traditional full-time jobs, "non-traditional" employment relationships are steadily becoming the norm, structuring how workers move through the economy.

In the free market, employers are not required to offer comfortable work, to provide opportunities for advancement, or to pay more than minimum wages. But watered-down regulations, long-standing rules that do not address the new "flexibility" of employment relationships, and limited support for enforcement set the stage for employers to engage in questionable and illegal practices. A prime focus for many worker centers that organize low-wage workers is wage theft, where employers fail to pay workers the full amount they have earned. The scale of the problem is vast—in 2012, employees recovered over $933 million through wage theft cases, and this only involves amounts that have been reported and recovered in forty-four states. Daniel Galvin puts this number in perspective: it is "more than the total amount lost in all bank, residential, convenience store, gas station, and street robberies put together" (2016, p. 327). While the full extent of violations is unknown, national estimates put the overall figure at $50 billion per year (Meixell and Eisenbrey 2014; Galvin 2016). This practice is prevalent in low-wage employment. A survey of low-wage workers in New York City, Los Angeles, and Chicago indicated that in a typical week, two-thirds of respondents experienced at least one pay violation, amounting to an average of 14 percent of their annual earnings stolen by their employers (Bernhardt et al. 2009). While some individual states have passed laws to tighten enforcement of these regulations, policies have varied widely in their effectiveness, and federal action has been limited (Galvin 2016). In such a policy vacuum, it is no surprise that issues like wage theft run rampant as it hinges on a practical incentive—more money for the employer.

While labor laws ostensibly protect all workers regardless of citizenship, immigrant workers can face some of the harshest conditions in an economy already defined by weak policy enforcement. The jobs held by immigrants are, on average, worse than those held by native-born workers, with the median earnings of foreign-born workers standing at 83 percent of that of native-born workers (U.S. Department of Labor 2017). Immigrants are concentrated in sectors with low wages, with over half of all immigrants employed in a low-wage job (Capps, Fortuny, and Fix, 2007; Passel, Cohn, and Rohal, 2015) Further, immigrants typically make lower wages regardless of the industry they work in or their seniority. Undocumented immigrants make lower wages than both documented immigrants and native-born workers, with scholars noting an 18-percent wage penalty for the undocumented, and surveys conducted by advocacy organizations show that they are three times more likely to be paid subminimum wages (Liu and Apollon 2012, Food Chain Workers Alliance 2012, Massey and Gentsch 2014). This research also indicates that immigrant workers are routinely denied opportunities for economic advancement and are passed over for promotions and raises that go to native-born white workers.

After Garrity Foods: The Organizational Growth of the CLP

Facing down this employment regime with the supply-chain strategy at its heart, the CLP notched a series of wins for workers in the sector, and Emma rattled off the victories at meat suppliers, warehouses, and beer distributors across the region. Alongside these workplace-justice campaigns were other efforts to assist low-wage immigrant workers, including programs to help with legal issues and immigration paperwork, and public policy efforts focused on greater accountability for companies engaged in illegal practices. One campaign at the Delori Company lasted almost as long as Garrity Foods, receiving a good deal of press and helping to amplify the visibility of the CLP. The supply-chain strategy at Delori successfully recruited over sixty buyers across southeastern Pennsylvania to join the boycott. All told, the organization won millions in back pay and damages for workers through legal suits and settlements across many different campaigns that fought against wage theft, harassment, and illegal termination.

During these years, the CLP was also able to scale up its resources. Starting with a small seed grant during the Garrity Foods campaign, the organizational revenue had grown to over $200,000 in the year I began at the CLP.[2] The organization further became a well-known entity in the city's movement landscape, winning social justice awards and garnering good press along the way. To access the appeal of the organization to the wider community of individual donors, one need only look to the fundraising gala that it threw every year. In its first year, the event brought in less than $3,000, but several years later they would reach a $75,000 fundraising goal for the night. While these numbers may seem high, it's important to note that they pale in comparison to labor unions and some of the larger, national worker centers with yearly budgets in the millions. Drawing from this mix of foundation grants and donations, these resources funded an office location and modest salaries for a handful of staff members.

Moving to more recent events, Emma explains to me that today the CLP has two active campaigns. The primary campaign that organizers are focused on hasn't yet gone public, and Emma wants to check with the staff before sharing the details with me. The second is an ongoing organizing drive at Finn's Distributors stemming from an earlier workplace justice campaign at the warehouse that had begun two years previously.

A group of workers had been hired through a subcontractor, one run by the company but employed in the same building as regular employees. These jobs offered lower wages and worse benefits than similar jobs directly under Finn's management. Further, workers were concerned about steps that new owners were taking to reduce their health insurance plan alongside abusive treatment by their direct supervisors. When the company refused to address these issues, a group of workers joined with the CLP to host a large march and rally where they delivered a petition to management. While the campaign did not reach the phase of city-wide leafleting and boycotts, continued engagement by the campaign led to important changes—the workers were able to have the supervisor moved, save their health care, and end the subcontractor employment arraignment.

Emma explains to me that part of the victory at Finn's Distributors included the establishment of ongoing meetings between the company president and workers, with the CLP staff acting as advisors. In having an open channel of communication, these meetings are meant to continue the process of dealing with issues at the worksite. She notes the role of these meetings in political education, leadership development, and expanding worker membership. Workers at Finn's must prepare to speak with their managers, which provides many opportunities to both receive leadership training from staff and to work in solidarity with their coworkers. The company had also recently agreed to give the CLP access to the building and to speak with workers in the break room. Emma saw this access as a crucial victory that allowed the staff to reach potential members and talk to them at the worksite.

Most importantly for Emma, however, is the opening that these meetings provide to continue organizing workers. Previously, a campaign victory marked the end of workers' membership with the CLP. Given the footprint that the CLP has been able to attain at Finn's, the power of the supply-chain strategy, and the excitement leading up to their next campaign launch, Emma remarks that the CLP is evolving beyond its traditional strategy of workplace *justice* campaigns that tended to involve fired workers and public engagement with employers using illegal practices. In a shift toward workplace *organizing* campaigns at places like Finn's Distributors, the emphasis is to not only organize workers into CLP campaigns but to train them to start and lead their own independent unions grounded in rank-and-file control and direct-action tactics.

When I ask about the genesis of this evolution and how the parts fit together, Emma begins by flipping her pages to reveal a multi-colored sheet. With the "CLP" distinctive font and color scheme, it reads:

Vision – "Sector Control"
   Our vision is an organization of workers who control the regional sector through worker-led organizing, direct action, and solidarity.

Mission – "Highly Valuable Membership Experience"
   By creating a highly valuable membership experience, our mission is to build an organization of workers who control their sector.

Gesturing to the sheet, Emma tells me that the old model is too limited. Rather than having a staff-led worker center do the heavy lifting of a campaign, she states that workers need to challenge their employers directly through a union without an organization like the CLP acting on their behalf. Most importantly, they need to do so at the worksite and in solidarity with their coworkers, using the inherent power that workers have in their relation to the means of production. Thus, the new approach of the CLP is to coach workers on how to do this. These rank-and-file–led unions will be the vehicle for workers to directly fight for better treatment, benefits at work, and ultimately worker control over the entire sector. The role of the CLP is to compliment this work, providing "advice and strategy, training on how to conduct campaigns, and resources for campaigns and legal support" to back the vision of independent worker-led unions. In practice this means that workers would join the CLP through a dues-free membership that simply involved participating in a campaign. From there they would receive the training and coaching necessary to start or join a worker-led union. As described by Emma, once successful, the realization of the vision would involve many unions all as part of a single, worker-led movement—training, litigation, and resources would be housed in the CLP, with rank-and-file unions as the heart of worker power at their jobsites.

As we wrap up, we spend the remainder of the day talking through the basics of any orientation at a new job: setting up my email and phone number, how to use the printer, and where Emma likes to go for lunch. As Emma describes it, the new, union-centric approach seems to be key to the potential of the CLP's mission and vision. It turns out I have arrived at the organization at a key turning point, where they hope to move away from the reactive workplace justice campaigns that brought them so much historical success and toward something different in the future.

Unions, Worker Centers, and the Evolution of the CLP

Reflecting on this orientation allows us to examine the story that the organization told itself and the work that this narrative performed in building an organizational identity. To understand why the CLP aimed to experiment with a novel form of unionization, we should set it in the proper context. Traditional labor unions were the historic force that set the standards for all workers in the economy; the trend has been consistently downhill since the membership peaks of 1954. The year 2023 marked the lowest figures since before the passage of the National Labor Relations Act, with only 10 percent of all workers in unions, amounting to 14.4 million total members (U.S. Bureau of Labor Statistics 2024). Between an entrenched neoliberal ideology in both parties that disregards or actively opposes union power, an economy that continually moves out of step with their legal and structural strengths, and a model that struggles to organize an increasingly low-wage and service-based workforce, unions face a tough external context.

Mirroring the discussion of workplace violations above, an important part of the story of union decline is the ability of employers to routinely flout labor laws without penalty (McQuade 2014). The data on violations is telling, where employers violated the law in 41 percent of all union elections during 2016 and 2017, illegally firing workers in 29 percent of all elections (McNicholas, et al. 2019). And when the federal government does address a violation, the legal remedies involve only posting notices about the nature of violations or rehiring of and paying lost wages to illegally fired workers. For an employee illegally fired for union activity, current statute does not allow penalties, damages, or civil suits, and in the time it can take to process a violation, workers often must move on to other jobs. Even after a successful union election, if a company refuses to negotiate a contract with a union, the power of the National Labor Relations Board is limited to simply ordering them to bargain more. As Schiffer puts it, such policies "don't sound like much because they aren't that much" (2005, p. 5). In such an environment, companies have profitable incentives to ignore labor laws that have no real teeth to avoid collective bargaining agreements (Logan 2006).

But unions themselves must share some of the blame for their own decline. Though the alarm bells have been sounding for decades, many unions have struggled to shake off risk-averse and conservative orientations and have generally fallen short in their attempts to widely organize new members. As then-AFL-CIO head Richard Trumka put it in 2013, unions have been "failing—failing miserably . . . by every critical measure" (Oswalt 2016, p. 20). Some critics tend to see traditional unions as structurally unable to escape their lot as "business unions" that merely collect dues, enforce contracts, and provide services to members (Levi 2003). In turn, the responsibility of members under business unionism is to simply pay their dues and act only when prescribed from above. Business unionism as a culture enables conservative, risk-averse strategies, and squelches labor activism in favor of the stability of contracts and peace with employers. Though leftist critics argue that rank-and-file militancy and shop-floor leadership must form the core of a successful labor movement, traditional unions—even if they shift to more worker-centric strategies—will face strong incentives to avoid the risks of direct action and may prefer to quell labor dissent (Fantasia 1988, Ness 2014, Driedger 2019). Many of these critics argue that we need to experiment with organizational forms that more directly center workers as the source of leadership, power, and legitimacy and are built to do so from the ground up.

Some have put their hope in newer structures termed *worker centers*, *community unions*, or *alt-labor organizations*. The CLP was founded as a worker center, which, unlike unions, do not formally represent workers through collective bargaining agreements. Worker centers are also generally organized as nonprofit 501(c)3s with self-appointing boards. In contrast, officers of labor unions, which are nonprofits organized as 501(c)5s, are directly elected by the union membership.[3] Instead of concentrating solely on individual worksites, worker centers typically prioritize specific geographical regions, often catering to particular types of workers and frequently emphasizing specific ethnic or racial groups (Fine 2006). And while worker centers may participate in political advocacy, legal assistance, and service provision, what sets them apart from other advocacy organizations is grassroots organizing among low-income workers. This entails aiding workers in addressing various issues at their workplaces, such as illegal termination, wage theft, discrimination, harassment, unfair hiring practices, and violations of labor laws and safety regulations. Worker centers often frame these efforts as "workplace justice campaigns," which involve significant public efforts by allied groups and activists who support workers by "naming and shaming" companies for bad workplace practices.

Although worker centers address diverse workplace concerns, the 501(c)3 nonprofit structure has important implications for campaign strategies and resource mobilization. Strategically, while unions are locked into a set of federal guidelines that structure their activities, the nonprofit form places worker centers within a different legal framework. Accordingly, worker centers cannot act as the collective bargaining agent on behalf of workers, cannot automatically collect dues from paychecks, and must be careful about the amount of political lobbying they do. But this also allows for tactical flexibility. Given that workers have the same federal protections to organize regardless of union membership—though they are often not enforced—worker centers can benefit from labor laws that protect all workers in organizing efforts even outside of union membership (Griffith 2015). Thus, when calling for strikes, secondary boycotts, community campaigns, and other confrontational actions, worker centers can face less organizational and financial risks than unions do when they engage in similar tactics (Rosenfeld 2006; Naduris-Weissman 2010; Duff 2013; Dirnbach 2019).[4]

But worker centers also face strategic limits. While workplace justice campaigns offer crucial support to low-income workers, they typically involve "hot-shops" that are characterized by illegal employment practices and where campaign victory means enforcing legal standards and punishing immoral employers rather than winning long-term, above-minimum gains (Fine 2006; Milkman & Ott 2014). Given the deterioration of state regulatory practices and the high number of violations, such campaigns are important. However, they still require long timelines and intensive resources of time and money, and having a compelling legal or moral argument does not guarantee victory. With this approach, worker centers have tended to see more success in one-time campaigns and governmental advocacy rather than growing a committed membership over time (Milkman 2014, pp. 16–17). And for many workers, the interest in membership outside of addressing acute issues remains low, creating a ceiling for worker centers that might wish to have a larger, more active membership base (Monforton and Von Bergen 2021). The conclusion for some is that the worker-center model is at its strongest when it is enforcing laws and influencing policy rather than fighting for long-term, above-minimum gains for workers (Jenkins 2002). For nationwide organizations such as The Restaurant Opportunities Centers and the National Domestic Workers Alliance, such challenges have led to the strategic abandonment of confrontational tactics at worksites in favor of policy advocacy, employer-centric, and market-based approaches (Frantz and Fernandes 2016).

The CLP historically struggled with similar challenges, where each new campaign required building a membership base from the ground up. As William, the CLP's Executive Director, later explained it to me, while the organization always had an interest in above-minimum gains, their historic strategy had been to combine worker-led public campaigns with lawsuits at hot-shop targets, classic examples of the workplace justice campaign. Calling this "CLP 1.0," William saw this earlier approach as "litigation plus settlements," where the legal side of campaigns would win back pay for workers and force the employer to agree to a code of conduct to follow labor laws. But this had its own challenges around membership:

> In that approach, membership would explode, but it would explode around campaigns. Then, no matter what their experience was, you would lose a lot of people [when the campaign ended]. [We were] basically setting ourselves up not to have an enduring membership base.

In turning their attention to the Fishtown Condiment Company, the "CLP 2.0" model aimed to combine what they saw as the most useful parts of the worker-center model with a union vision aimed at a lasting membership base of empowered, rank-and-file union members.

Partnerships between unions and worker centers are nothing new. And though the relationships between labor unions and worker centers can sometimes lead to disagreements over strategies and goals, the AFL-CIO itself has worked to provide funding and support to worker centers and bring their energy into the broader labor movement (Narro, Waheed, and Poyaoan 2015). Thus, it comes as no surprise to see union–worker center pairings across the country, such as Centro de Trabajadores Unidos en la Lucha (CTUL) and the Service Employees Industrial Union (SEIU) in Minnesota, the Warehouse Workers for Justice and the United Electrical Workers (UE) in Illinois, or Laundry Workers Center and United Steelworkers in New York (Greenhouse 2021). In fact, one of the first worker centers, the Chinese Staff and Workers Association (CSWA), formed its own independent union for restaurant workers in New York City.

As Emma noted, the heart of their union vision was rank-and-file power coupled with a strong distaste for bureaucratic or representational union models. While not completely opposed to collective bargaining agreements, a core tenet of their training was that workers should deal with workplace issues directly rather than by filing slow-moving grievances under the control of a shop steward. Contracts that used no-strike clauses or complex grievance procedures were understood to disempower the ability of the rank and file to make their demands directly to management. If there was a problem during the workday, workers should be empowered to collectively respond, as needed and in real time, to address the issue. As such, the model had little space for business agents, paid organizers, or other staff that took power out of the hands of workers. And while there was some openness to formally certifying a union through an election overseen by the National Labor Relations Board if needed, the vision of unionization offered by the CLP did not view employer recognition as necessary for legitimating the existence of a union, nor did it see a need to have a majority of workers involved for workers to fight for their demands. Similarly, there was little support to automatically take dues from workers' paychecks. Instead, committed members would voluntarily pay their dues, which would be modest due to the lack of paid staff or overhead.

While these strategic considerations played a role, the interest in this model stemmed primarily from the CLP staffers' ideological critique of business unions. Viewing the worker-center model as limited for mass mobilization, staff also saw traditional unions as complicit in weakening worker power and increasing economic precarity. They regarded the worksite as the primary site of oppression and believed that any effective model must affirm workers' collective power and prioritize their leadership. And while other approaches might secure union contracts, they overlooked the central aim of labor action—empowering workers to overcome oppression and exert control over their employers and the economy. Thus, the emphasis on worker leadership in the CLP's approach should be understood as equally ideological and strategic, as staffers were unwilling to make tactical decisions that could undermine workers' leadership in the movement.

Navigating the Relationship

The successful realization of this vision entailed CLP staff members supporting workers in initiating union campaigns and assuming leadership roles at their worksite. Once off the ground, these unions would be a vehicle for workers to assert power at work and, eventually, across the economy. And while the separation between the CLP and these unions fits into the narrative of worker leadership and business union criticism that drove the staff, it also had an important strategic role given the legal distinctions between worker centers and unions. Unions cannot receive the tax-free donations and foundation funding that are the lifeblood of most worker centers, while worker centers are barred from the revenue that stems from collecting dues through employers on behalf of a workforce. Creating distance between the two bodies was legally important, and the CLP was careful not to engage in any formal representation of workers to their employers.[5] But I should be clear that, while this served a legal end, it was primarily a political decision to embrace a structure that required workers to lead and for their unions to stand on their own.

In my initial time in the field, my understanding of the relationship between workers, the CLP, and the unions was somewhat murky. Like Emma's narration on my first day, the relationship was often discussed as one between established organizations. In reality, without a pre-existing cadre of worker-leaders there was no substantive union to speak of, having never evolved past the visioning and training phase. And while the hope was that a successful union drive at either Finn's Distributors or the FCC would change this, a worker-led union never emerged as a reality at either worksite.

There are two more complications about the history of the CLP that are worth discussing, ones that I came to better understand through conversations with allies and reviews of press releases and news stories about the early days of the organization. The first is that while many of the earlier workplace justice campaigns existed in the "CLP 1.0" framework, most were *also* attempts to incubate independent unions, turning to workplace justice organizing to win important benefits for fired workers when unionization seemed unlikely. In fact, the campaign at Garrity Foods that led to the formation of the CLP was one of several attempted union drives involving coalitions of workers and allies, some of whom would later join the CLP staff. The CLP was started, in part, to help advance legal claims in the wake of mass firings at Garrity, but the hope was that the campaign would end with a unionized workforce. But the union side of this history is mainly absent from public-facing narratives, focusing instead on problems faced by workers and the workplace justice approach of the CLP. As later chapters will show, one outcome is that many allies did not fully understand the union-related goals of the CLP.

Second, while the story presented by Emma was one primarily of organic worker leadership, the role of allies loomed large in the history of the CLP. Workers were crucial actors at Garrity Foods and CLP campaigns, and from what I could learn, they played important leadership roles. But outside organizers and activists were also essential in both organizing those workers and enacting the supply-chain strategy. This was especially true for tactics that used litigation, which required legal skills, experts, and the ability to access both. The presence of allies and non-worker organizers at Garrity Foods and other campaigns complicates narratives of a worker-founded organization running purely worker-led campaigns. Further, the supply-chain strategy of engaging the customers of the primary target did not need—nor exclusively use—workers to function successfully. As a staffer later explained it to me, you simply set up a couple of die-hard activists in front of a target, give them a box of pamphlets and enough time, and they will win the campaign. While it's challenging to run a labor campaign without *any* workers, allies were quite capable of effectively carrying out a strategy that did not require the unique power that workers have at the worksite.[6] For both the founding of the CLP and its core strategy of the supply-chain strategy, allies played important roles, providing leadership, resources, and elbow grease to campaigns.

How the CLP Worked

If the narratives of the CLP's history help to illustrate how the organization saw itself and its vision, attention to the internal workings of the organization brings attention to the logics and practices that were designed to attain that vision. On a day-to-day, infrastructural level, what did it look like to try to achieve the CLP 2.0 vision of worker-led independent unions? Much of what I learned the first few months was the product of simply being present in a small, open-plan office space without rooms or desk dividers. While I would eventually move into a larger role after my first three months, I was initially not invited to participate in staff meetings, and my interactions were mostly limited to taking direction from Emma. Nonetheless, I could overhear most of the conversations in the space, even if I missed some details, and Emma encouraged me to look through past meeting notes saved on the database. I quickly saw that while the CLP model has much in common with many grassroots activist groups, it was organized as a modern, metric-driven nonprofit organization.

The inspiration for the CLP model came from a diversity of sources. As would be expected, various handbooks and strategies from the labor movement littered both the office and strategic conversations. Additionally, books and jargon from the business world explained "How to Close a Deal," while Silicon Valley innovations were also present in processes like the "agile methodology" or the framing of the organization as a "start-up." Spliced together, the CLP approach combined the ideals and campaign tactics of the labor movement with a metric-driven approach that emphasized organizational planning and efficiency. At the heart of it appeared to be the staff's intent to build a labor organization that was highly structured and formalized, yet dynamic and responsive to both changes on the ground and opportunities to make that structure more efficient. To understand how this worked in practice, the next subsection examines how the CLP was internally organized.

Structure and Operating Areas

The CLP was divided into two departments: Program and Development. Each department consisted of two Operating Areas (OAs): "Organizing" and "Campaigning" under Program, and "Communications" and "Development" under Development. While these four OAs formed the main structure of the CLP, I saw little discussion of the two departments in my time there. Formally, Organizing was primarily concerned with workers: developing current members into leaders, bringing new members into the CLP, and helping members run their campaigns. Campaigning, where I was based, handled all other aspects of campaigns, including research, ally development, media relations, and overall strategy and tactics. If Organizing tended to look "in" toward members, then Campaigning looked "out" toward actors external to the CLP involved in each campaign. As far as I could tell, Development and Communications never functioned as separate OAs, and usually were referred to only as Development. Development generated revenue from two sources: foundation grants and individual donors. To the extent that communications played a role here, it was solely in the form of communications to and with donors or for fundraising events. Staffers in other areas typically handled campaign-specific communications on an ad-hoc basis.

While such a structure might suggest that the CLP was a large organization in need of precise job categories to coordinate staffers across projects, in fact the staff size was quite small. When I arrived, there were only five paid staffers plus Nathan, a full-time volunteer organizer. Besides William's position as executive director, Emma was the sole staffer in Campaigning. Alejandro was our Organizing lead and James the head of Development. Miriam split her time between Organizing and Development. In addition to the paid staff, I worked with Emma in the Campaigning area. Nathan mainly helped Alejandro and Miriam on organizing projects. Over the next year and a half, we usually had three to five interns working in the office and another volunteer working on website development. Of course, we would all pitch in for big phone banks around development drives such as the yearly fundraising gala, or campaign events like getting allies to turn out for public actions.

Critical Targets, Members, and Other Metrics

As discussed earlier, the vision of the CLP was one of workers exerting power at their places of work. The mission was the guide to enacting that vision: "By creating a highly valuable membership experience, our mission is to build an organization of workers who control their sector." On their own, the vision and mission can be guideposts for an organization but ultimately do not provide a tangible pathway for action. Meeting with a potential member or sending an email update to allies are both actions that fit into the mission, but to what end?

Listening in on staff meetings and reading meeting notes (and later supplemented with my own experience sitting in these meetings and preparing my own notes), I began to see the structure that staff members used to organize their work. It was heavy on metrics, jargon, and data. The overarching tools that enacted the mission were "critical targets," which were described in the following way: "Imagine it's a couple of years down the road and we have just spectacularly failed. If we ask, 'Why did we fail?' those are the critical targets." Also framed as "performance variables," the critical targets at the CLP focused the work of staff members onto specific tasks and outcomes, which were in turn used to design productivity plans for each staff member. The intent was to make the mission into a concrete set of measurable tasks, so that staff members were looking at these critical targets every day in planning their work.

Some examples will illustrate how critical targets worked in practice. A key critical target for organizers was bringing new workers into the FCC and Finn's Distributors campaigns. In designing the plan for this metric, the staff first determined what a reasonable goal would be for an entire year— how many workers could they bring into the organization as members, given the state of the campaigns and the capacity of the staff? This yearly figure was then broken down into monthly and weekly membership goals for Organizing, which in turn were used to design productivity plans with their own set of goals for each staff member: what were the daily and weekly actions that staff members could take to meet the critical target for the month and for the year? For Organizing, the most crucial campaign metrics involved tracking worker participation in the organization. Some of these were straightforward to determine: Has an organizer had a one-on-one meeting with a worker? Has the worker received a hard copy of the demands letter, and from whom? Keeping track of these metrics also helped organizers develop their productivity plans and meet their critical targets.

While bringing new members into the group is not a surprising goal for a member-based organization, this functioned alongside other critical targets in the organizing area such as retaining members, measured through meeting attendance; offering opportunities for members to take on leadership tasks, such as running a meeting, bringing a potential member to an event, or speaking with the media; and overall attendance in general meetings, which attempt to bring in "prospects," or potential members. Both the Campaign and Development OAs had critical targets as well. For its part, the Campaign OA included a formula for determining the "power asserted" by the CLP outside of the actions that members took, including emails and phone calls directed at campaign targets, attendance at events by allies and supporters, and coverage in the media.

A key part of Emma's productivity plans included "cultivating allies" and sending out campaign updates to prepare for possible actions. The Campaign area took responsibility for building groups of supporters to help with campaign work as well as for developing targets built to measure how many stores participated in a given boycott. For Development, the targets involved revenue sources—finding new foundation grants and donors as well as retaining and developing historic ones. Across the board, each critical target unfolded into subset metrics that drove the daily work of the staff.

As we will see, a particularly crucial metric was the "worker rating." Common in many labor organizations, this rating entailed assigning workers a numerical value from zero to five. "Ones" represented strong support for a campaign, mainly workers who were members of the Leadership

Committees (LCs). "Twos" were campaign supporters who did not show the dedication or regular participation of campaign leaders. "Threes" were neutral, while "fours" were workers who had expressed skepticism over the campaign, its aims, or the organization. "Fives" were reserved for workers who were actively working against the campaign, perhaps pressuring workers to not participate or informing management as to which workers are involved and to what degree. "Zeros" represented workers who had not yet been contacted by an organizer. In an ideal world, this allowed the CLP to quickly measure its support in each campaign. With a simple glance at a spreadsheet, organizers could identify which workers needed more attention to be "moved" up the ratings and which should be considered leaders who needed opportunities for leadership development.

Staff occasionally noted that a challenge of using numerical data in this context was that there was an incentive to "drive up the numbers" in ways that looked good on paper but might not reflect actual circumstances. For example, getting a member to attend three months of meetings may help critical targets on membership and member retention, but the act of attendance on its own does not win campaigns, develop members into leaders, or assure that members are experiencing the value of their membership.

During a meeting that occurred early in my time, staff members decided on the following four metrics for both the FCC and Finn's Distributors campaigns to guide their work through the sprint process: (1) the number of Leadership Committee members gained, (2) the number of first-time one-on-one meetings held with workers, (3) the number of follow-up one-on-one meetings held with workers, and (4) the number of confirmed home addresses of workers received. As William explained it, these goals helped to focus everyone's minds on the workers rather than the institution. As I overheard him state, "If we make our goal-setting worker-centric, the institution will take care of itself."

Nonprofits in the Labor Movement

The history offered by Emma highlighted the importance of worker leadership in how the organization thought about its own work. Similarly, the operations and infrastructure of the CLP illustrated a single-minded, data-focused approach to organizing—from operating areas to metrics to daily meetings, organizing workers into the CLP was the heart and soul of the work.

But attention to the strategic and tactical aspects of the CLP can underplay the crucial role of Development in the procurement of funding. Staffing was a good indicator of the importance of this, where roughly half of all paid staff time was devoted to Development. This introduces the third group outside of workers and activists who played an important role in the work of the CLP—donors and foundations. If the programmatic aspect of the CLP pushes us to reflect on the strategy of the CLP, the place of resources asks us to consider the impact of its nonprofit structure. In later chapters I will consider some of the deeper questions of representation and accountability that this brings up, but for the moment I will simply try to place the CLP in the wider debate on nonprofit movement work.

As discussed earlier, much of the excitement about worker centers stems from their strategic flexibility compared with the union model, a flexibility based in part on the nonprofit organizational model (Adler, Tapia and Turner 2014); Milkman and Ott 2014; Ness 2014. Alongside strategic considerations, the nonprofit model also changes the structure of resources. Unlike unions, whose monetary resources are constrained mainly to member dues, nonprofit worker centers typically exist on foundation grants, donations, and government funding for services with only some utilizing a nominal dues structure.[7]

While providing room for strategic innovation relative to unions, to the extent that foundations and other external actors are important resource providers, the nonprofit form can create and reproduce power relationships that place grant officers and organizational staffers above membership and mission. Nonprofit funding models can incentivize organizations to avoid confrontational dissent and perpetuate, rather than challenge, the structures and practices of modern capitalism (INCITE! 2007). Foundations—whose resources are often drawn from private wealth—do this by prioritizing certain kinds of programs and demanding specific forms of institutional practices. In her work on farmworker organizing in California, Kohl-Arenas puts it this way:

[Foundations] have promoted theoretical frameworks, institutional arrangements, and professionalized practices that constrain the work of organizers around notions of developing and integrating migrant leadership—but not to strike, organize, or challenge any aspect of agricultural production, and not to create alternatives to the predominant system. (p. 176)

Kohl-Arenas's research highlights the irony of how foundations aim to develop front-line community members as leaders only to channel their energy into neoliberal projects that are in line with elite values. Actors working in these relationships thus often have "to disguise, hide or shift priorities away from the root causes of poverty" (Kohl-Arenas 2016, p. 176). The outcome is the continued production of the "self-help myth" by foundations, which prioritize "funding individualistic programs that appear to address poverty but that in practice often avoid the root causes of the problems foundations propose to solve" (Kohl-Arenas 2016, p. 4).

By withholding funding from projects deemed too radical, direct confrontation with the causes of structural inequality are "organized out" of the debate in favor of placing responsibility on the behavior of the poor, a dynamic that has occurred among some of the largest and most well-funded worker centers (Frantz and Fernandes 2016). As Piven and Cloward put it in their canonical research on protest, "Organizations endure, in short, by abandoning their oppositional politics" (1979, p. xxi), a dynamic that seems especially powerful for organizations funded through the neoliberal logics of philanthropy.

But as Majic argues in her research on sex-worker organizations, nonprofit actors can sometimes "continue the work" of social movement based oppositional politics (2014, p. 5). This process of "resistance maintenance" requires that organizations strategically navigate the landscape of nonprofit funders and state-institutional actors in order to pursue radical social change (Majic 2014, p. 2). For worker centers specifically, Frantz and Fernandez show that some do retain oppositional political stances through a reliance on individual donors, small-scale grants, and some member dues (2016). These exceptions to the standard critique of the nonprofit model illustrate how social movement activity is more complex than visible public demonstrations and direct action, and that nonprofits can sometimes function as confrontational social movement organizations rather than disempowering charity or advocacy groups (Majic 2014).

Building on this scholarship, one conclusion of this book is that, under the right conditions, the nonprofit form need not spell the end of radical political action or ideology. By strategically navigating the institutional landscape, CLP staffers developed a funding vehicle that could advance their agenda of training workers to start rank-and-file unions among a primarily low-wage and immigrant workforce. To do so required couching their mission to donors in specific ways—deemphasizing the more confrontational parts of their mission and embracing a softer and more elite-friendly language of member-led campaigns against bad employers. These narratives emphasized the educational role of the CLP and did so in a way that highlighted the leadership and agency of workers. Such a framing is necessary in the foundation landscape where resources for direct action and organizing are limited.[8]

And yet I believe the professionalized logics of the nonprofit industrial complex did seep into the organizational culture of the CLP. For example, the "start-up" mentality often centered on finding the right metrics to guide the organization's work and address its challenges. As I discuss in Chapter 4, the real challenge during my time with the CLP was not determining what to count or how to count it, but rather how to measure complex relationships and interpret that data effectively for actionable insights.

Quantitative metrics are only as useful as the logic that underpins their measurement and the framework that informs their interpretation. For instance, one of the core goals of the FCC campaign was to move members up the member rating tracker—turning threes and fours into ones and twos. However, the interpretation of these metrics was sometimes lacking. As we will see, organizers rated workers as "ones" when they agreed to join the Leadership Committee at FCC, but there was no other mechanism for participation at the outset of the campaign outside of that Committee. Consequently, any worker attending a meeting was labeled as "one," regardless of their actual commitment or interest in assuming a leadership role. And while correctly recording a worker's rating was a topic of much discussion, at times the processes behind moving a worker up the rankings were less clear. If the ultimate goal was to cultivate worker-leaders who could run their own union campaigns, the reliance on tracking metrics sometimes overshadowed critical considerations regarding the methods for fostering this transformation. Thus, the organization's meticulous, data-driven approach frequently obscured more pertinent inquiries regarding the development of worker leadership.

As we have seen, understanding the orientation and approach of the CLP requires more than the historical narrative provided by Emma; it demands contextualizing a vision that aims to address the labor movement's failures in addressing an increasingly low-wage economy. By delving into the CLP's operational strategies and organizational evolution, from its inception as a nonprofit worker center to its transition toward union campaigns, we see the persistent tensions and hurdles encountered by worker centers in cultivating lasting membership growth and political effectiveness.

This chapter also explored the operational dynamics of the CLP, with a particular focus on the necessary work of securing funding from foundations and donors, an examination that extends beyond the organization itself to explore the broader landscape of nonprofit organizations within the labor movement. Nonprofits must navigate a delicate balance between strategic flexibility and potential co-option by external funders, and the CLP was able to remain secure in its commitment to liberatory struggle and confrontational politics. At the same time, the professionalized logics of the nonprofit industrial complex did seep into the organization's culture in important ways. As we move further into the campaign at the FCC, these historical and infrastructural dynamics will serve as an important backdrop to the mission, culture, and actions of the CLP and its staff.

3

The FCC Campaign

We now move directly into my experiences at the CLP as they prepared for the public launch of the campaign at FCC. Beginning with my attempts to recruit elected officials onto our side, we will also see an example of how staff members thought about organizing workers into the campaign. These first few months included important meetings with the Leadership Committee (LC) of workers who were nominally in charge of the campaign, as well as their initial delivery of a petition to management and the swift response from the FCC. Still in my early time with the organization, this narrative illustrates how worker leadership was understood by the staff as well as the powerful ways it was deployed with elected officials, the company, and with workers themselves. But this chapter also hints at the more problematic parts of the narrative. In conversations with the elected officials, important questions come up about the organization: how many members are there, and in what ways do they provide leadership and direction? Given the outsized importance of the LC not only for the campaign strategy but also for the ideological needs of worker leadership, why was it convened so late in the process and with such limited capacities? Later chapters aim to fully explore these questions; in this one, I lay the descriptive groundwork to illustrate how worker leadership was used in the run-up to the public launch.

The Campaign at FCC

A week after my orientation, Emma sits me down to tell me about their next campaign launch, which is set to go public in a few months "as soon as the workers are ready." Up to this point I have known that something has been in the works, but the staff wanted to get a better sense of who I was before they revealed the details. With raised eyebrows she tells me, "We're organizing the Fishtown Condiment Company." I sense she expects me to be impressed, so I try give an appropriate reaction. "Oh, wow! I guess I didn't realize they were local." Emma shakes her head and tells me she'd like me to read through the

Worker Centered. Biko Koenig, Oxford University Press. © Oxford University Press (2024).
DOI: 10.1093/oso/9780197784907.003.0003

company profile they put together over the past year to get me up to speed on the plan.

Later that day I talk with Emma about the campaign, and I am particularly curious about why the CLP is focusing on companies like the FCC. Emma explains to me that the Finn's Distribution campaign has helped the CLP understand the wider employment landscape faced by low-wage and immigrant workers. Apparently, there is some degree of a social network among these workers across different employers, so the Finn's campaign helped the CLP connect with workers at other companies.

Through the profile and campaign plan that Emma shares with me, I understand that the FCC campaign is part of a what they called the Regional Distribution Strategy, the goal of which is to organize the handful of larger companies in the city and suburbs. The focus on food warehousing and transportation was linked to the CLP's previous work in this sector, but also was a strategic choice for the evolution of the mission. The production and distribution requirements of foods branded as locally made—such as meat, pickles, seafood, hummus, baked goods, and beer—easily fit into the supply-chain strategy that had led to so much success. Furthermore, some of the packaged foods, sauces, and condiments sold under the FCC brand, which made it a favorite among grocery stores, had a limited shelf life. The perishability of these products contributed to their marketability as fresh and local. In a similar vein, the desire to market and consume locally grown and produced foods also required a short geographic supply chain.

From a labor perspective, Emma explains how this proximity between workers and customers offers two advantages for the CLP strategy. First, it allows workers to easily access customers for protest actions, something much more difficult when products are shipped from a distance. This also allows activists and supporters to engage more directly with workers and customers. Second, it reduces the possibility that employers will move production facilities to break a campaign.[1] This is especially true for companies that want to market their wares as locally produced. For nominally local companies, moving a factory overseas or to the southern states is often not an option given the nature of the products and the market.

Thus, the FCC campaign was the start of a new approach for the organization. Rather than waiting for "hot-shop" scenarios of fired employees or reports of illegal practices, the CLP was going to take a proactive approach to organizing across a clearly defined sector based on their experiences with Finn's Distribution and connections with workers throughout the industry.

The main targets all had industrial-sized facilities that dealt with products on a large scale for wholesale and retail across the city. These food factories employed not only the butchers, brewers, and bakers who directly handled the food but also the loaders, maintenance workers, and delivery drivers that kept the supply chain alive.

By the time I arrived at the CLP, organizers had already been working for months to lay the groundwork for a union drive at the FCC. The key target was their main facility in the city, only a short walk from the CLP office. The company was something of a fixture in the local food scene, successfully tapping into the growing consumer interest for handmade, locally produced food. After a small-scale start, the company grew to have accounts with grocery stores, restaurants, cafés, and wholesale buyers across the region. Their main packaging, warehouse, and distribution facility employed less than one hundred workers, including their own delivery drivers.

When I ask about the focus on FCC in particular, Emma tells me that some workers had reached out to them about problems at the company and were hoping to organize. She implies that this was through connections with Finn's Distribution workers, though she is vague on the details. Emma thinks that the visibility of the FCC's branding will help a campaign hold the company accountable to high standards and respectable treatment.

Explaining Membership

While the Finn's Distribution campaign simmers in the background, the main focus of the office is the upcoming public launch of the FCC campaign. Emma tells me that while the workers haven't picked a specific date yet, they are hoping to go public in roughly two months. Since I am attached to Emma, much of my work in helping to prepare for this launch is public-facing—drafting press releases, updating the list of journalists, preparing materials for allies, and developing a strategy for getting local elected officials to support the campaign.

Along with these tasks I help Emma with various other aspects of the launch. Like the entire staff, she is optimistic about the campaign, perhaps even excited for the fight that will occur when we take the campaign public. The campaign launch involves two steps. In the initial "soft launch," the Leadership Committee will deliver a demands letter to management that lays out their requests and asks for a meeting to discuss how to proceed. The assumption is that the company will refuse to meet, so the staff is planning a larger public action a week later. This will involve a press conference at the warehouse and a second delivery of the demands letter that will be joined with a support petition signed by allies. That day will also see a press release, the launch of the campaign website, and (hopefully) coverage in the media and signs of public support from elected officials.

The challenge is that we want to prepare for the launch without letting the FCC know that they are the target of the campaign. We work on a "save the date" email for close allies to be ready to sign the petition, but that doesn't include the specific information about the FCC, simply the date the petition will go live. This list includes long-time CLP supporters, labor groups, and other activists from around the city who would be willing to support the campaign without the details. I end up taking on the bulk of the planning around contacting elected officials. Our main focus is on those city and state representatives whose districts include the FCC worksite. The goal of the outreach is direct—William and Emma want to secure face-to-face meetings with representatives in order to talk to them about the upcoming campaign and secure their public support. When I ask how they fit into the campaign, William tells me with a "What can you do?" shrug that "the workers like it when a politician talks to the company," with the goal of encouraging management to seek dialogue with the workers. While none of us think very highly about the power of government actors in this context, this part of the strategy can be helpful if not ultimately critical.

Similar to the ally outreach, the challenge is to ask the representatives for support on a campaign whose details we are not going to divulge before the public launch. Emma points to the week between the initial demands-letter delivery and the press conference as an ideal space to try to schedule meetings. This is also the time we will make the ally petition go live. In this one-week gap, the workers will have gone public to management and we will be able to speak openly about the campaign to elected officials, but hopefully still leave a window of time for them to participate in the press conference or to issue a statement in support of the workers. If we can land meetings during that week, it should work perfectly.

In the end I secure two meetings with representatives. The first is with Greg, the chief of staff of a representative whose district includes the FCC site. Unfortunately, Greg is only able to meet before the soft launch, meaning that the campaign details are going to be kept secret.

Later that week finds Emma and me at a meeting with Greg, a tall man with an intense, focused attitude. The meeting itself goes quickly, as Greg peppers Emma with rapid-fire questions while I just focus on taking good notes. Luckily for my efforts, Emma's responses match her considered, soft-spoken nature. Seated in a small conference room, Greg is somewhat confused about who the CLP members are and what the organization hopes to accomplish.

"Are they mostly non-unionized?" Greg asks about the members, "mostly immigrant workers?"

"Yes...." Emma responds. While Emma tends to speak slowly and softly to begin with, this pause seems particularly long. "Our membership is mostly immigrant workers from Latin America."

"How about status? Are they illegal? Or, what's the word?"

"We say 'undocumented,'" Emma answers with a polite smile, "but it varies from member to member."

"And how many members do you have? How big is the organization?" Greg's brow is furrowed as he leans back in his chair.

Emma pauses, thinking. "About two hundred?"

"And what does a worker have to do to join?"

"Well...." Emma again pauses. "The workers have to join the campaign. They eventually join their own unions, but membership with the CLP is free."

"And you have won a bunch of campaigns already?"

"Yeah," says Emma, with a nod.

"So, ... is there a reason that you only have two hundred members at this point?"

Emma leans back in her chair, thinking. "It's still a small organization, and we focus on member-driven campaigns, and a lot of our focus was on these workplace justice campaigns. We recovered almost $2 million dollars, but recently we've moved onto workplace organizing campaigns."

Emma doesn't offer any details about the FCC campaign, so Greg isn't able to offer a firm commitment. Though he does indicate a willingness to help:

Well as you get closer to the date, you'll call us and let us know. Obviously, we'd be happy to help, we want workers to have a good job, and there's been lots of places around here that have screwed workers out of jobs. We can't commit anything without knowing anything," he laughs, "but we want to learn what's going on. We'd be happy to help.

On the ride back to the office I ask Emma about the membership number. Does the CLP really have two hundred members? While Greg wasn't clear why he thought the number was so low, I'm surprised it's that high, given that I rarely see workers in the office. With a smile, Emma responds that the CLP membership is not only free, but it's guaranteed for life. "That makes sense," I respond with a chuckle, though I'm not certain *how* it squares with the notion of worker leadership. The implication is that the CLP counts any worker who has ever been involved as a member in conversations like these. One of the staff members will later refer to this as a "vanity metric," since it helps the CLP look good to allies and funders but doesn't help with internal campaign goals and critical targets. But what does a vanity metric mean for worker leadership? I am not sure how the pieces fit together.

Regardless, the next week we are invited to meet with Michael, another representative in the district. In coordinating with the chief of staff, I learn that the meeting will be with Michael himself. While originally William plans to attend the meeting, the day before the meeting he asks me to go instead, and to go on my own. I balk, saying that I'm not sure what to say and that Emma should probably do it. William gives a laugh and says, "You're ready, brother!" Seeing my nervousness, Emma helps me to prep for the meeting with a set of talking points, sharing the ones she used for our meeting with Greg. Both she and William review them, coaching me on exactly how much I should share about the campaign (the sector, the general neighborhood information, and the planned launch dates) and what specifically to ask for (a public statement in support of the workers to organize). Emma tells me that, should it happen, we will ask all the elected officials to speak out against any illegal firings when the campaign goes public. This meeting is laying the ground for "the ask" that might come later.

I meet with the representative in a large conference room, where he sits at the far end, framed by a giant window looking out onto the street. An older man with a beard and glasses, he is exceptionally friendly in our conversation and seems quite open to my pitch. Reading from my laptop notes, I deliver the set of talking points that Emma helped me develop. They follow the earlier meeting with Greg closely—a brief discussion of our history with special note of the amounts of back pay we've won through campaigns, our links to other labor and progressive groups, a note about our two hundred members, and a presentation of the current campaign. Emma has me indi-cate that one of the main concerns is around healthcare costs, given Michael's interest in the topic. For the first time, I'm speaking about the CLP in a possessive sense: *our* history, and *our* goals. It feels genuine and exciting.

Michael is interested and attentive while guaranteeing nothing. Similar to Greg's response, without the details he is hesitant to commit, though he notes his general agreement to supporting low-wage and immigrant work-ers. As we wrap up, he even recommends that I look up "Songs of Freedom," a documentary about Paul Robeson that has just been released on iTunes. I shake his hand and thank him for his time as he gives me a big smile. "Good luck to you! And be in touch," he says. I return his smile, feeling that I have done an excellent job on my first independent assignment for the CLP.

On my return to the office, I jot down a few reflections in a lull between meetings. While I continue to feel like an outsider in the organization, my first two months have led to steadily, if slowly, increasing access to what the CLP does and how they do it. In trusting me to meet with Michael by myself, William and Emma have given me hope that they will bring me deeper into the organization as my responsibilities widen and I show myself to be a competent staff member. Further, I feel that it is starting to be *my* orga-nization as well: a thing that I am a part of and that I contribute to in a meaningful way. This is less a sense of ownership and more one of partici-pation and acceptance, since I know that the CLP isn't mine; it belongs to the workers.

At the same time, the growth of my knowledge about the organization has left some items less clear than when I began. While I was convincing in my presentation of the CLP membership to Michael, including the "two hundred members" figure, I am not entirely certain what to make of the membership question. How many workers *are* part of the organization, and to what degree? While the common refrain is "workers lead, the CLP fol-lows," what do workers actually do in terms of leadership and participation? At the time I note these as minor questions. Truthfully, the excitement and energy around the FCC campaign, with a public launch only weeks away, sweeps most of my concerns about my work to the side. Later, on the train toward home, I mainly feel that excitement, compounded with a sense of pride over the meeting with Michael and the trust that the CLP had in me. While I know it is one small piece of the larger story, the feeling that I am contributing something important to the workers' campaign at FCC leaves me satisfied.

How to "Close a 'One'"

While the staff has been working to confirm the specific date and time for the two actions with the workers' Leadership Committee (LC), Emma and I are busy drafting campaign emails, press releases, and tracking the RSVPs for the ally petition. Meanwhile, Alejandro, Miriam, and Nathan are continuing their work "building the LC," the committee of worker-leaders who will ultimately run the campaign. From my perspective, the energy and excitement around the campaign is palpable among the staff as the date gets closer, and the three organizers are a flurry of activity as they come and go from the office to meet workers and are constantly on their phones to schedule more meetings.

I know the immediate goal for the organizers is a crucial LC meeting that they are trying to schedule for two weeks before the soft launch. As I understand it, it is an opportunity to move a few more workers into leadership positions before the campaign goes public, when management will ostensibly learn which workers are active members. For the staff members, this means engaging with workers who were rated "two" or "three" on the worker tracking spreadsheet and working to "elevate" them into the one category reserved for campaign leaders.

I see this process of "closing a 'one,'" where organizers try to bring a worker into the LC, happen in real time one day in the office as I work on my letter drafts. Nathan, a full-time volunteer organizer, and Miriam, a staff member who splits her time between grant writing and organizing, are eating lunch on the couch, talking about a worker they want to encourage to join the LC. From my spot at the conference table, I listen in on their conversation. The worker, whose name I don't catch, has expressed some interest in the campaign but is unwilling to take a stronger position. Nathan has met with him in person and has a phone call scheduled in a few hours to "make the pitch" to join the LC. Nathan expresses his nervousness about the call and is concerned that he will say the wrong thing. Taking on the calm assurance of a mentor, Miriam offers him advice on how to manage the conversation, using a process that many organizers would find familiar. It begins by asking the worker about their frustrations and challenges at work and actively reframing these as problems that only the campaign can solve. As Miriam puts it, the CLP campaign and the worker-led union are "the only opportunity that he's going to have to get the raise that he wants."

The next step is inoculation, when Nathan can "defuse the workers' concerns about joining the campaign" while also equipping them with language designed to counteract arguments they might hear from management and anti-union workers. Miriam's examples range from abstract and historical arguments, such as "workers on their own have never won anything," to ones specifically designed to address workers' fears of losing their jobs, which includes informing them of their legal right to organize. Some she constructs to counter typical employer arguments about unions causing companies to close. For the FCC, Miriam points out the size of the recent warehouse expansion and the number of customers as well as the popularity and profitability of the company. The organizers designed these steps to provide workers with a conceptual and emotional pathway into the campaign. Finally, the "move to solutions" brings it all home and frames it through an organizational lens. A worker has problems, but the only true solution is going to be through collective action—an active group of workers who are striving together to form a labor union and win their demands from the employer. That is the sole pathway to securing higher wages, more accessible healthcare, improved treatment, and a better life.

Pep talk in hand, Nathan retreats to a corner of the office for the phone call. Everyone returns to their work, and even though I cannot hear his conversation, I silently root for Nathan to do well and I sense that everyone else is simply pretending to work while straining to listen in on the phone call. After about twenty minutes he ends the call, and Miriam stands up, asking him how it went. William also comes to the front to hear about it, as Nathan delivers the news with a big smile that the worker is going to try to come to the next LC meeting. William gives a hoot with a fist pump. "Go Nathan! That was very strong!" Nathan also brings some news—some workers are planning on "doing their own thing" and want to talk to management about their problems outside of the campaign. This worker is curious to see what these other workers want to do, and Nathan worries that the worker is not as committed to the campaign as Nathan would like, LC attendance or not. William encourages him that working on his pitch could help address this issue: "When employers have tried to push people outside of their union, to do something on their own, it's never worked." He suggests that next time, Nathan can inoculate on that point by offering up questions like, "Why do we need the union?" and "Why have workers historically sought to join them?" For the staff, the organizing process is a model for every worker at every workplace—the solution to all problems is to organize and unionize through a worker-led union.

Nathan's call marked my first opportunity to see the organizers in action, and the commentary provided by Miriam and William went far in illustrating the CLP organizing model. From what I could see, "closing a 'one'" was a process of bringing workers into the vision that underpins the political ideology and strategy of the CLP. A worker has successfully moved through the process when they have accepted that a worker-led union is the only way to address whatever problems they have at work, and that this specific model of unionization requires leadership and active mobilization on their part. At the time of this conversation, I note that this process of organizing seems to have an ambiguous relationship with worker agency. On the one hand, it posits the worker as *the* agent of change in the union, in the workplace, and in their own life. On the other hand, the process of a worker embodying that agency presupposes what workers should want and how they should go about getting it—a premise developed by non-workers.

At the time, I discount these reflections given my understanding that workers oversee the campaign and have been working behind the scenes to prepare the campaign launch. While the strategy of "building the LC" by cultivating workers into leaders seems appropriate, what I fail to see in these first months is that the LC has not actually had a single meeting by the time of this phone call, and that the staff, rather than the workers, picked the dates for the launch, a finding I develop in the next chapter. Further, there had been no formal meetings of workers to plan the campaign up to this point. Rather, organizers spoke with workers individually or in small groups, using those conversations to develop the campaign. It should be noted that the staff designed this plan intentionally through consultations with union organizers who had run historically successful contract campaigns among low-wage immigrant workers. Nonetheless, this made the upcoming LC far more important than a simple opportunity to provide leadership development, as it marked one of the last chances to get *any* workers trained to run the campaign as a group. While the tensions generated by this context will become clear in the next chapter, let us first attend to these meetings and the final days before the campaign launch.

The Leadership Committee Meetings—Preparing to Launch

The LC meeting scheduled for two weeks before the launch ends up spread over two days to accommodate the workers' varying shifts. While I was not invited to attend, I did help with some inconsequential parts of the planning, such as making sure we had food and coffee in the kitchen. Luckily, Nathan's notes for the meeting were incredibly detailed, peppered with quotes and capturing a good deal of the conversation. Between these notes and talking with the staff after both meetings, I had a sense of how the meeting progressed soon after it was held. The following section uses planning documents, notes, conversations with staff, and later interviews to reconstruct how the meeting progressed.

Both meetings shared the same agenda and had the same goals: encourage the LC to bring more workers into the campaign, make decisions about the launch, and develop the LC members into stronger individual leaders who are equipped to run their own union. Four workers attended the first meeting, and three attended the second. One of them included David, an English-speaking white worker, and this required translation from English to Spanish. Both opened with workers talking about their frustrations at FCC, naming concerns around the affordability of healthcare, a lack of raises, and "dignity on the job" related to treatment by supervisors. William followed this with welcoming remarks, in which he framed the campaign within the larger the CLP history and offered the following call to arms:

> There is no question that your campaign will be the most powerful and effective campaign in the history of the CLP. You and your fellow Leadership Committee members have undergone the most comprehensive leadership development process in the history of the CLP. The organization has done a more extensive research project on the FCC than any other company where we've launched a campaign. Finally, the CLP community of members, staff, and allies has never been stronger, larger, or more dedicated than today.

After these remarks, the meeting turned to the role of the LC. As Miriam explained it, the main work of the LC was to act as campaign leaders and to bring more workers into the campaign by developing a "list of six" workers for which each LC member was responsible for organizing. In addition, staff tasked the workers with identifying one worker on their list who had the qualities of a good LC member—someone who showed commitment, was trustworthy, and was of good character. The workers would then bring this person to the next LC meeting to help grow the core group of workers leading the campaign. Between the two meetings, this meant that the seven LC members had a goal of organizing an additional forty-two workers, of which they would invite seven to the next LC meeting, doubling the committee's size.

There was also a discussion about how the campaign would unfold moving forward, where Emma presented the campaign plan she had developed over the prior few months. It began with workers openly declaring their membership in the campaign and in their own union. From this point, she presented three phases of the campaign. First, she recommended that workers present their demands in a letter during the workday, a draft of which was prepared by the staff in advance of the meeting. The letter stated that workers are concerned with their pay, with healthcare that they cannot afford, and with treatment on the job. It asked that management agree to a meeting, with the CLP in attendance to support, to discuss these concerns and gave a one-week deadline for the company to respond. Emma also pointed out that the letter declared the workers' intent to form a union, which would offer them legal tools should there be any retaliation by the company. Assuming the company would not agree to meet, the next step would be a public press conference where workers would present the letter for a second time to management alongside an ally petition and with media members present. Assuming the company was still intransigent, the second phase of the campaign would involve leafleting at highly visible retail customers about the campaign and a wider media push to "poke holes in the company's story of itself." Finally, if the campaign were to drag on, or if workers were to face intense retaliation, Emma recommended "customer education," the supply-chain strategy where workers and activists would call for FCC customers to drop their contracts with company until the campaign was resolved.

During the meeting one of the workers asked about what might happen if the campaign lost. William assured him that his right to organize was protected under law, but that it was nonetheless a hard question to answer because the commitment of the organization was for "complete victory and nothing else." To this he added what eventually would become a slogan during the campaign: "We would rather lose everything, lose the organization, than lose a campaign."

In the discussion of the public launch, Emma recommended scheduling the public launch a week after the proposed letter delivery, giving us time to collect signatures on the ally petition and organize elected officials to attend the press conference. The workers agreed to this schedule, only recommending that the initial letter delivery be moved one day earlier to ensure that the head manager was in their office. Alejandro then offered a choice to the workers: they could do the press conference solely as the LC or try to add the base of workers who had expressed support for the campaign. The second way would involve more people but would take more time and effort in the next two weeks to prepare the other workers to be ready if the company were to resist the campaign. In both meetings, the workers preferred bringing the base into the public action, though two of the LC members expressed concerns that other workers were not ready. When the organizers recommended a target of eighteen extra workers beyond the LC to join in the public launch, one worker weighed in with, "I think it's good, but . . . I guess you guys [the staff] have a sense of how you will get those eighteen other people to be there. Do you think that's enough time to prepare them?" William responded that the staff had already had "hundreds of meetings" so that most workers knew about the campaign already, and that the LC would have "training on the best way to bring people on board to the campaign."

Both meetings ended with staff members prompting the workers about their inoculation points and reminding them that the company might target them specifically as leaders of the campaign. If they stayed together and kept their resolve, the company couldn't break them. Miriam told one group to think about how they would feel one year from now, recounting an initial meeting she had with one of the workers. She reminded the worker that he believed that conditions were finally changing because workers were no longer walking with their heads down, and that scared the company. Workers might have been afraid of getting fired, but the company was conversely afraid of them standing up and being united. At the second meeting, William reminded the workers of the power of the union model that these workers were building—the labor movement needed something new because the old way was no longer working, and these workers were on the cutting edge with their model. Workers needed to represent themselves and be willing to fight for what they believed in without staff like the CLP getting in their way.

When I later asked how the meetings had gone, the staff was positive and enthusiastic, and William told me that the campaign was looking "strong" with "extremely strong leaders." With the dates for the letter delivery and the public launch finally set, my next two weeks in the office were full as I followed up with elected officials, reached out to sign the petition, and helped Emma with the planning for the press conference. For their part, the organizers were barely in the office. I assumed that the LC was meeting regularly due to the editing I provided on the press release document, but otherwise most of the action seemed to be happening outside of the office.

The Soft Launch

Two weeks later the workers deliver the demands letter to the company, and I see a copy of it for the first time. Usually when the staff talks about the company, the language is sharp: Emma seems almost excited to "crush the company," while William talks about how workers "slave away in a dungeon" to pay for the vacation homes of the managers. Given these comments and the general hostility toward management, I'm surprised by the friendly, non-confrontational tone of the letter:

> Dear FCC,
>
> We're excited about the next chapter of the Fishtown Condiment Company. We have come together as members of the Clara Lemlich Project to respectfully request a discussion with you about how we can achieve even greater success for the company while guaranteeing that our families' futures are secure. We're incredibly proud of the products we make every day and hope you'll accept our request for dialogue in the friendly spirit it is offered.
>
> We would like to discuss:
>
> 1. Respectful Treatment from Management
> *The Fishtown Condiment Co. brand stands out for local, responsible production. Consistently respectful treatment is absolutely essential to make that promise real.*
>
> 2. A Fair System of Regular Raises
> *Predictable, reasonable raises are essential to supporting our families and maintaining a superb workforce.*
>
> 3. Health Insurance
> *Health benefits that we can access are critical to the wellbeing of our families and critical to the Fishtown Condiment Co. retaining highly-skilled workers over the long-term.*
>
> Our belief is that dialogue is always sensible. We very much hope for a positive response by this Friday. Thank you in advance.
>
> Signed by the Leadership Committee of the Fishtown Condiment Company

The letter fits neatly into the "high road" strategy that the staff designed as the first step of the campaign, though they assume that management will not respond to the letter without additional pressure from the workers. While none of the staff is present for the actual delivery, they begin to hear from workers later in the day about how the action went. Alejandro reports that five workers were present for the delivery, and that management seemed confused about who they were supposed to contact based on the text of the letter. The workers explained that they needed to call the CLP office to set up the meeting.

During this final week before the full launch, I listen to the staff as they prepare their push for the press conference while I work with Emma on media and ally outreach. The organizers are busy with two main tasks: preparing LC members for their public leadership at the press conference and getting signatures from workers for the second presentation of the demands letter. They track these actions with the usual combination of goals and metrics—out of roughly one hundred workers, the aim is to have forty total signatures on the letter by the public action and twenty workers present for the press conference. With the event scheduled for a shift break, the hope is that workers will exit the factory and join their coworkers outside. The day-of schedule includes opportunities for all LC members to have a leadership development opportunity during the action by taking on such tasks as speaking through a bullhorn, holding banners, or giving quotes to the media. The staff closely tracks these items, including the ratings of workers as they have heard more about the campaign and have had an opportunity to sign the letter.

Part of this final push involves an "outreach blitz," in which two staff members stake out the factory around the clock for three days. Emma joins Miriam, Alejandro, and Nathan to help, while I follow the routine updates of who they speak to and what happens via posts on our database. With an eye on the metrics, Miriam reminds the team to track which workers they have spoken with, who has taken a copy of the letter, and who has signed. He notes, "We can and will win over more workers and directly support our leaders if we win the war of words against the company. The way that will happen is through consistent, deliberate, and ongoing communication with the base." As I look through the daily updates and chat with the staff as they come and go from the office, the organizing blitz seems to be very effective, as the team meets with roughly seventy-five workers during that time. Multiple copies of the letter are handed out, and some workers ask for additional copies to hand to their coworkers. Though everyone is clearly tired from the long hours, the organizers fill the office with tangible excitement in anticipation of the launch.

"The Union Busting Has Begun!"

William is particularly excited about how the workers presented the letter on their own to management and has arranged for some of the members from the Finn's Distribution campaign to meet with FCC workers at the office and to lend their support. "That's the seeds of independent unionism!" he tells me, adding, "We're workers together, and they're bosses together!" Eduardo, one of the LC members, comes to the office on that Wednesday. His entrance brings the typical surge of energy into the space that happens whenever a worker pays a visit: all the staff members stop their work to give him big, warm greetings, offering congratulations on the letter delivery. With a shrug and a shy, prideful smile, he recounts telling the manager to "just pick up the phone and call us" to schedule the meeting.

Eduardo and William sit at the conference table as they discuss the campaign. Eduardo tells him that management wants to have a meeting with the workers and company lawyers but without inviting the CLP, something that Alejandro had already heard about during the blitz. William is indignant. "[They can bring their lawyers] but you don't get to meet with *your* advisors present?" Eduardo hints that some of the workers are open to that meeting, but William cuts in: "What they see is an offer to meet. What they *don't* see is a strategy to break their union. Never once has that type of meeting produced a good end." William changes his tone, growing excited. "If the letter delivery had been weak, they wouldn't have done anything! This shows that it meant something to them. Next week's march is going to be amazing. It's going to be unreal."

After Eduardo leaves, the energy in the room shifts as the staff holds a quick debrief. William is concerned that the workers might agree to meet with the company without the CLP. "[Eduardo] did really well, 90 percent. It's more than we could do on our own. But it would be great if they just drew a line in the sand and said, 'If you want to talk, call the CLP.' We need to make sure the leaders are inoculated and ready." His concerns mirror an all-staff memo he had sent to us earlier in the day, in which he emphasized that the workers' meeting with the company but without the CLP "is a very dangerous and divisive employer tactic. **We must reinoculate like crazy.** We have to deal with this message now; otherwise the press conference will seem unreasonable to threes and maybe even leaders who are still not fully convinced that the company will resist."[2] In the memo he develops an "inoculation rap" using a "problem/solution" approach. The problem is that the offer to meet is a "deceptive and classic tactic that all companies use as part of anti-worker campaigns. . . . Every CLP victory has come after negotiations led by workers with staff present in support using years of experience and training." The solution he presents is that by "firmly and without hesitation rejecting FCC's offer, they'll see that this deceptive tactic will not work and that the only way to resolve this campaign is to make real improvement and respect our membership in our organizations." The rap ends with a call to action: "Educate your co-workers about what we've discussed. . . . Stand strong and with total clarity to show the company that the only way to resolve this campaign is a real negotiation and acceptance of our membership in the CLP and our union."

With this strategy in hand, William and the organizers later discuss what the workers should do if the company continues to call for a meeting without the CLP, especially if it is a mandatory meeting held on the clock. Meetings like that are typical of anti-union campaigns, when company managers (often supported by lawyers and consultants) pressure workers to not join a union. Typically, they go to great lengths to ensure that they do not break any federal laws that make it illegal for a company to tell a worker that they cannot, or should not, join a union, though as discussed earlier, these laws are not well enforced. As such, these meetings are popular tools in the management playbook; since the meeting happens during an employee's workday, the employer controls the setting and the presentation, and since the workers are paid for their time, attendance is usually mandatory.

William recognizes that not attending such a meeting is risky but directs the staff to advise LC leaders and their "list of 6" to not attend any meetings called by management. He is also clear that if management is telling workers they are open to meet without the CLP, it's a problem for the organization's timeline: "One of our most important metrics is 'time to victory.' This kind of meeting shows that the owner isn't ready to accept the workers' demands, which just delays our victory." He implores the organizers to head this off so that we can meet the goal for winning the campaign on time. As I leave for the day, I hear William talking with Alejandro. He is surprised that there has not been any immediate pushback from the company, noting, "usually you give a punch and take a punch, but so far we haven't been hit at all!"

On the Friday before the press conference, I arrive early to the office, and only James is present. When Emma arrives later that morning, she gives me a big smile and announces, "The union busting has begun!" On Thursday, management held "forced anti-union meetings," where, as Emma puts it, the message was clear: "Wages are good, healthcare is good, don't believe the union's lies, and the CLP is terrible." As she puts her bag down, I do not completely understand why she seems excited. When I ask if she is worried about harassment or firings, she pauses and smiles. "Well, we'd just crush the company if that happened."

Later that afternoon Alejandro returns from trying to meet with workers, and he, along with William and the organizing team, discuss more of the details he heard from people in the field. All the LC members went to the meetings, with none of them taking the staff's advice to not attend. The company held two different meetings to cover workers on different shifts, and management encouraged the workers to do their own research while hinting that signing onto the letter could get them fired. They also raised the specter that a union contract could force the factory to close. After reading a statement in English, a worker was asked to read a Spanish version as well. From what Alejandro has heard, no one asked any questions in either meeting. William is initially heated in his discussion of the meeting, stating that it is illegal for the company to imply they might close the plant in the event of a contract, but he eventually starts laughing. "This is great for our campaign! Beloved company threatens to close to fight against worker's rights!"

When Nathan expresses that he is nervous for how the action is going to go on Monday, William reassures him. "Don't worry, we've got better numbers than we've ever had. We're doing great and we're going to win this!" At this time, we hope for a well-attended press conference to mark the public launch of the campaign, with hundreds of signatures on our ally petition and several attending in person to support the twenty workers who signed their names to the letter. The stage appears to be set for a dramatic launch on Monday.

4

"We're Getting Our Asses Kicked!"

As luck would have it, I am unable to attend the press conference that publicly launches the FCC campaign. I head to the office a few hours after it has wrapped up to check in with Emma about our next steps. Now that the campaign is fully public, I have a big workload, including plans for a social media campaign, media notices to send to reporters, and follow-up calls with elected officials to bring them further into the campaign. I know it is going to be a packed couple of days for the entire organization.

I open the door to the office and walk directly into a full staff meeting led by William, who stands with his palms pressed into the conference table at the front of the room. Behind him the whiteboard displays some scribbles in William's handwriting, and from the look of those scribbles the meeting has only recently started. I make eye contact with Nathan and Alejandro, who offers me a tight smile as I close the door. Miriam is at the far end of the table, leaning back and listening to William, while Emma sits with her back toward me. William offers me a quick nod, turning back to the group to finish what he was saying before I walked in. "We're getting our asses kicked!" he says, straightening up and gesturing to the whiteboard. "When you go public and your level of support goes down 80 percent, it means we're losing . . . we're losing our first real campaign. We have to be real with ourselves that the organization is not performing. If we lose FCC, we might as well close up shop."

I am completely stunned, stopping in my tracks in the middle of the room. When no one invites me to join the meeting, I step over to the couch, pulling out my laptop with the intention of doing some work. In the end I simply watch and listen to the meeting from my spot a few feet away. I jot down what William has written on the white board, which looks like a debrief of how the action went that morning. GOOD and BAD columns at the top of the board, with much more text under the second category. The GOOD notes that there was a strong ally participation on the petition and that workers took the lead in speaking at the podium and talking to media. The BAD list is much more concerning. While the organizers had a goal of fifty signatures

Worker Centered. Biko Koenig, Oxford University Press. © Oxford University Press (2024).
DOI: 10.1093/oso/9780197784907.003.0004

on the demands letter and twenty workers in attendance, only twenty ended up signing the letter and only six attended the press conference. Further, several workers went to management after the event to ask that their names be removed from the letter, though I am never able to discover the exact number that did so. The hope that workers would leave the factory and join their coworkers did not materialize, though many watched from the breakroom windows. The notes also say that the staff feels the action itself was rushed and disorganized.

As the meeting continues, it sounds to me like there were concerns among some workers that the CLP was looking to "destroy the company by driving away customers." To make matters worse, there are rumors that the company had lost a large account the very morning of the press conference. Taken together, I assume this means that the meetings the company held with the workers last week were more effective in structuring the terms of debate than we had given them credit for.

Miriam makes several sharp observations about the state of the campaign, noting that all the organizers will have to double down with their contacts to ensure that they don't pull away from the campaign in this moment of "backlash." She also points out that there was "no strong strategy for converting the energy of the blitz—or even the twenty signatures on the letter—into solid membership and a solid base. Some people who signed weren't really brought into the fold of membership." In response, William wonders if everyone should have focused more on the twenty people who signed the letter, but he offers no concrete solutions. William and Emma share their concerns that the next deadlines in the campaign plan may not be met on time, including an in-person ally mobilization and a planned social media event. Miriam pulls them back, reminding everyone that the workers must be brought back into the campaign first. "Things like the website, tweets, etcetera, don't matter if the base isn't solid."

William also calls out Alejandro and Emma for not catching these problems earlier. For Emma's role, William feels that we spent a lot of time contacting allies and activists for the public launch, including my work with elected officials. "Biko did a lot with the electeds," he says as he looks my way, then back to Emma, "but maybe Biko wasn't directed well." In the end, he notes that we did not actually get any elected officials on board and may have been wasting our time. For Alejandro his concern is directly related to turnout. "We wanted twenty workers but only had six. Why did this happen? What can we do?" There is no clear answer.

One of William's concerns is about measurement—the focus has been on the number of meetings rather than their outcomes in terms of quality and results. From my perch on the couch, I think to myself that this is a good point, though there is no discussion about what an alternative measurement might be, and I choose not to speak up given the tension in the room. Nathan offers that he would like to have a prep meeting with Miriam or Alejandro before he meets with a worker. William nods, and adds that the organizers should think about training LC members to accompany organizers in their initial meetings so that they can add a "second voice to the pitch."

With this, William turns back to the whiteboard to sketch out what the next steps are. The first is re-investing in the Leadership Committee (LC) and bringing workers back into it. He says that we need to focus on building a strong LC even if it's a smaller group than we would like, since after today we are not going to have a majority anytime soon. The plan he proposes is to "get deeper" with the existing members, hold follow-up meetings with three workers who recently joined, and plan out the next two "waves of committee recruitment." The staff identifies four new workers to bring in during these waves. The LC will become the space where this group runs the campaign, though it's not clear to me how this strategy is any different from what has been going on up to this point.

The second step William sketches out is to decide which workers the staff needs to talk to, and how to control the narrative of what happened this week when speaking to them. He directs the following frame that staff should use: the company had an opportunity to listen and to meet but instead spent their resources on hiring anti-union lawyers and holding forced meetings. The launch underscored the widespread support of the community and media for the workers' cause, while also signaling to the company that they cannot evade the campaign and must address its demands. This demonstration reinforces the effectiveness of the CLP model, revealing that the truth about the company is reaching the public. But to truly engage the company to address their demands, workers must actively engage in the campaign. This framework is in line with the problem/solution framing that William used earlier in the week and mirrors the organizing approach of channeling worker concerns into the campaign.

William continues to write on the board, narrating his outline. The next step involves Emma making sure that the newly launched campaign website is up and running, including a tightly managed set of outreach emails to encourage campaign allies to visit the website. Additionally, William wants to get an elected official to call the FCC and make a statement in support of our campaign. His frustration clearly visible, William directs Emma to call the local city councilor's office to not only request a meeting but to also make a specific ask about intervening in the campaign. Turning back to the table, William chides the whole group that they need to "wake up every day like we're trying to win this campaign!"

William lets out a sigh and turns back to the whiteboard, writing down the next topic, Worker Campaigning. "What is going to build the LC?" He brainstorms a few tactical suggestions. Another worker delegation to management, but stronger? Holding a leafleting action in the neighborhood around the worksite to generate local support? Scheduling a general meeting for all workers? The main goal, as William sees it, is to accomplish "regular, well-attended LC meetings." Miriam offers a position in favor of a general meeting for all workers, in that it "allows people who are interested in the campaign to come to the office and have an experience with their co-workers outside of the shop." She also notes that these meetings need to come first in the process. "If we have problems getting people out to a meeting, how well can we get them to a direct action?"

William writes down four different options, ranking them in order of how well they "show the power of the workers." The first could be a direct action inside the plant, such as a new delegation to management or something that occurs during a shift. The second could be a low-impact action that would occur outside of the worksite, involving workers who were off the clock, perhaps another letter delivery or a small rally. A third option could be a staff-driven media campaign, which William notes would "have permission from the workers." Finally, he proposes a general meeting for workers, with one-on-ones scheduled in advance. Miriam and Alejandro feel that the last choice seems the most likely to happen, given the current circumstances. William says they should determine goals as a soon as possible: "Always do a numerical goal sheet as soon as we start thinking to get our juices flowing. Without goals we don't learn. The general meeting is an excellent example of a place to do this."

Finally, William says that he is shaking up the hierarchy, and from now on Miriam will act as the supervisor for both Organizing and Campaigning, which includes everyone except William and James. William expects everyone to have one-on-one meetings and weekly check-ins with her, and he states that Alejandro and Emma need to discuss how to "empower the staff" to support the work that they are doing. Leaning over with both hands on the table, he tells everyone that they can't miss their work deadlines anymore. Further, to stay engaged, he directs, "Don't be late to meetings!" and do not look at your phones when you should be working "Third, we need relentless prioritization—we have to know what we need to accomplish every day." Finally, we need a "strong leadership presence" that doesn't let the structure of the organization get in the way if things aren't going right.

Straightening up, William ends the meeting with an inspiring speech about how we are on the cusp of transforming both the food and the labor movement. "What's unique about this group is its culture—we're driven by our passion and our message." He tells us that difficult moments like this are necessary for the group to "grow in its resolve," and the plan now is to turn "defeat into victory."

The meeting ends with William's words hanging in the air, as everyone quietly disperses. From my vantage point, the failure of the public launch comes as a huge shock. How could a strong, worker-led campaign, with clearly defined targets, innovative use of technology, and "great numbers" perform so poorly on the most important day of the campaign?

As an organizational insider, albeit a new one, I was stunned that the campaign launch could go so poorly. Only three days before, the staff had been touting their strong campaign metrics and the leadership of the workers. At the time, I could only chalk it up to the opposition from the company, though the anti-union meetings had not seemed particularly intense at the time. It was only sometime later, with the clarity of hindsight, campaign notes, conversations, and interviews, that I began to understand a different story about the launch. Before we move on to the later phases of the campaign, let us take a moment to explore what happened over the eleven months of organizing in the run-up to the public launch.

In the remainder of this chapter, I follow two lines of thought. The first is a deeper exploration of the FCC campaign plan, where I pay particular attention to the challenges that organizers faced in bringing workers into the LC, the aspirations of the wider Regional Distribution Strategy, and some reflections on how the campaign was pursued amid these challenges. Attention to these details offers a more complicated explanation of why worker attendance at the public launch was so poor: not only was there resistance from the company, but worker support for the campaign was never very high to begin with. While these reflections are important to understanding the outcome of the public launch, they do not fully explain why a metric-focused organization would be so caught off guard by the outcome. And while some might explain these outcomes as simply the result of poor planning, the historic successes of the CLP, the vast experience of the staff, and the care with which they developed the plan suggest otherwise. I do not think we can explain what happened in the FCC campaign in terms of staff mistakes or organizational misconduct, especially in a movement landscape where even the best resourced unions consistently lose campaigns. Planning, strategy, and data are all important parts of the story but do not tell it in full.

Thus, the second line of thought returns to the narrative of worker leadership held by staff members. Here I illustrate how their ideological commitment to this leadership provided crucial energy for staff members, was a key tool in how workers were organized, and yet obscured some of the challenges faced by the organizers. In the end, the commitment to and a desire for worker leadership on the part of the staff may have overpowered the metrics provided by campaign data.

The Practice, Strategy, and Ambition of the FCC Campaign

The CLP had struggled at the basic level of meeting workers and getting them involved in the campaign from its beginning, roughly a year before the public launch. A note from a meeting five months before the launch shows that only a few workers had joined as members at that point, no new members had been organized in that month, and it ends with an all-caps sentence: "WE NEED TO BUILD THE LC!!!" The zeros across the board for critical target outcomes were the theme throughout the initial months of the campaign, with only an occasional worker becoming a member. About three months before the launch, when I came on board, only three workers at the FCC were considered active members of the campaign. As a comparison, the Finn's Distribution campaign was in better shape owing to its successful workplace justice campaign the year before, with twelve active members, though this number did not increase, either, in the six months before I arrived.

By the staff meeting held three months before the public launch, only three FCC workers had joined the LC, and at this point the LC had not held a meeting. Like previous months, all the goals for the month were far under their targets. While meeting notes state that the organizing work saw some success in "moving workers into the campaign," there was also a concern that staff members were struggling to meet workers and needed to spend more time planning "how to reach our goals." Looking ahead to the next month, the Sprint Plan called for similar organizing targets with the aim of holding the first LC meeting by the end of that month.

The discussions coming out of the weekly Regional Distribution Strategy planning meetings help to partially explain some of the breakdown in the FCC campaign. For one, all the organizers had trouble with visiting workers at their personal residences—sometimes workers were not home, or addresses were incorrect. While the work that Emma, the interns, and I performed using public records to narrow down addresses helped to some extent, it was nonetheless difficult to find a worker at home for an unplanned meeting when you were unsure where they live. Regardless, after ten months of effort, and on the eve of the first LC meetings, only four workers were marked as LC members. This led to a staff discussion about how to ensure that the goal of the first LC meeting would be met on time: should "strong twos" be invited? Should there be a pre-LC meeting instead, or a call on current LC members to each bring a person? The staff decided to use this first meeting as an attempt to move twos into leadership. Ultimately, this first LC meeting, described above, was pushed back to two weeks before the public launch.

While the organizers struggled to find workers to attend the LC, other work on the campaign continued forward, driven by adherence to the campaign timeline. This included the work that Emma and I did to reach out to elected officials to endorse the campaign, drafting letters to FCC customers, and getting the campaign website in order, which, two weeks before the launch, was still missing worker stories and pictures. From my perspective, the work on these deadlines provides for some of the largest gaps between the performance of worker leadership and the role of the staff. At no point did I participate in any discussions that explained that these deadlines were from a staff-generated schedule or that the LC—the supposed leadership body of the campaign—had never met to make decisions about the campaign. Simply put, without a functioning LC there was no campaign infrastructure for workers to lead.

About six weeks before the soft launch, the organizing team combed through their notes to assign a rating to every worker they had met with up to that point. Through the first eleven months of the campaign, organizers had met with a total of 64 of the roughly 120 workers they knew about at the factory. Six were ranked as "ones," eight as "twos," thirty-nine as "threes," ten as "fours," and one as a "five." The remaining were rated as "zeros," as they had yet to be contacted. This didn't include workers from the factory for whom they had no contact information. If, as the CLP does, we measure "campaign support" by the sum of "ones" and "twos," this means that only fourteen workers were supporters at this point.

The Sprint Review at this time stated that "we currently have six confirmed and four pending" members of the LC. The notes illustrate that membership in the LC, and thus leadership in the campaign, was primarily measured by willingness to attend this meeting. "Pending" membership in the LC was reserved for workers who were not yet convinced they wanted to join the campaign at all, a surprisingly low bar for what was deemed worker leadership in conversation. As I observed in the office, the staff spent almost all their time building toward the success of these meetings and ensuring that they were properly planned. Not only would these be the first time that the workers had met together as a group, but a successful meeting was also critical to keeping the public campaign launch deadline on track.

As we have seen, the organizers secured commitments from enough workers to schedule the first LC meeting a few weeks before the launch. And of the eight invited workers, some still expressed concerns about the campaign or skepticism about joining. Yet in the Sprint meeting that occurred just before the first LC meeting, staff described the state of the campaign in optimistic terms: "With robust organizational support and increased solidarity, the workers will launch their campaign next month." The timing of this illustrates how the staff scheduled the launch of the campaign before workers had even held their first meeting, while at the same time performing a narrative of worker leadership in the office. In the energy around scheduling the LC meetings there was little discussion about how the worker contact targets for that month were missed by a wide margin, with an average completion rate of only about 40 percent.

Here I want to emphasize that the staff had put a great deal of time and effort into developing the campaign, including working with two prominent union consultants to help them develop the overall strategy. Two key decisions informed by this consultation stand out. First, the plan called for the accelerated timeline we see above between the first meeting of the LC and the public launch. Second, before the first meeting of the LC, organizers would not tell other workers who was involved with the campaign. Both decisions were intended to keep management from learning about the campaign and retaliating against suspected members. This logic was drawn from the consultants' successful experiences in organizing unions in the face of intense employer resistance and was considered especially sound at a company like the FCC which employs low-wage workers. It also played into concerns that one of the workers was about to be fired, which I discuss below. Going public as soon as possible was designed to protect workers from illegal termination and harassment. But while these decisions were born of best practices by longtime union organizers, those organizers came from traditional union structures rather than the direct-action vision of the CLP.

The challenge of the accelerated timeline is that it required workers to be significantly bought into the campaign by the time of that first meeting. In the FCC campaign, attendance at the later LC meetings indicates that this did not seem to be the case. While the energy coming out of the first LC meetings was high, the subsequent meeting held the following week was poorly attended. As discussed earlier, while the seven LC members were each tasked with bringing a new member, for a total of fourteen LC members, only four workers confirmed they would attend the second meeting. In the end, only two appeared. The final LC meeting, held three days before the public launch—when Miriam hoped to discuss which workers would handle which leadership tasks and prepare them for speaking to the public, also had only two members in attendance. This was on the same day that William assured the staff, "We've got better numbers than we've ever had."

The Ambition of the CLP

The CLP's own plans, documents, and later interviews with staff members show a campaign that consistently struggled to bring workers on board, an existential challenge for a worker-led organization. These struggles included the wider Regional Distribution Strategy, the industry-wide plan to organize employers across the city. My own introduction to the strategy was through the FCC research profile that Emma presented to me in my second week. While there were some hints about other targets, I was unaware of any details beyond the campaigns Finn's Distribution and the FCC. When I later looked at the notes regarding the original Strategy work plan, I saw an ambitious attempt to organize multiple shops across the sector in a single year.

Beginning with Finn's Distribution, the CLP developed plans to help workers organize LCs at three other companies over the course of two years, with plans to take a new campaign public roughly every six months. The plan included a further goal to research and begin organizing workers at several other companies in the year after these first four. Given the small size of the organization, with only one full-time and one half-time staff organizer, a plan to organize three major shops in a twelve-month timeframe seems impossible. But the organizing model of the CLP was rooted in a strong belief in the interest of workers in starting unions, the power of workers to lead campaigns, and the overall efficacy in the union model they proposed. The intent was that, after an initial group of workers were brought into the fold and staff helped develop Leadership Committees, the CLP would shift to providing support, training, and resources for workers rather than directly organizing new members as the staff moved onto the next campaign.

My review of the records shows that within only a few months the plan was already off course, with the first public campaign launch pushed back six months given an "unrealistic timeline." A month later, two of the campaigns were dropped entirely, leaving only Finn's Distribution and the FCC as active sites of organizing. The staff made this decision because workers at the other sites had either left their jobs or stopped showing any interest in starting a union at that time. In the following months, organizers worked to build the LC at the FCC, where the combination of low levels of worker interest, the strategic decision to keep the campaign secret from workers, and the inability to hold a first LC left many workers feeling as though nothing was happening in the campaign.

Pressures to Launch

In the move toward workplace union organizing and away from the CLP 1.0 model of workplace justice campaigns, the energy to support a campaign had to come from sources other than fired workers or public fury over illegal practices. This was especially true within a strategy that held off LC meetings until the last moment and kept workers separate from each other. So where did the staff find the motivation to press forward with the FCC campaign? The first source of energy was a straightforward belief in the campaign strategy, and that, regardless of low numbers, once the LC finally had its first meeting and the campaign went public, things would get back on track. With the veil of secrecy lifted, workers would gravitate into the union based on the clarity of the campaign messaging, the reputation of the CLP, the conviction of their coworkers, and a shared desire to stand up to their bosses for a better life.

The FCC as a target was also a source of campaign energy. Some staff were excited about the possibility of organizing at FCC over other companies in the sector due to the company's regional name recognition and the promise of holding a highly visible company accountable to community standards. A win at FCC would also help prove the CLP model to a wide audience, and the publicity generated at a highly visible target would help sell the model to the movement. As one staff member put it after the campaign, a victory would enable the staff to develop their economic and social capital as leaders and innovators in the labor movement. If the CLP were able to offer a new, successful vision of how to organize low-wage immigrant workers, the staff would be the author of that vision. But it would also demonstrate to other workers that they had the nascent power to not only start and run their own unions, but win.

Institutional factors also played a role in keeping the campaign alive. In later interviews, I found that staffers had some apprehensions about low membership numbers but were equally concerned about missing the internal deadline for the campaign launch at FCC. After the other Regional Distribution Strategy targets were set aside, staff felt the FCC campaign was the only company available to run a viable campaign. If this too was canceled, the CLP would have nothing to show for their efforts after an entire year of work. This would further translate as individual failures of staff members to meet critical targets and work plans. Thus, the usual high stakes and anxiety that we might expect to accompany a campaign launch were amplified by concerns of personal and organizational failure.

A staff member later told me that the decision to go public not only alleviated their anxiety surrounding the campaign but also galvanized the office as they transitioned into taking action. With the date decided, organizers could focus on the concrete goals of running the outreach blitz, getting workers to sign the letter, and preparing for the press conference. There was a sense of relief in the "no turning back" of the campaign date and how it concretized staff activity around a firm deadline with clear deliverables.

The pressure to continue the campaign also came from a response by the company. About six months before the launch, the company had caught wind that some sort of union drive was underway. In response, management had circulated a letter to all the employees with a solidly anti-organizing message, signed by the owner and founder:

Dear Employees,

We have recently learned that union officials have been visiting employees at their homes. We want you to know that we, at FCC, value our employees' privacy and have not provided any one from the union with any information about our employees. We also want you to know that you have no obligation whatsoever to talk to these officials, to listen to them, or to let them into your homes.

That being said, it is clear to us that this union has targeted FCC. If you haven't already been approached by a union official, you may soon be approached. You may be asked to sign a membership card by the union with the promise that the union will get you higher wages or better benefits, anything you want if you just sign a card.

The decision to sign or not sign a card is your decision. All we can do is urge you to find out what this union, or any union, can and cannot do for you once you sign a card. Don't fall for the promises the union officials will make. Get the facts. Make your decision an informed decision.

In the recent past, actions by this union put a very well-known company out of business, DelPenn Shipping. The employees of the company blindly followed the union's leadership, and as a result, their company is no longer around. You might ask yourself, or the union officials, what did the union promise the employees of DelPenn Shipping. If they promised the employees higher wages or better benefits, those were clearly not promises that the union lived up to.

This week we celebrate the anniversary of the opening of FCC. Over the years our biggest goal has been to provide a great place to work. We pride ourselves on providing our employees with good wages and nice working conditions. We think we have done a good job and we hope you recognize our efforts by telling the union officials that they are not needed at FCC, with their promises they cannot fulfill.

FCC Management

The letter was incorrect in terms of who was sponsoring the labor activity at FCC, as the Teamsters ran the DelPenn Shipping campaign with no involvement from the CLP. What was clear is that the FCC did not appear interested in having a union shop or union activity among its members and was willing to invoke the possibility of closing the factory in order to stop it. As I learned through later interviews with workers, some, having read the letter from management, had assumed that the Teamsters were in fact trying to start a campaign at the company and had reached out to that union to get involved.

After management released this letter, the staff became increasingly concerned that the company would fire a worker—a concern not shared to the same degree by all the organizers I spoke with. This fear put pressure on the staff to "go public soon, or drop it," but this pressure did not translate into results.

Pressure and Performance: Enacting Worker Leadership

With much of the evidence presented above drawn from the staff's own planning documents alongside conversations and interviews, it is clear that they were not oblivious to the low rates of worker participation. Further, the confidence that the public launch would signal a turning point in the campaign should not be discounted as naivety or ignorance on behalf of the staff. With a strategy designed in part by union consultants with stellar credentials, an experienced staff, and a history of successful workplace justice campaigns to draw on, it makes sense that CLP staff would remain committed to the FCC campaign. But optimism about the launch, however well placed, does not tell the whole story. And while attention to the membership numbers above helps explain why the campaign fared so poorly on the day of the launch, it does not explain why organizers were themselves shocked at the low turnout and lack of worker involvement. And if worker support was indeed low, why was the staff consistently so optimistic about worker leadership?

To understand this puzzle, we must move beyond looking at how many workers attended the LC meetings or signed the petition and move to an examination of the underlying logic at play among staff members. How did they make sense of the campaign, the place of the workers, and their own efforts? I take up these questions next by exploring the role of the worker-leader narrative in the campaign, both its internal logics and practical outcomes as articulated and enacted by staff members. Attention to this will help to illustrate how it influenced the organizational work of the CLP, leaving little room for staff to discuss campaigns outside of a powerful, worker-centric moment of grassroots mobilization. I first discuss the ideological need for staff to understand the campaign as worker-led, a need that both empowered staff to act and obscured the impacts of staff leadership. I then turn to reflect on how the narrative influenced the staff's interpretation of their own data. All told, the discourse of worker leadership was a powerful tool used to envision—and intended to enact—a novel form of unionization, but in practice it may have hamstrung the staff in their efforts to organize workers. These insights will help to set the stage for later discussions of strategy, power, and worker leadership at the CLP.

Ideological Needs and Internal Contradictions

As I discussed in Chapter 3, the commitment to worker leadership was rooted in the political values held by staff members. Not only did they hold strong critiques of advocacy organizations and business unions, but they also saw worker-led activity as more effective. This outlook was regularly framed as foundational to the organization as well as individual staff members. Further, building a strict organizational firewall between the CLP and the worker-led unions was not only consistent with this ideology but was necessary given the legal distinctions between unions and non-profits discussed earlier. But while it involved strategic elements, it is not enough to think of worker leadership at the CLP solely in terms these terms. To be a legitimate actor in this part of the labor movement meant to hold the tenet of worker leadership as a high priority, making it problematic to understand a campaign, a staff member's work plan, or an organization as something other than worker-led. Worker leadership among staff was thus performative in the deepest sense of the word—the social practices of staff members were intrinsic to the production of their own identities as allies.

This illuminates a significant inconsistency in FCC campaign, where staffers could record low membership numbers while also optimistically touting "the best numbers we've ever had" in internal conversations. In pointing out this contradiction I do not intend to single out the CLP as a special case—ideological and moral contradictions abound in the movement world as in human life more generally. This is especially so for actors who have sharp critiques of capitalism but must act within it to affect change. Rather than critiquing the existence of this contradiction, we should try to understand its logic and the work that it accomplished. Staff were genuine in their expression of worker leadership as a thing that existed in the present at the same time as they worked toward that leadership as a goal for the future. Yes, this is a contradiction, but a useful one that served many purposes. It enabled staff to understand their work as politically legitimate, it provided the pathway for tactical flexibility as the campaign struggled, and it facilitated the beliefs that the model both would prevail in the future and was successful in the present.

Returning to the first LC meeting offers a helpful example of how the narrative operated with staff. Whereas I had assumed that my presence in the office would provide access to conversations about the "real" state of the campaign, this was complicated by the ongoing narrative of worker leadership and participation on the part of staff members. What I failed to realize at the time was that the LC meetings held a month before the launch were the *first time* that workers had met together. Of course, this was part of the overall campaign strategy. But based on how staff had discussed the LC as something that already existed and was actively providing leadership, my assumption was that the first meeting was one in a long line of moments where workers were making decisions and planning the campaign. For example, in the process of scheduling the press conference, the staff would frame it to allies, to myself, and to each other with language such as "the LC hasn't decided on the date yet," or "the workers are still thinking about what the best date will be." Technically, this was true. But at the time, there was no LC in functional terms, and "the workers" as an organized group capable of making decisions as such were an abstraction. These phrases could be better thought of as intra-staff performances that both reinforced the ideological commitment to worker leadership while prefiguring what the organized, worker-led campaign would look like once it got up to speed. And, to be exceedingly clear, even the realization of the details of these meetings did not change my own orientation about worker leadership in the campaign.

Beyond this particular example, the performance of worker leadership was crucial in a campaign with little evidence of workers taking an active part in the decision-making processes. The internal structure of the CLP, the rank-and-file–led model of the union, the development of the Regional Distribution Strategy, the choice of the FCC as a target, the campaign tactics and deadlines—all of these pieces were developed by staff members with minimal worker input. The instances of actual worker participation that staff members held up as worker leadership were in fact highly structured moments that were based on decisions made by the staff without workers. This occurred in several ways. First, there were instances where the staff would present workers with a recommendation for action, such as the date to go public. Not surprisingly, workers agreed to this date, though they did decide to move it one day earlier. Similarly, staff members would offer workers a choice between a set of options, such as to go public with only the LC or to invite the base to the press conference. A similar option was given in dealing with having a public figure reach out to the FCC, either a politician or a popular grocery store. In these examples, the action itself and the choices presented are determined in advance by staff members who also provide the structure for thinking through the trade-offs between the options. None of these are examples of substantive worker leadership. I observed a similar dynamic in a meeting between Finn's Distribution workers and management, where staff characterized strong worker leaders as those who followed the recommendations of staffers. In these cases, staff members have a clear proposal of which choice to make—proposals that are tactically sound and informed by the staff's rich knowledge of campaign strategy—and the workers tend to go along. That workers made a choice is presented, however, as evidence of worker leadership under which the LC decides when and how to go public with the staff acting as mere advisors.

Let me hasten to add that I do not believe these practices are problematic as such. It would be unfair to expect a worker who has no experience in the labor movement to be able to navigate the design of a campaign without the help and recommendations of experienced organizers. In fact, staff organizers take on explicit leadership roles in most traditional union drives, even those that aim to center workers within a campaign. The CLP itself hoped to one day only provide training and support to robust LCs and unions that would function as self-determining groups of workers. My interest in this dynamic is not to condemn but to examine the impact that these commitments had on the campaign and the organization. To do so requires exploring its failure to galvanize the workers at the FCC alongside the lack of reflection on the part of the staff about this performance in practice.

Part of this dynamic can be understood in prefigurative terms, where the CLP offered workers a rank-and-file–led model of unionization that reflected not only their political commitments but also their vision for the future. But we typically call movements prefigurative when they have developed a concrete, working example of the future they are working toward, such as the Black Panther Party's free-breakfast program or the Occupy

Wall Street general assemblies. Given the lack of worker leadership at the CLP, its prefigurative aims were mostly rhetorical, what we might think of as *representative* or *declarative* speech acts (Austin 1975, Searle 1975). Such utterances illustrate how the speaker believes the world to work, such as William's insistence that "workers lead, and the CLP follows." But we must complicate these "statements of fact" with their simultaneous existence as goals to be achieved. In many ways, such speech acts were attempts by staff to will a particular world into existence. They were creative endeavors that aimed to make space for workers to experience new ways of thinking and being, laying out a pathway for workers to reconsider their place in society while alleviating the tension that staff experienced from the reality of their leadership roles. And while the staff struggled to fully enact this vision, it would be incorrect to explain the narrative as pure fiction or as an ideology that runs counter to reality, as that "reality" is itself structured by the creative energy of the dominant ideological frame of capitalism. When workers articulated their respect for their employers or their aversion to labor conflict, it was not necessarily an expression of the "truth" in opposition to the "false" goals of the worker leadership—workers develop pro-employer positions within the ideological structure of capitalist relations.

The power of the worker-leader narrative enabled the staff to navigate the struggles of the FCC campaign, simultaneously asserting worker leadership while working toward it as a goal. One practical problem this solved is that the depth of the staff's political commitments left little direction for how the organization should function without worker support. In fact, their commitment to worker leadership foreclosed the possibility of the CLP existing as an explicitly staff-led enterprise, instead casting staff members as trusted advisors or mentors who take their cues from the membership. In doing so, it smoothed over the ambiguous nature of leadership within the campaign, within which the power of staff members to frame the entire project—including their desires of proper worker behavior—was obscured and rendered apolitical.

If we return to the FCC campaign plan specifically, there is a surprising lack of tactics that utilize the economic power that workers have in relation to the means of production. Of the sixteen possible tactics designed for the campaign, only one—a one-day strike—placed the workers and their union at the center of power. All other options, from the mild tactics of social media campaigns and press conferences to the top-rated tactics of secondary boycotts and holding demonstrations at the homes of managers, required only some degree of worker participation and are not based in the unique power of the workers themselves. Drawing instead on the historic success of the supply-chain strategy, these tactics stem from the associational power of campaign allies to use their public voice to hold companies accountable to legal and ethical standards. Of course, the CLP would have preferred to have an organized workforce capable of shutting down a plant without *any* help from allies, and ally tactics do help to insulate vulnerable workers from termination and harassment. But for a radical, worker-led model, the campaign plan expected very little of the workers and their union except to participate and lend their legitimacy to tactics outside of the workplace. This speaks to the ongoing conflation of staff and non-worker activity with that of worker leadership.

Further, the strategy of keeping the campaign secret does not sit easily within a frame of worker leadership. Again, this decision was developed in consultation with union organizers who had found it to be a successful and powerful strategy: Build the LC in secret, have a public launch after the second or third meeting, and prevent the company from retaliating before the campaign has gotten started. But the union consultants had developed this strategy in a very different context from that of the FCC campaign, one where the goal was to quickly organize workers as a company was in the process of being sold to ensure that the new owner would face an already-organized workforce. Further, the goals of these campaigns were to pressure companies to agree to majority card checks and contracts with workers represented by a traditional union, all supported by union organizers, researchers, lawyers, and other staff. This approach was not in line with the model of unionization that the CLP staff attempted to train workers to build. Regardless, the decision to keep the campaign secret from workers made the campaign staff-centric. One can only frame this as worker-led from within the strict ideology of worker leadership.

Thus, we return to the central contradiction of the worker-leader discourse and its more nebulous effects. In the absence of functional worker leadership, staff initiative took the place of concrete worker direction. In practice, this collapsed the distinction between the voices of workers and staff—staff members articulated what they believed workers would want, what would be best for them, or what they assessed was best for the goal of worker leadership. As a normative commitment that dictated how the organization ought to behave, it encouraged staff members to frame moments of staff leadership as worker leadership. This was grounded in critiques of business unions and top-down campaigns, which frames staff leadership not only as an undesirable quality but as *the core reason* that the labor movement was in shambles. Thus, the ethical and political claims of the narrative were tightly woven into the norms and practices that it generated. There simply wasn't conceptual room nor communicative space for committed staffers to discuss their work outside of worker leadership.

The Place of Metrics

The metrics that the organization collected and interpreted were a key part of the CLP's organizational culture, often framed as a search for the right quantitative metrics to guide the work of the organization and solve the problems that they faced. Exploring the subjectivity of these metrics, and how worker leadership informed how staff collected and understood the information, helps explain why a data-focused staff would nonetheless be surprised by the outcome of the campaign launch. One example was the problem of "membership churn," where workers would join the CLP but not stick around long enough to be developed into union founders. The data held by staffers noted that when members churned, they typically did so after their first meeting. Here, a staffer explains the role of data in how they considered the problem:

> The major leakage in the member journey is right after they sign up. So, what I came up with is a set of experiments to score. If that's where the major leakage is, what are the things that are going to keep members from churning? A better orientation? A buddy system with senior members? Is it the messaging? Are we signing people too quickly? The data gives you a "This is what I expect to do" line in the sand, which allows you to know what moves the line and is actually valuable. If we do experiment X over time Y, will it decrease churn by one-sixth? I set a line in the sand, this is what I expect, then you do the one easy experiment, then an assessment of that experiment, so once we know that, we can say some strong things about what works.

This style of logic was at play throughout the CLP's approach to data—so long as the staff can figure out the right things to count, staff could test different options to determine the best outcomes. The quantitative critical targets of worker one-on-ones, follow-up conversations, and committee membership (among others) were important guidelines for understanding the efficacy of organizers and the general state of the campaign. I also saw the desire for clear data in how meticulously staff members tracked worker ratings. As in the discussion of member churn above, the sense was that the right data measured in the right way would help staffers execute their organizing plans. And though the organization struggled to bring in workers, it was not my sense that it was due to bad data.

The challenge that came up over the course of my time with the CLP was not what to count but how to navigate the complex, subjective, and qualitative goals that formed the core of their vision and mission. How would one assess a better orientation from a worse one? What about a buddy system would address member churn? What was missing from the attention to metrics were serious reflections about the assumptions at play in what was measured and, more importantly, how it was interpreted. The energy around the outreach blitz that occurred between the letter delivery and the press conference is a good example of how this played out in the campaign.

With an around-the-clock coverage of the worksite over the course of several days, the staff kept detailed notes about who they spoke with during their attempts to secure more signatures for the second letter delivery. During the blitz the positivity and excitement in the office was high, even considering the long and early-morning hours required across the board. As William noted on the final day, while he expected the momentum to shift to management after the first letter delivery, "your [the staff's] push and the leaders' push was so determined that the ball still moved forward!" We all thought of the blitz—which led to several new worker contacts and letter signatures—as a tangible victory and a clear step to a well-attended public launch the following week.

Yet, a close examination of the details of the blitz does not leave much room for excitement. Of roughly seventy-five interactions with workers—some of whom staff members spoke with for the first time and many only for the second—less than ten involved workers who were interested in signing the letter or learning more about the campaign. About half of those ten were workers already tapped to join the LC. Of the remainder, about forty-four interactions were neutral, involving workers taking a copy of the letter or asking for more information, but neither offering a signature nor holding extended conversations with organizers. The last group of about twenty-three interactions was negative, with workers refusing to take a copy of the letter or declining to speak with the organizers. The worker tracking information reflected these numbers, as only a single worker became a "one" and three workers became "twos," while three workers each became "fours" and "fives" and nine new workers were added to the ranking of "three."

Further, while the overarching goal of the blitz was to lay the groundwork for a worker-led union with strong membership, this was measured primarily through signatures on the letter. In the first instance, the goal was fifty signatures, a number that required a sizable proportion of workers rated as "zeros," "threes," "fours," and "fives" to sign beyond the seven LC members. Organizers directed the LC members to get their "group of six" to sign onto the letter, and the main goal of the blitz was to gather more signatures. That organizers only obtained twenty signatures—and some of the workers reneged on their signatures after the launch—shows that the process of developing campaign support had been flipped on its head. Whereas in an ideal scenario, the established commitment of a worker would translate into the act of signing the letter, staff members seemed to conflate the signing itself as a commitment to the campaign. In the campaign debrief, Miriam was explicit about this problem, noting that signing a letter did not, on its own, translate into real membership or support for the organization. But this was only clear in hindsight and did not lead to reflections about how to build "real membership."

This approach to metrics, and the tactics such as organizing the LC and the letter blitz, focused on the inputs and outputs of campaign tasks without much discussion of the underlying processes of worker politicization. Signing a letter or attending a meeting does signal some degree of commitment or interest in a campaign. But what does it mean to be an LC member or a "real" worker-leader? What does it take to turn a "three" into a "one"? Neither of these is easy to assess or to accomplish. In the FCC campaign, staff assigned "ones" to those workers who attended meetings, regardless of their opinions about the campaign or their interest in becoming organizers. In the end, these metrics did not help staff understand which workers were the leaders they wanted.

This chapter has been mainly retrospective, drawing on later conversations and interviews I held with staffers and a review of the campaign data I conducted at the end of my fieldwork. In practice, there was little room to reflect on these issues within the organization in real time. As we will continue to see, staff members would eventually acknowledge the lack of worker support, but it was not on the tip of their tongues. The debrief after the launch was an example of the dilemma—it was clear that "we [were] getting our asses kicked" and that it had something to do with a lack of worker involvement. But there was no deeper reflection on the overall model or the role of worker leadership in the campaign, and the discussion of solutions was thin. Organizers needed to "get deeper" with the base and needed a new strategy for "identifying leaders" and "moving them along." In the next chapters I examine the details of what these shifts looked like. But for the most part, the message was to stay the course, ending with a celebration of the CLP culture for its "passion and resolve."

Given the strength of their convictions, why would we expect any different? William's admonishment that it was "better to lose the CLP than to lose the campaign" echoed a deep commitment to a particular vision of worker organizing that no amount of failure could shake. As staff members continued to enact the rhetoric of worker leadership, the CLP continued to pursue the campaign in the same manner in which it had begun. Over the next few months, the campaign continued to slide, with active membership falling to a single worker six months after the launch, one who would soon quit their job. At the same time, the CLP was nonetheless able to turn "defeat into victory," or a victory of sorts. While still struggling to organize workers, the CLP leveraged the notion of worker leadership to convince the FCC to attend a meeting by organizing actors outside of the workplace. I continue this story in the next chapter.

5

Performing Worker Leadership

The month after the public launch at FCC would bring two important changes to the dynamics of my experience in the field, changes that would pull me deeper into the discourse of worker leadership. First, though I remained unpaid, I was promoted to Campaign Associate with a corresponding increase in organizational responsibility and access. Second, I soon found my time split between two organizations, the CLP and the Philadelphia Labor Justice Alliance (PLJA). In the remainder of this volume, I continue the story of the FCC campaign from these two vantage points.

My promotion to Campaign Associate expanded my understanding of the organization, affording me a seat at the table in staff meetings and planning conversations as my responsibilities grew. Over several months, the mechanics of worker leadership in the organization became clearer to me as I was able to observe how staff members negotiated low levels of worker support. From the distance generated by time away from the field, this seems like an easy dynamic to explore. When staff members reported low numbers of worker support and then immediately shifted to a narrative of worker-leadership, the assumption might be that they were knowingly deceiving each other or intentionally performing an onstage discussion that obfuscates some other truth that they "really knew." In practice, this distinction was not so simple. In the office and in later interviews, we continued to engage with both positions regardless of their apparent contradictions. The foundation of this dynamic lies in the role played by the worker-leader discourse in shaping the connection between truth claims and political identity, rooted in the vision that the discourse presents of the world. Just as nationalist discourses create narratives of patriotic righteousness and democratic discourses ones of equity and fairness, the truth claims generated by the worker-leader discourse framed the practices of staff members as worker-led.

This allowed staff members—myself included—to hold onto the vision of worker leadership even when it was functionally absent. We filled this

Worker Centered. Biko Koenig, Oxford University Press. © Oxford University Press (2024).
DOI: 10.1093/oso/9780197784907.003.0005

void with our own conceptions of what worker leadership would look like and what we believed workers would want, or, more accurately, what we as staff members wanted workers to want. In practice, there was no conceptual room to imagine workers who did not espouse the vision of bottom-up worksite control, militant unionism, and an aggressive desire to "fight the boss at work, everyday" as leaders. At the same time, the exaltation of worker leadership meant that campaign failures were never the fault of workers. Instead, blame was cast at either the counter-campaign of the company or the inefficacy of the staff.

My own experience illustrates the practices of the discourse. During my initial months as Campaign Associate, I too heard the numbers on worker leadership, and I too understood the campaign as worker-led. I held these positions in an unreflective manner during the course of my time with the organization, caught up in the day-to-day work of the campaign and the consistent narrative of worker leadership. During this time, my responsibilities expanded to include managing the relationship between the CLP and the PLJA. It was here that I actively deployed the performance of worker leadership in a routine and consistent way. Only upon later reflection would I realize that when I told the PLJA that I would "check with the workers" I was simply getting direction from William, Emma, or Miriam. In turn, they would consult the staff-written campaign plan or their own assessment of what workers "were ready for." When I presented information to PLJA members, I would frame the workers as the authors of the campaign. Taken together, my practices constructed the truth of worker leadership in the campaign while I simultaneously constructed my own political identity as a labor radical.

In this chapter, I show that while the CLP staff struggled to motivate and organize workers, they concurrently recruited the PLJA into the campaign with an eye toward leveraging additional power against the company. As I describe herein, this collaboration was part of an ongoing relationship between the two groups and was enabled by the PLJA's desire to lend support to a worker-led campaign. Examining how the PLJA came to be involved in the campaign allows us to explore the practices of worker leadership among CLP staffers, PLJA members, and workers themselves. Taken together, these two threads allow me to consider the logic and impacts of the worker-leader discourse among and between these different groups.

The Philadelphia Labor Justice Alliance

I began volunteering with the PLJA, a grassroots organization made up of progressive union members and labor activists from around the city, around the same time as I had begun my research with the CLP. By the time I joined, it touted only a handful of members who regularly attended meetings, but its wide support among labor allies was illustrated in an impressive history of mobilizing people to support strikes, workplace justice campaigns, and various progressive causes in the region. The first PLJA meeting I attended was characteristic of this regular business of the organization. Their work on different labor campaigns involved tasks that would be familiar to many activist groups—signing petitions, sending members with the PLJA banner to protests and events, and lobbying local politicians.

In that first meeting I was also surprised to see Emma in attendance acting as the representative from the CLP. Afterward, she explained how the PLJA and the CLP already had something of a working relationship. When the Alliance was first forming, the CLP was engaged in the drawn-out campaign with Delori Food Supply discussed in chapter 2, where workers had been fired for speaking out about unpaid overtime and harassment by management. While CLP staff, allies, and members had been leafleting outside of grocery stores calling for a Delori boycott, they had struggled to find any success. Emma heard about the new PLJA and asked them to join the campaign, and with their help convinced the first store to drop their Delori contract, which reinvigorated the campaign. After two years and many successful boycotts, the relationship between the two groups was solidified. Over the next several years, the PLJA became a staunch supporter of the CLP.

Not only did my first meeting illustrate the work of the PLJA and its ongoing relationship with the CLP, but it also led to me taking on the role of Communications Coordinator, in which I would be responsible for managing the email and taking notes for our meetings. As I began dealing with the communications for the PLJA over my first few months, it became a regular occurrence to share a notice about a protest or a petition. "The Coalition of Immokalee Workers has as a National Day of Action at the Wendy's restaurant near the hospital, can anyone attend?" "The National Domestic Workers Alliance is having a fundraiser for its Domestic Worker Bill of Rights Campaign. Is anyone interested in going? We could buy a block of tickets as a PLJA, please email Megan if you're considering attending."

Across all these events, a small group of activists were able to use the cache of the PLJA to punch above their weight. Given that, at the time, there was no particular campaign that occupied the Alliance's time, one item that was clear to me early on was a desire from the group to do something more meaningful than pass information around and send members to events. Indeed, even in that first meeting we discussed ways to formalize our relationships with labor groups and to think creatively about how to support workers. As my luck would have it, these conversations would lead my two field sites to overlap in some significant ways.

Bringing the CLP and the PLJA together

Soon after the public launch of the FCC campaign, I am back in south Philadelphia for the next PLJA monthly meeting. With three months of meetings and a handful of political actions with the alliance under my belt, I feel a real sense of belonging in the meeting. I take a seat and open my laptop to take notes as Susan kicks us off with a discussion of the FCC launch from a few weeks past. She notes that, in the wake of such a successful press conference at the public launch, the CLP has asked us to consider getting more involved with the campaign, and she then looks to me for an update about where we might be going.

Earlier in the day, Emma and I decided that we could get by with only one of us attending the meeting, and I volunteered. Since it would be my first time representing the CLP in public, Emma helped me with my talking points, giving me specific instructions about what to report about the campaign and the "ask" for the PLJA moving forward. While I am still shocked from the failure of the public launch, the staff has been a flurry of activity in the recent days following the public launch. From what I can surmise, the outreach and engagement with workers must be quickly bringing the campaign back on track, and I trust that everyone knows what they are doing. For the time being, I feel inspired by Emma's request to represent the workers at the PLJA meeting and understand how crucial that group's help could be in winning the campaign.

Reading from my prepared notes, I confirm Susan's point that the day was a resounding success for the workers. "The FCC workers felt the power of the community behind them and know that they are on a path to improving the conditions at their jobs." For the next stage of the campaign, I share that the workers are asking the PLJA to join in the social media campaign, and I also explain that the workers would like the PLJA to think about how the Alliance could take a more public stance in support of the campaign, including ideas like releasing a public support letter or holding an event. While there is much to discuss, the Alliance likes the idea of doing something with more intention. As we finish the CLP business, Susan states that she is going to plan a small meeting with William and anyone else from the PLJA who might be interested in order to discuss next steps for the two groups to work together. While other people nod in support, I am the only one to volunteer to attend.

And with that we move on to the rest of the crowded agenda. Though the meeting runs well over two hours, the number of events makes the time move quickly. Everyone has something to discuss, from arrests at the recent Walmart action, to plans for the PLJA's annual member celebration, to our potential membership with a local chapter of a national network of labor organizations.

Two weeks later finds William, Susan, and me meeting up to discuss how the PLJA might work more closely with the CLP on the FCC campaign. We decide that a committee of the Alliance could focus specifically on the FCC campaign, and that another press conference, one organized by the Alliance with allies and organizations vocally offering their support of the campaign, could kick off the partnership. Together, we decide that the next step should be a meeting between this committee and the FCC worker Leadership Committee, to hash out what the relationship should look like moving forward. As we clink our beer glasses, I wonder aloud about the possibilities of a bottom-up, member-led consumer group working together with a similarly bottom-up, worker-led labor group.

The Promotion

The excitement I feel coming out of the meeting with William and Susan, and the formal decision by the PLJA to start an FCC committee, is tempered by the two months it takes to schedule a meeting between the committee and the workers. I anticipated that it would be a high priority, given the concerns coming in the wake of the public launch and William's interest in the press conference as a tactic. While I try to keep it on the agenda in my discussions with Miriam and Emma, at this time I just assume that the workers have more important issues going on. At the same time, the end of my six-month commitment to the group is coming up soon, and I feel like I have little to show for it in terms of my own research or the impact of my help on the campaigns.

One day, both Miriam and Emma approach me while I work, and Miriam asks me if I am free to go to lunch so that we could all have a "conversation about your role here." While I agree with a smile, my heart rate jumps. Was I being asked to leave? Over lunch, it quickly becomes clear how wrong I am. As the three of us sit in the rear sunroom of a trendy cafe, Miriam offers me formal praise for my "hard work" and "commitment to the campaign." As she says this, Emma hands me a sheet of paper with a slight smile. Rather than being shown the door, I have been promoted to the position of "Campaign Associate," under Emma as Campaign Director. The sheet outlines my formal responsibilities, mainly the strategic research and campaign planning I am already doing. I will also be taking over more responsibility with the interns. Emma tells me that even though I am an unpaid volunteer, the formal title will make it easier for me to represent the CLP.

For the rest of the meal, I try to engage with Miriam about her background and her perspective, since this is the first time we have had the opportunity to talk outside of a staff meeting. When I ask her how the campaign is going from the organizing perspective, she offers a blunt "stagnant" with no follow up. Even with Miriam's reticence to share, the promotion is a breath of fresh air. Part of my new responsibilities involve attending the weekly Regional Distribution Strategy (RDS) meetings as notetaker and having more one-on-one meetings with Miriam and Alejandro to ensure that all the staff is working in concert. As I ramble on about my excitement and surprise to Miriam and Emma, I silently decide to extend my fieldwork to see where this new position might take me.

In the end, my new role led to a ten-month extension of my time with the organization. The promotion marked a critical turning point in my experience at the CLP, as my increased participation with staff members and within the organizational infrastructure allowed me a wider perspective into the ebb and flow of the campaigns and how the staff members interpreted those changes. This access was especially crucial in the weekly RDS meetings, where staff members would discuss most of the important campaign items. As I began experiencing a closer familiarity with the work of the campaign, I was initially convinced by the narratives of member leadership and accountability presented by staff members. It still would take some months away from the organization before I realized the deeper ambiguity created by the ongoing performance of worker leadership, by which time I found that I too had embodied the discourse, enacting it through my conversations with other staff members and allies. In retrospect, the time it took for these realizations to dawn on me is surprising given—as illustrated below—the routine reporting of low worker involvement.

Reporting the Numbers

Each weekly RDS meeting began with a rote accounting of the worker ratings for each campaign. As discussed previously, this metric assigned each worker a number and allowed for a quick review of support. Workers labeled as "ones" were strongly committed to the campaign, which was usually measured by membership in the Leadership Committee (LC). "Twos" were in favor of the campaign but not as active leaders. "Threes" were neutral, while "fours" were workers who had expressed disinterest or had told organizers to stop contacting them. "Fives" were workers who were actively working against the campaign, and "zeros" were workers whom organizers had not contacted.

An example from three months after the public launch is emblematic of how these discussions went.

"Ok, FCC member ratings," says Alejandro, looking up from his agenda.

Nathan reads from the spreadsheet on his computer. "Two ones, seventeen twos, thirty-three threes, twenty-one fours, two fives, and twenty-four zeros."

There is a long pause while Alejandro and Nathan look around to see if anyone had comments. On my laptop I note that this means nineteen workers were in support, twenty-three were against, and thirty-three were neutral, with another twenty-four unaccounted for. Both Emma and Miriam are on their computers, and I am not clear if either has been actively listening.

Alejandro notices that the numbers have changed from the week before, asking what happened. Nathan notes the names of two workers. "I moved them from threes to fours, and you moved another from three to two." Alejandro nods. "Oh, right!"

They both look around, and after another moment of silence, Alejandro lets out a sigh and moves onto the next agenda item.

And that marked the end of the conversation about ratings, an empty recounting of the numbers, which happened every week but rarely sparked deeper conversations about the state of the campaign until much later, as I discuss in the next chapter. To me, the numbers always appeared bottom heavy with "threes," "fours," and "fives." At the same time, workers who wouldn't come to meetings could be left ranked as a "one" or a "two" for weeks, seemingly overstating the amount of support.

At other points, the staff would signal problems of worker participation by discussing the challenges of scheduling meetings with workers. In our weekly meetings, it was a recurring item that the organizers would need to re-schedule a meeting due to lack of participation or worker cancelation. Similarly, in a later one-on-one, Miriam made it clear that "the chain of the campaign [had] come off the bicycle," telling Alejandro, "All you can do now is try to put the chain back on so that you can move forward, even in a small start." Soon after the meeting just discussed, Alejandro was blunt about the two campaigns: "We have a dead LC at FCC, and Finn's Distribution is not going well." Between these discussions and the worker rating reports, the staff clearly was aware that something was going wrong. And yet there were no concrete discussions about the implications for our model and processes in the absence of active worker leadership. Staff members could recognize and discuss the challenges the campaign faced, but only within a narrative that asserted the leadership of workers and insulated them from criticism.

The Bank of America Letter

I observed the outcome of this lack of reflection as we nonetheless continually tried to mount tactics in the campaign with the aim of encouraging the company to accept the presence of a worker-led union and to hold a meeting. While we had a long list of planned actions to hold after the public launch, with the campaign plan indicating at least one action per week, almost all of them were successively canceled due to a lack of worker participation. I will offer one example that was emblematic of the process.

It is three months after the public launch, and Emma and I are planning an action that involves sending a letter to the Bank of America branch that had lent FCC a Small Business Association loan. Our plan is to have two workers author the letter that would explain their problems at the job and their request for FCC to meet with them to talk. The remainder of the letter hints at the possibility of legal action, profit losses, and credit risk for the company if the campaign were to escalate to a supply-chain strategy. Tactically, the goal is to win a meeting with the bank where we can offer to end the campaign once the company agrees to a meeting. This would in turn cause the bank to request that the company meet with the CLP.

We began working on the draft soon after the launch, but by the RDS meeting three months later, Miriam admonishes us for not putting enough time into the letter. In a discussion of how the letter fit into the larger campaign strategy, she tells us that we "need to fuck with the company" by thinking like "a military general": What are the strategies that would most directly engage the company? How could we come up with a plan for building support? How does this tactic fit into the wider strategy?

The following week, we again discuss the letter. Alejandro and Nathan share their plan for holding a training with two workers to go over the text, understand the tactic, and to help author it. Partway through their explanation, Miriam weighs in on the discussion and attempts to adjust their approach. "Imagine if we weren't available. How could we make it so that members could both write a letter like this, and also understand how it fits into the wider strategy of the campaign?" She sighs in what seems like frustration. "They shouldn't just approve the letter, but be instrumental in its writing." Looking at Alejandro and Emma, she continues. "Obviously, our goal is to not just tell them [what to say], but work with them to write it. Pretend that this is the only opportunity they have to work on this, so what would you do in this time?"

After a pause, Alejandro looks up from his notes to ask, "So should we bring them a finished draft?"

"In an hour meeting," responds Miriam, "they should spend half an hour on the details of the strategy and half on the revisions. They won't be able to revise unless they grasp the purpose of the letter. [When I talked with these two workers before] they didn't understand the concept, you know?"

However, the two workers do not show for the training, even though Emma designed a strategy training, completed a full draft of the letter with their names on it, and Alejandro had worked hard to confirm their attendance. In the following weeks, the organizers attempt to get a handful of other workers to author the letter, to no avail. When no one comes to a final meeting to work on the letter, Miriam directs Nathan that "all the other leaders should see it and review it before we send it out." In the end, those meetings are never successfully scheduled, and Emma simply signs her own name on the letter. We do not follow up on the letter, and as far as I know we never receive a response from the bank.

This tactic illustrates how the staff was stuck between two competing pressures. On the one hand, the core of our mission was to advise and train workers to found their own union and run their own campaign and, in doing so, provide direction for the CLP and other allies in our attempts to support that campaign. As Miriam put it, workers should not only approve but also generate plans and tactics. On the other hand, the staff was concerned about keeping the campaign alive and meeting their own deadlines for tactics, all part of a multi-month campaign plan designed by staffers. The outcome was that Alejandro and Emma tried to split the difference between writing a letter in the name of the workers and finding a way for them to develop the process on their own.

This tension between worker and staff leadership in writing this letter was never fully resolved for any of the tactics that the CLP used. Even Miriam's call for the workers to be "instrumental" in the process translated into a thirty-minute review of a finished draft. Further, when workers did not participate, the staff still needed to implement these tactics out of fear that the campaign would lose even more momentum, and that they would face the ire of their supervisors for not meeting deadlines. Pressures like these ended up prioritizing the goals of the campaign, the organization, and the staff over that of workers who, due to their lack of participation, were never in a place to articulate clear goals in the first place.

In the end, the absence of worker participation did not stop the letter from being sent. Worker leadership in this case was pro forma, as workers might "see" and "review" the letter before Emma put it in the mail. And yet, in the tension between the need for worker leadership and its absence, campaign work nonetheless continued within the frame of worker leadership. While Emma signed the final letter, it spoke on behalf of workers, using the "we" pronoun to collapse the CLP and the workers into a single voice.

Staff Failures versus Worker Leadership

According to Miriam's analysis, the issues with the letter stemmed from inadequate leadership and planning by staff members. An implication in this analysis is that workers were willing to take the lead had staff members only been organized enough to give them the chance. But if workers do not come to meetings, do not show up to trainings, and do not return phone calls, how are workers supposed to offer leadership? There is perhaps a different question to be asked about the viability of the campaign, or our skills in persuading workers to join the campaign, but these were not how we framed the problem. Instead, workers hadn't been given the opportunity to lead. As a staff member would later put it, a core concern throughout the campaign was of "staff initiative displacing worker initiative," as though the CLP staff was eclipsing what would otherwise be more deliberate involvement by workers. From what I could see, workers did not seem apt to display initiative regardless of the space that staff members tried to create for them.

The Bank of America letter and many other tactics we canceled all faced the same layers of problems. First, getting workers to take part in the actions or simply approve them was a challenge on its own. This happened in a general context where worker support was marginal and where organizers struggled to simply hold regular meetings. Second, staff members recognized this issue while simultaneously advancing the campaign plan and emphasizing that its tactics were driven by workers. This was imperative because the CLP could not engage in explicit top-down or staff-driven strategies without facing an existential crisis. Their vision of the labor movement was as much about worker leadership as it was about explaining the failures of the movement within top-down, advocacy-based, and staff-driven approaches to organizing. Staffers could not conceive of their own work as part of these historical failures.

The implications of the worker-leader narrative were many. In the first place, this context left little conceptual room for real reflection and discussion about what to do when workers were not leading. Sometimes tactics were adjusted but not halted, as in the Bank of America letter. In that instance, while workers were not involved in the writing of the letter, the CLP spoke *for* them, substituting assumptions for what workers would want if they were involved. Typically, this is what happened throughout the following months as worker participation dwindled to zero. In its own way, this was another unspoken assumption about workers. They are—or should be—leaders, but they are not responsible or accountable to the campaign when they are not. To put it differently, we were loath to critique workers for missing deadlines and instead criticized each other for our perceived deficiencies.

This politics of worker representation came to a head in what Emma described as an "ugly argument" between William and Miriam. Part of the campaign plan involved leafletting actions, the first step in the larger supply-chain strategy. For this tactic, allies and workers from the factory would hand out leaflets about the campaign to customers coming and going from a popular boutique grocer. This "customer education" would not explicitly call for a boycott, but would use a high-road tone to inform people about the what the workers were asking for and why.

As part of the strategy, Emma, Miriam, and William had been working on a letter that workers from the FCC would give to grocery employees during the leafletting to explain what was happening. While the staff members were not interested in organizing these workers, they wanted to limit the amount of conflict between the two groups. Like most of the letter writing in the office, this process involved multiple drafts between the three of them, which is where the conflict began. As I wasn't present for the actual argument, Emma and Alejandro filled me in on what they saw happen. What started as a disagreement over the protocol for the correct order of staff revisions turned into an argument about representation. Miriam felt that the letter was overly professional, read "like a credit card statement," and wouldn't resonate with workers of color. William, who is white, felt that as a former food worker he knew what would work, and accused Miriam, who is Latinx, of trying to speak for all workers of color. From there it escalated into a shouting match until Miriam left. That evening, Miriam posted to her social media account that she had never encountered white male patriarchy like she had in this conversation, particularly in a work setting, emphasizing her refusal to tolerate it as a person of color.

Setting aside the nature of the conflict, it underlines the logic of the worker-leader discourse. The core disagreement was over who gets to speak on behalf of workers, yet within in a framework that valorizes worker leadership and agency. Both Miriam and William made claims based on their own identities and experiences. Workers did not participate in the writing of the letter or the planning of the action. That this might conflict with worker leadership was never up for discussion, while the question of who can best represent and speak for the absent workers became the topic of debate.

These examples show how we managed the performance of worker leadership within the office. My deeper access to this foggy set of relationships did not immediately present me with a clear idea of who was leading, or when. Rather, the outcome was that I was also drawn into the performance of worker leadership and did not think critically about the rhetoric of worker leadership and the practice of staff direction. As the relationship between the

CLP and the PLJA deepened, my responsibilities expanded to manage communications between the two. In practice, this meant that I too would soon be in the thick of the worker-leader narrative.

Organizing the PLJA

As mentioned earlier, the CLP staff had been trying to schedule the PLJA–CLP meeting since Susan, William, and I had met for drinks. The main obstacle was finding a worker to attend, a challenge that was reflective of the wider problem of member involvement in the campaign. In the end, Miriam was finally able to schedule Miguel, a worker she had been speaking with but who had not yet agreed to be part of the LC.

The day begins with a contentious RDS meeting between Miriam, Alejandro, Emma, Nathan, and me. Nathan starts the meeting with a succinct summary of changes from the previous week: "Our support [ones and twos] went down from nineteen to seventeen, the middle [threes] stayed the same, and against the campaign [fours and fives] went up from twenty-three to twenty-four."

After a long pause Alejandro adds that "two of the workers I moved to fours were against the campaign a long time ago. . . . They even blocked me on Facebook!" He laughs in disbelief.

Again, there is a long pause, as Miriam stares at her laptop and everyone else waits to see if there will be any questions. Eventually, Alejandro moves to the next agenda item of FCC departmental meetings. As they have struggled to get workers to attend general LC meetings, the organizers have been instead trying to hold meetings by work departments. The logic is that since workers in the same department will routinely see each other at the factory, there will be more accountability and mutual support among the workers. The strongest foothold seems to be among a group of overnight workers.

"Next is departmental meetings," says Alejandro, letting out a sigh, "and the night shift meeting was canceled due to lack of support."

Without looking up from her laptop, Miriam replies with a critical edge to her voice, "Did you follow the protocol we discussed?" She is referring to a strategy of confirming workers to attend these meetings, and asking them to check in with each other to ensure that people will show up.

"It didn't work," Nathan responds, pulling back into his seat with tight smile as he looks to Emma.

Emma speaks softly: "David didn't reach out before he went into work." David, a white activist that Emma knew before he worked at FCC, is a committed member of the campaign but only works part-time at the company.

Miriam looks up from her computer, looking at each of them in turn with a disappointed frown. "He was supposed to inform his coworkers, then confirm them again?" Emma nods yes, and Miriam adds, "And what were you guys supposed to do?"

"I was responsible for two workers to also reach out to them," says Nathan, "and I made flyers for Jalen, but he didn't communicate to other workers . . ."

". . . and he was refusing to distribute them this week," Emma adds, finishing his thoughts.

Miriam interlaces her fingers, leaning onto the table. "Efforts have been made?"

"Yeah," says Nathan.

Emma asks Nathan if he talked to David. "We need three people confirmed by tonight for the next night shift meeting to happen." Emma looks around. "David said he would call everyone. . . ." She trails off into a long pause.

After a moment, Miriam leans back in her chair, looking at the ceiling. "I feel sympathy for them. Everything is dissolving around them, and we can't put everything on David. It was a scramble on this; why did we bottleneck the process?" she asks, looking around at the staff. "Why did we excuse ourselves from this?"

"We didn't. . . ." Nathan's response trails off.

Alejandro and Nathan talk for a moment about how to get the workers confirmed for the meeting before Miriam cuts in, letting out a sigh as she types something on her phone. "Can you just ask the other workers involved in that department?"

"OK," says Nathan, "I'll do that."

Alejandro responds to Miriam: "Have you talked to workers in that department?" Miriam shakes her head no. "Are you going to?"

Mildly, Miriam says, "I have to coordinate with Tomás," referring to another worker on the night shift.

"Do you want to set a goal?" Alejandro asks. I wonder if he is trying to turn the tables on Miriam, but she doesn't meet his eyes.

Looking at her laptop, she responds with some finality. "My goal was to get Miguel to the PLJA meeting today."

I keep my mouth shut until Alejandro reads the agenda item "ally organization." Miriam states that this refers to the PLJA committee meeting, which is happening this evening at our office. Miguel is supposed to arrive an hour before the meeting, where Miriam will prep him.

Alejandro gives a sigh. "It would be stronger to have someone from the Leadership Committee present."

"David said he might be able to come," says Emma quietly, turning to Miriam, "... unless that's counterproductive?"

Again, Miriam doesn't look up from her laptop when she replies. "When did he say this?"

"Monday," says Emma, which is two days ago.

"Can he make the four o'clock prep? If so, that's fine," is Miriam's reply.

After a pause, I chime in with the proposed agenda: an update on the campaign, a discussion about accountability to the workers, and some discussion on the press conference tactic. We had agreed to provide the PLJA with talking points and a draft plan, and Emma asks Miriam if she has had the chance to read the draft we put together. She shakes her head no, and Emma suggests we let them see the draft, as the PLJA is going to edit it anyway. Not looking up, Miriam gives a non-committal grunt and we move on with the meeting.

Two Member-Led Organizations

Miguel arrives at the office little before four o'clock. He and Miriam sit at the head of the conference table, where they speak Spanish in hushed tones too quiet for me to hear. From the tone of the conversation, I guess that Miriam is prepping him for the meeting, a practice I have seen a handful of times. Many of the workers have never spoken in public before and are sometimes nervous to do so. The staff views opportunities like this as part of leadership development, and they usually try to have a few hours of prep time with the workers to help them develop what and how to say certain things.

Around five o'clock Susan, the PLJA co-chair arrives, and I make introductions between her, Miriam, and Miguel. Emma joins us and all move to the conference table, and after some small talk and some awkward silence, we get down to business. Miriam starts by asking if we should speak in Spanish or English, and that she can translate either way. Susan says that she speaks Spanish, so that would be no problem. I agree that Spanish is fine, but I might need help translating my own words. Emma nods in agreement.

We begin with formal introductions, our names and positions. Susan gets us started by sharing her own background and her hopes for the partnership. While she works in health care, she has a long history in the labor movement and underlines the importance of having worker-led, as opposed to staff-led, campaigns. This is part of the reason she is excited for the PLJA–CLP relationship.

She then talks about the history of the PLJA and the type of work that the PLJA does. In particular, she says that the PLJA wants to take on the FCC campaign as a major focus, and they are committed to doing so in a manner that is accountable and answerable to the workers who are running the campaign. She underlines the point that the PLJA is not interested in taking on leadership positions themselves and wants to support the workers in whatever way they can. In fact, one of the reasons the PLJA has decided to focus on the CLP campaign is that it is "explicitly-worker led." Miriam favorably nods along to this.

Miguel has been listening to Susan with a somewhat neutral expression during this and is curious to know how the PLJA could support the campaign. Susan shares that they are open to suggestions, but anything that allies could potentially help with, including attending actions, making phone calls to the company, coordinating social media campaigns, or speaking with politicians, is a possibility. After a pause, Miguel asks Susan how much it will cost the workers to join the PLJA for this support. Miriam laughs and quickly explains that PLJA isn't asking the workers for anything in return, they just want to help. Miguel gives a surprised laugh, clearly relaxing at that response. With a smile, Susan offers that the PLJA, like the CLP, is a member-based organization, that anyone can join, and that there are no payments or requirements. FCC workers could join if they wanted to, and are always welcome to come to meetings, but they don't need to.

Susan then adds that one thing the PLJA could also be helpful with is public outreach and education, since the organization has a history of having events and actions about labor campaigns. Nodding along, Miguel responds that he is open to having the PLJA work with them, though he will need to talk to the other workers. To this, Miriam adds that the best thing to do is to keep communication open between the FCC workers and the PLJA members, and I offer to do that since I am in daily contact with each group anyway. Everyone agrees to this, with Susan adding that the PLJA members and FCC workers probably do not all need to meet together anytime soon, but that it is always an option. Susan asks if there is anything the PLJA could be working on now, and Emma brings up the press conference, passing out hard copies of a plan for the action we have been working on. Emma also has a list of possible attendees from across the wider region, and she says we can share it with the PLJA to get the ball rolling on participation. Susan nods, and says we have a PLJA member lined up to begin working on the outreach effort. Our shared hope is to have the action ready to launch in a couple of weeks.

Susan thanks her and looks to Miguel and Miriam to see if there is anything else to talk about. We all stand, exchanging handshakes and smiles as Miriam states that this was a good meeting. As she is putting on her coat, Susan again invites Miguel and any interested workers to attend our next meeting in two weeks, and looks at me to indicate I will keep everyone in the loop. I agree to touch base with Susan later in the week to talk about the next PLJA meeting, and she heads out.

I hang around the office for a while longer to finish typing up the meeting notes. Miguel leaves shortly after Susan, shaking my hand with a broad smile and thanking me for my help on the campaign; though I will hear his name a few more times, I will never see him again during my remaining eight months with the CLP.

My hope was that this meeting would mark the beginning of a unique relationship between two member-led organizations. The coming months, however, would find the CLP shifting to a more staff driven, top-down, and ally-centric approach in the hopes of keeping the campaign alive. The discourse of the campaign did not shift with this change. The meeting between Susan and Miguel helped to keep the notion of worker leadership alive for the PLJA. But while we would eventually see workers, staff, allies, and the FCC management meeting at the negotiating table, the ally-driven tactic of the PLJA press conference would play a crucial role in pressing the company forward. For the next significant chapter of the campaign, staff and allies would lead in the name of worker leadership—but workers themselves would be mainly absent.

Worker Leadership and Ally Support

Having the PLJA hold a press conference began as an off-the-cuff idea by William. After the meeting between Miguel and Susan, the tactic came more clearly into focus. Emma and I drafted a set of talking points that detailed concerns about labor problems at FCC while also supporting the CLP campaign and the worker-led union at the company. Similar to the petition that FCC workers delivered to the company during the launch, the tone was intentionally "high-road." This was a clear attempt to activate allies and expand the scope of conflict beyond the worksite, as it engaged the company from a new direction.

We developed a plan about which media outlets to approach, and to push the PLJA in that direction Emma and I provided the PLJA with a carefully cultivated database of outlets to contact. Further, William wanted to hold the action as soon as possible after the initial meeting between Susan, Miguel, and the rest of us. An important quality of this relationship was the amount of control that the CLP retained over the work of the PLJA. Throughout the process of drafting the talking points, designing the long-term strategy, and deciding who to invite, the PLJA was kept on a short leash. What made the relationship work smoothly was the commitment that the PLJA had to worker leadership, and the ability of the CLP to invoke that leadership through our rhetoric. This required the PLJA to trust the organization, especially since workers were never the points of contact after the initial meeting with Miguel. It also required that the CLP—primarily through my role as intermediary—continually reference the idea of worker leadership.

Support and Trust

The next PLJA meeting was scheduled a few weeks after our meeting with Miguel, and Susan could not attend. She asked if I would be willing to report on our conversation, and I agreed to do so, again working with Emma to go over my talking points. I reported on the agreement between Susan and Miguel, and the establishment of our new committee to focus on the FCC campaign, and I explained the purpose of the press release as I passed out copies of the draft plan and talking points. I explained that the new committee would need to edit and approve the plan and, after approval, volunteers could use the contact list that Emma and I had put together for outreach. Using the language that Emma provided me, I explained that if there were any major changes to the plan, we would need to check with the workers for approval.

As I finished, Megan, who acted as PLJA co-chair with Susan, asked me to go over the concerns of the workers, and other members nodded that they were interested. From memory, I noted the main talking points of the campaign: fair wages, affordable healthcare, and respect at the workplace. In response, several people asked questions about these demands. What is the wage they are asking for, and how much do they make now? Had the Affordable Care Act changed the health care plan? Have the workers talked to the Teamsters or another union? Someone asked if the CLP has thought about bringing an established union on board, since they had seen several union signs at the public launch. I took a breath and waded in, trying to explain that the CLP members at FCC were forming their own independent union, one based on a model of direct action to try to push the company to meet their demands. I hadn't prepared answers for other questions, and some of the details I simply didn't know. I ended up deflecting with vague responses that invoked the workers. "The workers want a clear and fair system of raises," and "The workers think the current health care plan is too expensive."

Over the course of the next week, Susan and I organized the members who volunteered to do outreach for the action. In an email where we planned an upcoming conference call, Susan laid out the main purpose of the committee:

> "Our role is not to speak on behalf of the workers in any way but rather to understand well what they want us to do in solidarity and support. So, our "ask" is right now very simple: that management should engage in productive dialogue with the workers to hear their grievances and work toward solutions. The workers are still determining all the ways they want our support, but this one request is clear."

Only later, with the perspective gained from hindsight, did I realize the incongruity of these conversations. How could the PLJA express such dedication to the FCC campaign without an understanding of the key problems? It seemed odd that we had a conversation about basic demands months after we had made the decision to develop a committee in support of the campaign, and at the same time I couldn't clearly articulate these answers even as a CLP staff member. I believe that the answer is the same reason members were satisfied with my vague responses to their question—trust in the CLP and the shared the commitment to worker leadership soothed any concerns that we all might have had. The PLJA's interest in supporting worker-led organizing combined with the CLP's position as a worker-led group meant that, in practice, we were willing to back campaigns without much reflection on the details. And it is worth noting that in later conversations with PLJA members there was not much concern that the campaign had low levels of worker participation or was primarily staff-led. The vision they shared with the CLP was enough to make it the right thing to do.

"I'll Ask the Workers."

The partnership between the PLJA and the CLP had real effects on the campaign, as we will see in the next two chapters. The formalization of the press conference and the larger relationship building with the PLJA is a clear example of the coalitional power described by Brookes, especially the logic of expanding both the scope and scale of the campaign (2013, pp. 191–194). By taking the campaign out of the worksite and into the public arena, the CLP attempted to shift the balance of power away from the employers by leveraging the influence of organizations that were previously external to the campaign. Through the PLJA, the CLP shifted the scope to include more and different types of actors and expanded the scale to include players outside of the worksite. Yet it also moved the center of the campaign even further away from the agency of the workers.

PLJA members, for their part, supported the FCC campaign wholeheartedly at the same time that they were not all entirely clear about the goals of the campaign. This dynamic, which we will see again in later chapters, may appear at first blush to suggest naivety on behalf of PLJA members. But I think it would be incorrect to frame their work in this way. First, the belief in worker leadership in the FCC campaign espoused by Susan and other members reflected the discourse of worker leadership among CLP staff. When combined with the shared history of the organizations, and the initial meeting between Susan and Miguel, this belief makes sense. Further, the work of allyship in these situations is often one of low information, mitigated through a mix of trust and political ideology. I am sure many readers have had the experience of signing a petition or attending a rally for an issue where the political boundaries were clear even if the details of the issue were not. When labor groups are agitating against a company, not much additional information is needed for labor activists to lend some degree of support. Indeed, both the CLP and the PLJA would lend public support to even those traditional unions that they offered critiques of in private. This is facilitated by the relative ease and low risk of the tactics that are asked of allies, who are not likely to face arrest, harassment, or unemployment due to their participation.

In different but overlapping ways, the CLP staff, PLJA members, FCC workers like Miguel, and I all embodied and enacted the worker-leader discourse. This system—grounded in the environment of the FCC campaign and the organizations and actors involved in it—produced context-dependent truth claims bound up in relationships of power. The practices of this narrative, described above—designing campaign tactics, authoring letters to banks, disciplining staff members—were actions that aimed to win the campaign at FCC in a way that valorized worker leadership. And when we performed these practices of worker leadership, we aimed to create a worker-led campaign while simultaneously constructing our own political identities as actors who support worker leadership. To abandon the narrative of worker leadership, even in the face of low worker support, would have amounted to an existential crisis for CLP staff and the organization as a whole. My own inability to understand the tension between the practice and the performance of worker leadership illustrates how the narrative was embedded into the construction of our own political identities.

6

"It's Good to Be Back Out in the Streets."

Eventually it had become clear to everyone that the campaign was in shambles as the FCC campaign was down to a single worker—David—who was participating in any meaningful way. That David was a part-time worker who happened to be both white and already a political activist lent its own set of challenges to an ostensibly immigrant-oriented campaign.

The catalyst for the WFIO discussion from Chapter 1 was a Regional Distribution Strategy meeting where we were, for the first time that I experienced, transparent and reflective about the lack of campaign support. After Alejandro reported the worker ratings at the FCC, noting that there were thirteen workers in support, Miriam responded, shaking her head.

"So, thirteen in support . . ."; she pauses. "That is probably quite generous based on conversations I've had. Any thoughts?"

Alejandro sighs. "I agree that it's a generous description. Some people are listed here that we haven't interacted with at all for a long time."

Emma brings up that the standing Monday meetings for night-shift workers have not been going well, with only David attending, who is himself getting frustrated by the challenge of getting people on board.

"That makes sense," Alejandro says, nodding. "We had a moment with the campaign, and had a growing interest with the night-shift workers . . . but it's kind of demoralizing for David that he's showing up and other people are not."

"I did meet with Marcos yesterday," says Miriam, referring to another worker who was once involved with the campaign, and Alejandro perks up. "Oh, good!"

She shakes her head. "Oh, not that good! He said there's no talk at all about the campaign. It appears dead to most people, and most people don't want anything to do with it."

Alejandro sighs, looking down at his note pad. "Just like Jorge."

"Have you asked anyone about the strategy for the month to engage the company at the Bank of America rally?" Alejandro asks. He is referring to a tactic to hold a march and rally at the Bank of America location that made

Worker Centered. Biko Koenig, Oxford University Press. © Oxford University Press (2024).
DOI: 10.1093/oso/9780197784907.003.0006

a loan to the FCC, planned as a follow-up to the letter discussed in the last chapter.

"Marcos doesn't think that's a good idea at this time," says Miriam, shaking her head, "since there's not support or interest in the campaign. Jose said something similar; his take on the leafletting tactic was similar, that it would alienate people since there is a rift between the organization and the workers."

I'm surprised to hear Miriam's stark analysis of the campaign, but she has seemed more openly critical of the campaign since her argument with William.

She goes on to explain that the workers she has been speaking with "had thoughts about historical problems or errors in the run-up to going public. . . . Both of them felt like they put in a lot of effort and that they're the strongest leaders, but that the response from their co-workers—and from us—wasn't satisfactory. . . . They're not opposed to organizing or moving forward, they wouldn't stand in the way, but they are extremely doubtful that anything would move forward at this point. . . . For them it's much worse now than it was immediately after going public; it's one thing to hear negativity, opinions, or shit-talking from co-workers, but much worse when you don't hear anything about it." She sighs. "For Jose, it's the wreath on top of the casket."

The meeting ends with Alejandro asking William if he is free that afternoon to help the staff figure out what to do next, with Emma providing the prompt: "How can we act in our roles as advisors given the state of the campaign?" and Alejandro explaining how the base has become distant from the organization. William's answer: translate the feeling of WFIO to the new strategy of the militant minority. In this renewed vision we would take the campaign in an aggressive new direction, as William told us. "As much of a militant minority that we can muster to lead Phase II and Phase III of the campaign. Phase II being hitting the consequential, but not critical, relationships that the company depends on with the media and customers, and Phase III hitting the critical relationships that the company depends on, with wholesale buyers."

From Defeat to Fight

The WFIO conversation was an important turning point. It became part of the mythology of the campaign, as William would often remind us to "remember WFIO," the moment where the campaign changed from

"accepting defeat" to "fighting for victory." As a charismatic and thoughtful leader, he continually drove this point home over the following months,
often welcoming staff into the office with greetings such as, "We're finally
gonna do some damage today!" or "Biko, you excited to help fight the bosses
today?" It also worked to elevate the morale of the staff and help focus their
work in a new and concrete direction. In this way, it was similar to the
decision made to take the FCC campaign public amid low worker support—
simply having a concrete plan helped to alleviate some of the anxiety that
staff members were experiencing.

Having lost practically all its momentum and membership in the
five months since the public launch, the campaign was in dire need of a
strategic readjustment. Clearly, there were no easy answers at this point, and
William was probably correct in noting that many organizations would have
likely called it quits in such a context. The "core strategy" of a militant minority of workers leading street actions to amplify the visibility of the campaign
was the staff's attempt to rescue the vision of a radical, worker-led union at
the FCC. The logic at play was to engage the company by any means necessary, explain that engagement as the result of a worker-led union, and use the
example to illustrate to the rest of the workforce that the company could be
moved and that the campaign—and thus the power of workers—was effective and worth their time. The communication strategy employed by the
CLP would both keep workers in the loop about these developments and
consistently name workers as the primary agents of change. "When the company flinches," went the idea, "it is because you, the workers fighting together,
are the ones throwing punches." Combining successful actions with a consistent narrative would spark solidaristic thinking among the workers, and any
pushback from the company could be both re-framed as shared grievances
among the workers and refashioned into moral arguments against a target
with a strong public brand. While this approach would not guarantee success, the overall logic fit the direct-action model the CLP used and offered
a clear road map to jumpstart the campaign, relying on the tried-and-true
supply-chain strategy developed in earlier campaigns.

The conversation also opened the door to a frank conversation about
the lack of worker support and what that meant for the campaign. Staff
members had to vocally acknowledge the situation and make clear decisions about strategy in this context. As expressed by all the staff members
in the above-mentioned meeting, only a handful of workers were interested
in the campaign; many would renege on commitments to attend meetings

or planning calls, some expressed resentment about how the CLP has managed things, and most were wary of the tactics that staff members had been trying to schedule. While these were hard realizations to swallow, they did open space for transparency.

And yet we just as quickly closed that door as we moved toward an aggressive strategy that was still articulated within a narrative of worker leadership. It is worth underlining that in this single conversation the staff stressed the need for worker democracy and leadership, understood that workers had real concerns about the tactics under discussion, and nonetheless committed to a plan that emphasized these tactics. This is as clear an example of the performative practice of worker leadership as any, where staff explain their work as accountable to worker leadership while dictating the activity and subjectivities of workers. The result was a context where staff members projected their own desires for what workers should do onto the workers themselves. Jose and Marcos might have thought that aggressive tactics against the company would not work, and yet staff members believed that workers *should* want to take up these tactics and, crucially, that they *would do them*. They would become the "militant minority," defiantly taking up "asymmetrical power" to "resist wage slavery" and start their own union. The implication was that the campaign would draw them back into what the CLP thought was best for them. In sum, this logic of worker leadership allowed the organization to make a functional turn toward a staff-driven campaign that emphasized the external power of allies while still understanding it as worker-led.

Finally, this conversation marked a period of transition for the organization. Miriam, perhaps the staff member who had developed the most critical voice about the direction of the campaign, began to withdraw from the CLP. This had begun with her argument with William over the retail letter described in the last chapter, and I believe it is why she offered no real resistance to William's plan. She would quit less than a month later. Her critiques of the history of the campaign and the organization itself would grow sharper over her final month, though they would have no real impact. This was especially true when she and Alejandro failed to even get the four remaining worker members to agree to a meeting over the next two months. Soon afterward, Emma informed me that she was also planning to quit soon. Outside of a part-time development assistant to help with the upcoming yearly fundraiser, we made no additional hires. Alongside Nathan's departure a few weeks earlier, this left the staff as William, Alejandro, James, and me, along with a handful of interns. With James devoted wholly to fundraising and Alejandro our sole organizer, William took over as our direct supervisor while my responsibilities grew to replace some of the work that Miriam and Emma once performed. Much of this focused on administration and operations, including the bookkeeping and infrastructure needs for the CLP. I also ended up managing an ongoing policy campaign and directly supervising our interns. From this point forward, I was drawn even more deeply into the organization as I participated in all staff meetings regardless of topic as William, Alejandro, and I routinely met to discuss campaign strategy.

The Press Conference

Meanwhile, PLJA members work on finalizing the details for the press conference. In one of our staff meetings, William asks about the status of the press conference, and I proudly report that the PLJA hopes to hold it in the next two weeks. His eyebrows rise in surprise as he looks up from his laptop, "The workers aren't ready for that." I have no response, since this is the schedule that he originally designed, though I know that Alejandro has not yet been able to get the workers to meet in the seven weeks since the WFIO meeting.

I ask William what we should do instead, and he calls Alejandro over while sketching out a plan for the campaign and directing me to take notes. First, using similar language from the WFIO conversation two months prior, he notes that the next step is for the core workers of the "militant minority" to meet and determine how they can best form their union and hold their employer accountable to higher standards. Then, the workers will start to hand out leaflets and talk to customers with support from the staff. After this, the PLJA will hold the press conference. Finally, once we gauge the company's reaction, we will start going after a select set of high-profile customers to encourage them to drop FCC products until they agree to meet. The strategy is to order the tactics such that they progressively increase the campaign's engagement with the company, and that a street action at a store should come before the PLJA's action. Together they will be a "one, two punch" of different kinds of engagement.

William makes an off-the-cuff suggestion that someone from the PLJA could call FCC management before the action. He strategizes this on the

fly. "They should say that 'we are preparing to make our concerns publicly known.' It lets the company know that they need to come to the
table and start a dialogue. It could make them nervous, you know? More
attention will be paid to it because you're scared of it coming out." He
smiles. "The threat of the tactic is sometimes more effective than the tactic
itself!"

Organizing the Core

While Alejandro continues to push for a meeting of the "core," it seems
more and more clear that David is the only committed member. Alejandro
nonetheless continues to try to schedule a meeting with four workers, and
eventually we are on the cusp of our first grocery action. In an all-hands
meeting two days before the event, William again frames the tactic as being
worker-led. "So a couple of workers want to restart the pressure against the
company on Wednesday," he explains, turning to Alejandro, "which is great
news; congrats to Alejandro and to everyone else who helped workers get
out of the fear zone, which the company imposed. So that requires member
mobilization, and you have a good game plan for that, right?"

There is a pause as Alejandro hesitates. "Yeah . . .," he laughs nervously, "I
need to re-confirm with them. I confirmed last week, with three of them." He
sighs, adding quickly, "I mean it's a little difficult to get in touch with them
now."

Over lunch the next day, Alejandro confides to me that only David had
confirmed his attendance, and that two other workers have dropped out of
the campaign altogether and do not want to talk to him. One complained
that the campaign didn't have enough backing among the workers. When
Alejandro told him that he would have lots of community support at the
grocery action, the worker noted that allies didn't have to take any heat at
work for attending. Clearly frustrated, Alejandro is not sure what to do.

We decide to hold the action anyway. On the day of the event, I spend
the morning printing the flyers for the action and meet up with our group
on a corner a few blocks from the grocery store. William is giving a pep
talk about what to expect as everyone stands in a circle. David is the only
worker present, joined by the CLP staff members and a small group of labor
activists who have participated in previous CLP campaigns, most of whom
I have only met once or twice before.

For an ostensibly worker-led action, I find the event puts allies, rather than workers, at center stage. After two people unfurl our banner, David goes into the store to deliver the CLP-authored letter to the workers at the register—the same letter that Miriam and William had fought over months before. When I ask him how the delivery went, he tells me that the workers were not really interested in talking with him. After this, David takes a marginal role in the rest of the action, quietly handing out leaflets on the sidewalk. William stands in front of the store window, holding the door open for people as they come and go, chatting up people as they walk by, and making jokes to the rest of us. The attitude is a mix of excitement and intensity, and most of the volunteers throw themselves into the spectacle of a street action, singing songs, poking fun at people who don't take flyers, and talking about the details of the campaign to those who are interested.

After an hour, we run out of flyers, and we pose for pictures with David standing in the center of a group of raised fists with our banner prominently displayed in front. Two blocks away, we hold a quick debrief, William's excitement standing in contrast to David's more muted affect. While David remarks that he thinks it "went well," William laughs as he imagines how many calls the FCC must have received during the action. He lets out a satisfied sigh, looking around the group. "It's good to be back out in the streets."

Reaching Out to the FCC

The next night finds Alejandro, William, Susan, and me meeting at the bar. As the drinks arrive, William gives Susan an update on how the campaign is going, focusing on the leafleting action from the day before. "Oh, you should have been there," he says with a broad smile. He and Alejandro go on to explain how powerful the action was, how many volunteers turned out, and how we ran out of flyers much sooner than we had planned. He emphasizes how the workers delivered a letter of support to the grocery workers, and with a laugh describes how he could see the manager on the phone holding both a copy of that letter and the leaflet. With a smile he adds, "Oh they were definitely rattled. The FCC now knows we're back on the offensive." When Susan asks about worker turnout, William responds that many workers are still afraid to participate but are clearly interested, and a core group of workers is making sure the campaign "has enough push to raise the stakes." Susan smiles and apologizes for missing the action, asking what the PLJA can do to help.

When the second round arrives, William makes his pitch for Susan to call the company directly before holding the press conference. Susan should explain that the PLJA has some concerns about labor issues at the company. As such, they are reaching out directly to the company with the hope of coming to a resolution rather than making their concerns public. With the threat of bad publicity lingering, William hopes that a conversation with Susan can help "guide them to the meeting" by making a personal connection with the company.

For her part, Susan is game to make the call the following week. While there is some hope that this might get the company to finally relent and agree to a meeting, none of us believes that it will be enough on its own, and we plan out the next steps for the PLJA side of the campaign. Assuming the phone call will make no difference, the PLJA prepares to release a notice announcing the date and location of the press conference. William also asks us to prepare for an eventual supply-chain strategy at the FCC. This could be the first salvo in a drawn-out boycott campaign in which we would "engage the company" at their customer base.

The next ten days are a flurry of false starts as Susan tries to reach the lead manager. At one point we assume that they simply aren't going to return the call. After a round of phone tag turns into an email exchange, they set a time to talk the following Monday. Nonetheless, William wants us to be ready to release it the moment it is clear that the phone call is not enough to encourage the company to meet.

When Susan does finally speak with management, the outcome is less than straightforward. In Susan's email report of the conversation, she indicates that their talk was polite and open, with management expressing concern that the company treats their workers very well and that they "saw no need for a 'third party' (i.e., the CLP) to be involved or invited to any meeting." They felt that the FCC was being unfairly targeted, and that their wages were very good for the industry, and that the healthcare plan was the most that they could afford to offer. Susan responded by positing that "many workers, based on their own experience as well as that of friends and family, feel intimidated by the threat of retaliation to just speak their minds, and that there is strong consensus within the worker community (including PLJA) on the principle that workers should have a right to invite whom they choose to a meeting." While management is concerned that the CLP is simply looking for a fight, Susan assures him that this is coming from a cooperative spirit, and that they have "nothing to lose in having a meeting and finding out for themselves." By the end of the call, they agree to reconsider their opposition to having a meeting, but also request some time to think it over. With some nudging on Susan's part, they agree to send an update in two days. Susan suggests that William join the PLJA on our planning call to talk about next steps.

That call is well attended, with William joining everyone who has been working on the action. While the PLJA has been working on the campaign for months at this point, the call begins with some surprising confusion about the campaign. For example, one member asks William how close he thinks the campaign is to winning a collective bargaining contract for the workers. I cringe a bit when the question is asked. With a sharp laugh, William says, "No no no, there's no contract!" He instead explains how the model the workers are using is about using direct action and a motivated union to hold employers accountable and to make changes as needed.

As I take notes on the conversation with my phone cradled precariously between ear and shoulder, the significance of the contract question sticks in the back of my head. The most immediate reaction I feel is that I must be failing at my role of go-between. Perhaps my reports to the subcommit-tee have not been informative or thoughtful enough. Upon later reflection, however, I come to a different conclusion. My reports to the subcommit-tee have been meticulously prepared before I deliver them, with Emma or William checking my work and my phrasing of important issues. As with earlier conversations I had with PLJA members, it seems that some only have a vague understanding of the campaign. Yet what they know has been enough to encourage a sizeable organization of volunteers to commit time, resources, and institutional power. At the same time, our characterization of the demands has been somewhat vague, offering few details besides better wages, more affordable healthcare, and respectful treatment. For the PLJA, the notion that a group of workers wants to join a union and hold a meet-ing with their employer, and that the employer is resisting these efforts, is enough information for activists to know where to put their energy.

While I mull over these questions, the call continues. What becomes clear at this point is that the press conference tactic has shifted, because Susan has been able to open a direct line of communication with the company. As William explains it, the threat of the tactic is now the stick to Susan's conversational carrot. William asks Susan to communicate a clear timeline for the company as to when they need to have responded. Susan agrees to the plan, and we wait to hear what the FCC will say.

Re-framing the Campaign Narrative

The planning for the press conference illustrates the power that allies wielded in CLP campaigns. Using outside tactics that vocally demand that a company live up to community standards for employees is a classic part of the CLP's supply-chain strategy. And when workers were unable to muster enough power on their own to convince the company to meet, this coalitional power was crucial to keep the campaign afloat and the militant-minority strategy alive.

But the tactic also illustrates how the CLP secured the support of the PLJA through the performance of worker leadership. Outside of the initial meeting between Susan and Miguel, staffers (myself included) invoked worker leadership to the PLJA even when workers were not involved. We would use language such as "the workers decided . . ." or "we need to check with the workers at the shop." This language was effective in keeping the PLJA involved, but the worker-leader discourse also involved other categories of actors. Staffers themselves were both key players and audience members, though by this point the staff consisted of William, Alejandro, James, me, and a few interns. While the staff's re-framing of the militant minority and the street actions as worker-led were clear examples of this internal reframing, we also began to actively re-tell the story of the campaign to ourselves.

Sometime after the street action, the full staff is sitting for a quarterly meeting, including interns who have been invited to see what the process looks like. The presence of the interns and James—our development lead—allows for a more-transparent-than-usual conversation about the state of worker participation in the campaign.

When we move to talking about FCC, Alejandro explains that even though we planned three actions at different retail stores, he has struggled to get workers interested in the campaign. So far only David has attended an action, and Alejandro canceled the second when David could not make it at the last moment. For the third action, staffers and activists leafleted a store without any workers present.

"I'm hearing that it's been difficult to engage the workers," says James. "Is there a plan moving forward to do that? What's the plan?"

Alejandro sighs as he looks down at his agenda. "Yeah, so the plan moving forward is to continue engaging with David. We explained to him how important his presence is, that his presence is so important, and asked if we could be helpful in any way. So, moving forward, we continue to try to be engaged with David in the streets, but [are] also trying to provide him with support to speak to co-workers. And if I can help David focus on just bringing *one* person, just *one* person to a leafleting action. . . ."

After a pause he continues. "It's been . . . it's been very hard. When I can actually get a hold of people, on the phone, or house-visit attempts, it's hard to find people sometimes, most of the responses have been 'so and so is not participating and probably won't.'" He lets out a big sigh, leaning back in his chair. "That's been the most common. . . . If they are friendly and open to a conversation, most of them are saying that 'I don't want to be isolated or identified as a person who is campaigning. I don't want to be retaliated against, my co-workers are going to make fun of me.' That's the typical response. Or 'Why should I fight for everybody else? Why should I risk myself if they are not willing to risk themselves for themselves?'"

Here William jumps in, explaining to the interns how their attempts to bring workers into the campaign in the first six months after the public launch went terribly. "We were dead, we were lost. If we were a normal group with any sense we would have walked away, said, 'You know what, we lost this one, we got beat.' But, as hopefully you have heard, the second most important principle after accountability to members at CLP is commitment to victory. So we don't believe in losing. We'd rather lose everything than lose one campaign, because the working class has already lost enough. So we stood at the whiteboard and we said, 'WFIO, we're fucked, it's over.'" He laughs, pointing at the whiteboard. "So we discard our old strategy, we had a campaign that was completely defunct, so we said we're going to have a 'core strategy.' . . . We will take the leaders who are still more open, who have some hope, and work with them to restart the engagement after six of seven months of zero action, and *use* that restarted pressure to help them start their union. Essentially, it's a restarted narrative, it's a restarted story. So instead of the story being that the campaign was launched and went dead, the story is that the campaign was launched, workers patiently waited and hoped for the employer to come to the table, the employer hasn't, so workers, because they're committed to making work better, are escalating their engagement with the company until their power builds to the point where the company comes to the table and makes the improvement that workers need. So the strategy has the core build that power and use that power as a narrative. So we went from dead, to alive."

After a moment one of our interns asks, "So, actually . . . is it just David who is involved? Just a question!"

William's voice is sharp in his response. "The campaign was defeated, so we had to resurrect the campaign. David is the only leader that has taken action, right? Alejandro is meeting with others, who are interested, who are committing, and then they are getting scared. So only David has taken action." He takes a breath, and some of the edge leaves his voice. "What we're doing now, is using the story, of these recent actions, and the fact that David hasn't been killed, to duplicate that movement, from being scared and on the fence, to being active. That's the strategy. So a dead campaign, to a live campaign, but, a very fledgling campaign. So it's a credit to the workers who are interested in fighting, and it's a credit to our organization that the campaign is alive. The good news is we only need like five or six workers. Right? Our original goal was to have eighty workers at this point probably, or something like that. All we really need is five or six, because the strategic choice workers have made is very powerful," he says, referring to the supply-chain strategy. "It doesn't require a lot of workers, that's just the nature of the strategic choice being good."

In a similar meeting a few weeks later, William again underlines the need to re-frame the story of the campaign. "We have to start a story over again, change the story from 'We're dead, this will never work' to 'Workers, after being very patient with the boss, and not doing anything, being very generous, are starting to grind the company, *so tight*, that the company will have to come to the table.' So that's the heart of our current strategy. Utilizing the restart of our engagement, to help create space, and diminish the fear of reprisal, that workers feel to participate."

This approach is intentionally designed to address why the workers are hesitant to join the campaign. William explains the analysis in the following way: "The three top barriers [to workers joining the campaign] are one, futility. This employer, even if God rains down on the company, will never come to the table. Second is fear of retaliation, that if I step up, I'm going to be fired. Third is, concern about intra-co-worker drama." If the tactics of the retail actions and press conference successfully get the company to meet with the campaign leaders, prevent anyone from getting fired, and are understood as the outcome of solidaristic worker leadership, the strategy will go far in addressing these concerns.

This new campaign story is initially designed for strategic purposes, as the image of generous and patient workers waiting for their boss to do the right thing is far superior to one of organizers struggling to get workers to return their calls. But even in our initial telling, the narrative begins to take on the role of the internal truth of the campaign, one used to accurately describe what has happened and what will happen next. In the narrative that staff members use, the militant-minority approach is not something thought up by the staff but, rather, is the outcome of "a couple of workers [who] want to restart the pressure against the company." It becomes the story of the campaign that we all use, not only in the meetings discussed above but also in Alejandro's conversations with workers and my conversations with allies. As we all deliver letters, hand out leaflets, and tell their stories, the discourse of worker leadership produces a social world characterized by the power of workers and populated by people who only follow the lead of those workers.

"The Power that Workers Have"

Eventually it seems that the conversation between Susan and the company may have stalled. At the same time, a national news piece about labor activism across the region includes a discussion about the FCC campaign and includes quotes by both CLP staff and company management. In tone and content, the reporting is a clear win for the campaign, laying out the CLP's demands at the FCC and hinting at an upcoming boycott strategy. In the article the company notes that they have an "open door policy" for their well-treated workers, and that the CLP is simply looking to create conflict where there is none.

Perhaps it should come as no surprise to me when management emails Susan a few days after the article is released, indicating that they are open to holding a meeting. The tone of the email is somewhat defensive, which perhaps makes sense given that a prime component of the campaign strategy has been to call out and shame the company. In their talking points, management writes that the company has offered health insurance since its inception and is in the process of providing a new plan they hope will be more affordable. While open to meeting, the email pushes back against the campaign demands as outside of what the company can afford. They further request that the social media attacks on the company be suspended as a requirement for meeting, and they frame the proposed dialogue as a potential win-win. In closing, management asks for a draft agenda, a list of who will be in attendance, and a neutral meeting place for the meeting.

When I flag Susan's email announcing the meeting in a morning where only the two of us are in the office, William is ecstatic. He laughs, pounding his desk in excitement. "Oh wow! The proof of the pudding is in the eating, right Biko?" He gets up and starts pacing the room, giving out rhythmic claps like one would hear at a sports game along with loud whoops. "You see," he says as he turns to me, "that's the power of *organization*! That's the power that *workers have* in an organization!" After laughing for a moment, he abruptly shifts his mood, scowling as he stabs his desk with a finger. "Eighteen years! *Eighteen years* they never acknowledged their workers! Eighteen years they told a story, this Garden of Eden fucking story, working for me is like the Garden of Eden. And that's the *truth* of our organization, that's the *truth* of the worker's movement. The truth is powerful. It's hard to *get! it! out!* You know? But once you get it out its powerful."

He and I return to the email and look again at the news article, trying to deduce how it might have pushed the company to respond. Sitting in his chair, William leans back, looking at the ceiling. "There's a long way to go. But this is huge to go from outright busting to the table?" He leans forward again, looking at me across his desk as he draws out the words. "Huuuge, *huuuuuuuge* milestone. Still, you're gonna still see a lot of ups and downs and deceptions and manipulation, but!"—he shakes his head, smiling—"this is the path." I nod along, smiling too. "It's like a story," he continues. He gesticulates with his hands as he narrows his eyes and speaks softly. "The beginning of the story is, once upon a time, there are decent human beings who got to earn a living, and then, came capitalism. And the bosses like FCC who exploited the workers. The workers put up with it, suffered, one day they started to . . ."—he shrugs, raising his hands—"to *consider* fighting it, then they decided to fight it! They train, they build, they launch, they launch a struggle, the employer fights the struggle, the employer ignores the struggle, the employer marginalizes the struggle, but *then*," he smiles, getting quiet. "The workers reach to a higher level of power, and then, the boss comes to the table." He exhales in satisfaction.

At this point James opens the door behind William, speaking into his cell phone. William claps him on the shoulder, enthusiastic. "Hey buddy! Good to see you, my man!"

James, somewhat confused by William's energy, smiles back with a raised eyebrow, "Yeah long time no see."

"We've got some good news today, man!" exclaims William, and he proceeds to give James the update, drawing him into the conversation as I listen from my desk.

William continues in his celebration, with hand claps and fist bumps. "And it's a real validation of our strategy, because our strategy is centered on this idea that *worker voice* can influence the marketplace!" He gives a huge smile, turning to me. "And you know we just noticed in the article right before the FCC paragraph"—he starts to laugh, gesturing to my computer where we had the article loaded—"it says right there, 'The CLP knocked out seventy-five customers for Delori!'" This refers to the long-fought boycott campaign that the CLP eventually won. Reading it again, he laughs. "You know, the FCC only has maybe 200 wholesale customers. With the debt they have on the warehouse they can't survive on 125!" He laughs again. "And the workers, man, the workers sticking it out, sticking it out, you know? I didn't even think we had muscled the company enough to get them to the table."

James and I listen as William continues, his voice gaining intensity. "Now we just have to power the track, hold through the ups and downs and deception, and wrest open space for workers to assert their authentic personality without fear of reprisal!" He takes a breath. "And I'm proud of the CLP institution. We didn't do like, no names mentioned . . ."—he puts his hands up, with a laugh—". . . some of our friends in the worker center community who, when things go wrong, they, ha ha ha, that campaign just gets deleted from the website!" This causes him to laugh very loudly, gasping for breath. "And you don't hear a lot about it! Or they run to the foundation trough for more money for a losing strategy, you know?"

Narrating Worker Leadership

Throughout this chapter, we have seen several examples of worker-leader narrative in action. In this world, worker leadership is both a goal to be worked toward and one that has been achieved. We performed and explained their practices from within this narrative while devoting serious energy to strategies designed to win over workers and bring them into the campaign. William's extended monologue offers several insights into the social world produced within the narrative, one that we all lived in and actively constructed. William was clearly excited about the news, as we all were, and as we should have been—an offer to hold a meeting is a tremendous milestone for the campaign. At the same time, our framing of the victory continually references workers as the prime actors in the story. The CLP and the worker-led union are the sites of their power and the vehicle for their struggle. The decision by the company to meet with the workers is evidence of the power of the workers, and therefore the power of the CLP. This is an uncontestable fact to those involved in the campaign. This intersection of workers and the CLP in this narrative collapses the two into a single actor—the workers are the CLP and the CLP is the workers.

To explain the process of truth construction, we need only to look to the changing nature of the new campaign narrative that we deploy. While it begins as part of a communication plan intended to inspire workers of the power of the campaign, when the FCC agreed to meet, the narrative transformed into the truth of the campaign. Where earlier we recognized that the "campaign was dead" but needed a more tactical way to explain the lull in activity, now our truth is that workers *have* been waiting, *have* launched a struggle, *have* reached a higher level of power. Narratives of worker leadership are actualized in these practices as they re-constitute the CLP and the FCC campaign as successful examples of worker-led union activity. In staff meetings, conference calls, and on the streets, the performative practices of the actors in this story create context-dependent knowledge and meaning, building out the truth-claims of worker leadership that enable further rounds of action within the framework provided by the larger discourse.

But this narrative was not merely rhetoric, as it opened up new possibilities for action that would have been otherwise excluded, enabling us to act in ways that we would not have otherwise. A campaign that staffers pronounced "dead" was moved from "We're Fucked, It's Over" to "a real validation of our strategy" and a meeting with the employer. Perhaps it could also move to new sources of funding and resources for the organization. Nonetheless, it was the activity of allies that provided the power. As we will see in the next chapter, for all of its strength, this ally power could not spark a greater interest in unionization among the workforce.

7

The Meeting and the Aftermath

In the immediate wake of the response from the company, morale among the staff was high. The next day we held an all-hands meeting where William, Alejandro, and I strategized about next steps while also going over the campaign with our interns. Midway through the meeting, one of the interns asked about the ultimate campaign goal of a worker-led union at FCC, wondering how it fit into the overall strategy.

"You arrived at the operative term!" William responds with a smile. "That's the essence of the goal. The goal doesn't say to make the FCC sign a contract with the CLP. It doesn't say the goal is to beat the boss, or a $25 wage, or free healthcare. It could have said that."

He takes a deep breath. "A rank-and-file–led union is the goal, that's the end state, that's the vision. A living, breathing organization of workers on the factory floor. An organization of workers that can, from the start and for years to come, decide on their demands for the workplace they desire, can formulate strategies to make those big picture improvements, can resolve more individualized or smaller scale abuses, like 'my paycheck didn't have the right hours this month,' or 'this manager called me a jerk,' or whatever." He smiles, looking at each of us. "So that's a very specific and meaningful choice, to say the goal is a worker-led union, one that isn't run by us or anyone else who isn't a worker." His voice rises a bit as he gets excited. "Because it means again, a living, breathing, organization, an organization of workers! Now it's part of a bigger movement, of other workers, in the industry, but the union is the micro unit, it's the building block, at their job."

Later in the meeting, I ask if we should be concerned that most of our engagement with the company is coming from outside of the workforce.

"Well, the militant-minority strategy is designed to deal with this!" William responds with a smile. "With the most important problem of the campaign, which was the defeat of the Leadership Committee! So absolutely! That's the essence of whether the strategy succeeds or not. We know we can go around and hammer any company if we want, we have a dedicated group of allies who want to go and fight for workers, you know? But that's

Worker Centered. Biko Koenig, Oxford University Press. © Oxford University Press (2024).
DOI: 10.1093/oso/9780197784907.003.0007

not our theory of change. Our theory of change is that workers themselves have the decisive power to change the world."

In discussing the offer that the FCC has made to hold a meeting, William and Alejandro emphasize that we need to see this not as a victory in itself, but rather as an opportunity for the campaign to "create space for workers to engage and organize. How can we leverage this opportunity to create more space and provide more room for the workers to build their own union?" In this context, the feeling is that it is an opportunity ripe with potential to bring in more members.

"If we had the meeting with the company tomorrow, it wouldn't make sense," says Alejandro. "We could have a meeting tomorrow, but we would have only one or two workers. But if we think this through, and do it carefully, and use this as an advantage for building the base. . . ."

Two tactics come out of this meeting. First, since the company has asked the CLP to draft an agenda, Alejandro will use this request to reach out to workers who used to be involved with the campaign. "The company has asked! That's perfect, because that shows acknowledgment of their force in their union," William smiles, "*The FCC* has asked . . ... that *you* as members, and *workers* at the FCC, draft the agenda! Because that's their request. That's good, that's great. Because that also shows acknowledgment by the opponent."

The second tactic is in response the request that the CLP suspend the "attacks" at their retail customers and on social media. We decide that we should do so only if the company circulates a letter to all employees that encourages their participation in the CLP and guarantees there will be no retaliation for joining. If management agrees to make this statement acknowledging CLP membership, this will be a tremendous step for the campaign and show that the militant-minority strategy has borne fruit.

Somewhat surprisingly, the company agrees to circulate a letter to the entire workforce. Throughout these discussions of the letter and scheduling the meeting, we continue to invoke the need for "workers," "worker-leaders," and "worker negotiators" to assess, discuss, and approve decisions. But regardless of the level of worker involvement, a letter asserting that workers can join the CLP along with a planned meeting between the CLP and the company are huge milestones in a campaign that seemed dead only months before.

Given our excitement about the response, I expect the meeting to be scheduled quickly. However, the first meeting does not occur until three months later. Some of the delay is due to simple challenges of finding a date and picking a location. The biggest reason that I can see, however, is the struggle to find workers who are willing to represent the campaign. In the intervening months Alejandro uses the promise of a meeting with the company as the incentive to bring workers in, run a training on negotiations, and set the agenda based on their demands. But after two weeks he is only able to secure David to attend.

In his opening comments of the meeting with David, William again offers the new narrative of the campaign we have developed in the months after the public launch:

> Last month, under the leadership of David, we restarted our engagement with leaflets at a retail customer, and then at the same time we asked our allies to communicate with the company via email and phone. It worked. Our engagement has now changed the position of the employer who would not acknowledge the right of workers to have their own organization, and they sent an email saying that they want to come to the table. It's a wonderful sign of the power that workers have in this campaign and just generally, and a very unique opportunity for workers to get to sit face to face with a powerful campaign and to start and win their demands.

While David provides a few preferences for things he is concerned about, we as staff are instrumental in developing the final package—full healthcare coverage paid by the company, $3-per-hour raises for all employees, longer paid breaks, and freedom from retaliation for joining the CLP or the union. This meeting does help to develop a set of demands that the staff will use alongside the letter from the FCC to schedule another training with workers. But Alejandro is concerned that he could only get David to attend in the first place. In a further blow to the campaign, we learn soon after that he has also decided to leave the company, leaving us with no workers fully committed to attending the meeting.

Preparing for the Meeting

A few weeks later, the tenacity of Alejandro's attempts to reach workers leads him to think he can get five workers to commit to attend trainings and the meeting with the FCC. We finally set a date for the meeting, and the company sends the following letter out to the employees with their paychecks:

To the Staff at Fishtown Condiment Co.:
Last year, some of our employees joined the CLP and signed a petition to have a meeting with me and the management of the factory. Now we have decided to meet with the CLP to explore our mutual goals, and we plan to have that meeting soon. We want to let you know that any employee is free to join the CLP; it is your decision. It is your right to participate in this process and there will be no retaliation for those who do participate.
Sincerely,
The FCC

As the staffers explain it to me, this letter is a huge victory for the campaign. First, it underscores the right to freedom of association—if workers are worried that they will be fired simply for joining the campaign, this letter explicitly removes that fear. Perhaps more importantly, workers who think the campaign is weak or futile now have clear evidence to the contrary. The leadership of the workers has finally convinced the company to come to the negotiating table. But even with the letter, Alejandro still struggles to get more workers on board, eventually scheduling a meeting with three workers to prepare for the upcoming negotiation. Two others express interest but cannot attend the entire training. Given the ongoing struggles of getting workers involved in the FCC campaign, this meeting is one of only a handful of worker meetings in which I participate.

The content of the meeting also illustrates the distance between how the workers think about the campaign and what the CLP would like them to do. The CLP model and much of our rhetoric describes an aggressive working class who are ready to fight their boss, defend their colleagues, and exert their power at the job site through collective direct action. But much of what the workers want to discuss are the details of their individual problems at work and how to fix them. One worker is concerned about how he is paid as a delivery driver, including a lack of transparency for route payments and problems about getting tickets while dropping off deliveries in the busier sections of town. He explains that the company has a questionable—and possibly illegal—pay scheme where drivers receive two checks for their work, one of which is a personal check rather than a company check. Another is worried about the costs of the health insurance plans, for which he pays an entire week's pay for a month of coverage.

But the training sessions go well, and the workers are excited about the upcoming meeting and feel confident that the company will listen to them and make the necessary changes. They seem less inclined about organizing with their co-workers or using direct action. Some even suspect that once they have the meeting, getting what they want will be easy. Alejandro and William work to remind them that they are only in this position because of the work they have done to get the company to the table. Alejandro puts it like this in his introductory remarks:

> As you all know, we want to congratulate everyone for the progress that you have all made, because if it was not for you guys, if it's not for the workers, the campaign does not exist. In reality, having a date confirmed with the boss to speak about how to make the workplace better, to speak about disrespect, things that can go better for you, having that date and knowing you are going to have the opportunity to do something, that is huge. In the letter that you all received, that the FCC is going to come to the table, that they are accepting membership of the workers in your union, that's huge. They really do not want to, but they have to do it because at the end of the day the campaign is not convenient for them. On the contrary, the campaign will continue to be strong, and it's so strong because you all are professionals and deserve to be treated as professionals.

William also frames the campaign in terms of worker power:

> Do you all know about the CLP and where it comes from? The CLP came from the idea of the workers that work in unjust places, they are leaders and have the voice and power to change their situation for something better. It is your voice, it's your power. So what does that mean? It means that we are going to support you to be professional negotiators to be able to have the same ability as the other side. FCC is going to invite their lawyers, and they are preparing. And so are you. You are going to have the same ability, because a meeting like this is part of the campaign. You can say it is part of the struggle. It can be at the table, not only on the streets, not only in the press, but it is part of the fight. They are very afraid to think about running a company with a voice of much stronger and more independent workers. It's very different for them. They never thought of having a situation like this.

William still hopes that they might attract upwards of twenty workers to the meeting, about the same as who signed the letter during the public launch, and the workers are themselves confident that a few more workers will sign onto the campaign very quickly. In the end, these three are the only FCC workers who attend.

The Meeting

When I first joined the CLP, my research goal was to explore how worker-led, direct-action labor groups were winning campaigns and reshaping the labor movement. Through my participation at the CLP and the FCC campaign, sitting in on the first meeting between workers and their employer would have represented an amazing opportunity to see how workers wielded their power in practice. More than a street action or social media campaign, the idea of workers at the table embodies the ideals of a worker-led movement—no business agents or meetings behind closed doors, but workers themselves making demands for their own lives.

As the date for the meeting with the FCC neared, I had no idea what to expect from the meeting given the challenges we had faced. How would the three workers who had agreed to attend try to command power with a relatively weak campaign? What would the practice of worker leadership look like in this context, and how would it be understood?

Since the company does not want to meet at either the factory or the CLP office, we instead meet at a conference room in a nearby church that I had rented for the morning. FCC management sits on one side of the two tables that I have pushed together. On the CLP side, William is joined by the three workers who had attended the trainings. Alejandro sits on one end of our side to provide translation, I sit on the other to take notes, and Susan sits at the head of the table, having been invited as a neutral observer.

After introductions and handshakes, the conversation begins with William inviting each of the three FCC workers to present opening remarks in turn. Their comments are similar: gratitude for the opportunity to work at FCC, their personal stories of immigration, and the importance of collaboration between management and workers to strengthen the company further. In response, the managers express their commitment to creating a positive work environment where employees feel comfortable speaking up.

They also acknowledge the importance of addressing workers' concerns and express readiness to continue the conversation.

William then steers the discussion toward the three main issues raised by workers: respectful treatment by management, fair raises, and healthcare. The company acknowledges that while the pay system is complicated given the variation between the routes, it is also transparent. The workers, for their part, offer counter-examples of how their routes have changed to include more stops or longer times, but their pay has not increased in kind.

Management also shares, to my surprise, that a group of delivery workers had approached them with these concerns some months ago, and that the company was in the process of developing a new pay plan for the drivers. I hadn't known that workers had been meeting with the company outside of our campaign. This sets off a discussion that quickly gets heated, as people on both sides start talking over each other. In the first instance, William wants to see the new compensation plan for drivers. Management offers to share the plan when they have finished developing it, though they do not have a deadline yet. William presses them to agree on a clear date for when the plan will be ready, but the company pushes back, saying they are being accountable to those drivers who offered the complaints in the first place.

"I appreciate that," Willian nods. "And that's a wonderful thing, and I certainly hope that nothing we say here would impugn on the work that's being done there. I just hope that we all assume good intentions, on both sides, otherwise what's the point of dialogue, and our framework here is mutual gain. You know, all I honestly hear is 'How is my pay calculated?'" He laughs. "I consider that a pretty reasonable question. If you don't feel comfortable sharing the current system, maybe there's some problems with it you've identified; I'll see how folks feel about that. Personally, I feel if folks are OK, but if you feel uncomfortable. . . ."

Again, the company refuses to agree to any firm commitments. William takes this as resistance to the process of workers joining the CLP. When he finally asks again for the company to set a firm date as to when they could make the plan available, management offers to let them know when they can set a date to say when it will be ready. As the conversation gets tense, people leave no time for translation, so the back-and-forth has happened in English with Alejandro struggling to keep up.

William slaps both hands on the table. "Ok, we're going to have to take a moment." He looks around, "Friends? Let's go outside." The workers stand with William and Alejandro, and William taps me on the shoulder to join them as we go into the hallway. Speaking quickly in Spanish, he lets out a string of curses before getting to his main argument. "We asked a very clear question, very basic, how do I calculate my pay?" He strikes one hand with another to emphasize his point, his words an intense whisper in the hallway. "I wonder what we're going to do about this, if they're not going to give us a concrete answer, then they're not taking the process seriously. Not taking it seriously. If you're not prepared today? No problem, just tell us when you're going to send it. I recommended they give us a date." He looks around at all of us, and toward the workers. "It's your decision, friends, but I would want them to give me a date." The workers agree.

After we return the room, one of the workers emphasizes that this problem needs a solution and that it has been over five months since the company told the drivers that it would address the issue. William speaks up, stating that while perhaps the driver payment system is going to be solved, and that he believes everyone is there in good faith, "We can't accept this idea that you can't commit to a simple sharing of information." The response from management is unchanged—the plan will be shared "soon."

"The workers, as leaders of the Clara Lemlich Project," responds William, "need to see the plan so that they can decide whether it's something they can celebrate, or if it's something they're going to have to take a different path on, right? So the reason we're here," he laughs, "is to maximize the ability of celebrating FCC. Look, it's incredible, what I've heard these workers say, all the workers I've talked to at the company. Everyone says 'My goal is to give my all to this company. To take it to the next level.' That's not propaganda, that's not spin, you know, one might argue, you might talk to workers who are trying to make some changes and they might not have such loyalty!" He laughs again. "I've actually been very moved by that, everyone says, 'I have two goals: grow my family's well-being, and grow the company.' Right? So, we're not here to play gotcha, but we're here to try to celebrate... We're just looking to continue that same process." Eventually the company agrees to a one-week deadline to tell us when the plan will be ready.

The rest of the meeting follows this pattern. As we move from wages to healthcare to respect for the CLP membership, a worker will offer an opening comment based on their personal experience and William will take up the conversation from there. Workers will occasionally interject with comments or questions about their pay or the cost of health insurance. But at many points, the speed of the conversation is too fast for Alejandro's efforts at translation. As emotions rise, people forget to pause or to slow down, though I am unclear how much this impacts the ability of the workers to follow the conversation, given that they have some proficiency in English.

For the most part, the company shares vague information about the state of their economics: costs have gone up, they haven't given raises out this year—apparently for only the second year since the company was founded—and while they are rolling out a new insurance package, they realize that many workers will struggle to afford it. At the same time, the managers claim that it is increasing their own costs without providing better health options, but that it is all they can afford. But no details are offered. In addition to the significant delays in addressing the drivers' plan as noted by the workers, my analysis of the company's response is that it is largely limited to vague assurances and superficial statements, offering little substantial support or concrete solutions to address workers' concerns.

The final part of our agenda is scheduling the next meeting, which takes the company by surprise, as they did not anticipate needing to meet again. From the perspective of the campaign this meeting is only the beginning, an opportunity to collect more information and to organize more workers. But the underlying goal is to eventually win all the points on the initial demands letter. The company does not seem to understand this, and the conversation once again gets tense as FCC continues resist having another meeting, expressing skepticism as to why it is necessary, and William continues to point toward resolving the petition that workers delivered.

Eventually, the question of representation comes up as management asks about the membership structure of the CLP—who constitutes its membership and how does one join? William explains that becoming a CLP member involves filling out a simple document, which is free and accessible to all. But the FCC still expresses some confusion, perhaps strategically, about the role of the workers in the meeting. Are there other members? William clarifies that the three workers in the meeting are the delegates authorized to represent and speak on behalf of the campaign at FCC.

"Well, it's not a representational model," William continues. "That's important to point out, that it's a delegate model, but they have a mandate to speak, so it's not like a politician representing anybody. There is a petition that was signed [the letter workers submitted at the soft and public launch], which one could refer to, and as I think"—here he changes the topic—"probably both sides are sort of feeling each other out, which I feel is very healthy, and I know that campaigns have a lot of emotions involved on both sides, but absolutely, we can move to a place where there's complete transparency and dialogue going forward."

The discussion to schedule the next meeting continues to spark disagreements. William asks for it to happen in two weeks, while management asks that they agree to meet in principle but set the date in one week when they send along the date to share the driver compensation plan.

I jump slightly in my chair as William slaps the table, raising his voice to a high volume, "We have a worker who has given fifteen years of his life to this company . . . so what happens to the future of the brand is very important, we all have to safeguard it, so I understand if—." Management balks at the idea that the CLP has the company's best interest in mind. "We have to safeguard it," William responds, "because our members are the ones who pack and deliver the products and care for their families. So we're very flexible on dates. We're trying to set up a date here. I haven't had any problems with dates so far. . . ." Eventually management agrees to get back later in the day with possible times.

While both sides eventually agree on the details, the back-and-forth includes an argument where William hints that if the company doesn't agree to negotiate on the driver compensation agreement, the campaign would be back on. "And absolutely, you could unilaterally impose the new terms, and then we can decide whether we like it or not and respond." The managers resist this, citing that they want to speak to all the drivers. William adds, "I mean, we're here to try and solve these problems and make FCC better, but if you want to call it whatever you want to call it, that's fine with us, we don't care. But if you don't want to try and make FCC better with us, then we can take a different path."

After two hours, both sides agree to meet again, and the CLP will share their proposal for concrete next steps to resolve the campaign the day before the meeting. As we are getting up to leave, Susan speaks up for the first time, taking an agreeable and positive tone. "If I could say one thing, it would be the PLJA's vision is something that everybody shares in this room, communicated in different ways, to have a worksite that respects the workers. I think we all agree on that. I'll just say, beyond these principles and philosophies, that my personal experience is that as intense and uncomfortable as these conversations can be, they are far better than the alternative! I would encourage you all to think about, 'What is this process?' and I think it's fine that it's not entirely clear yet. Just keep in mind that it could be defined." She adds with a laugh, "And to keep it going!"

Processing the Meeting

Later that day, we convene for a full staff meeting, where the conversation swiftly shifts to discussing our session with the FCC. James, who didn't attend, states that the workers must be feeling great after the conversation. We are all feeling pretty elated, and William answers with enthusiasm:

"Oh yeah, they're feeling good, right? They saw that *you're* in the driver's seat! The company isn't in the driver's seat, *you* fought the company, *you're* telling them what they have to do." He pauses, leaning back in his chair. "It's a process, leadership development is something you go through and it's a process. It's really something to teach, and I wrote this down, stay silent after your questions! It's not on you to justify it after you've already justified it. You asked, 'How do you calculate my pay?' Just ask, and when they don't answer, push them to do it. It's little things like that."

I ask him what happens next. "What we wanted to do was get some valuable information so that workers can now formulate the final proposal, get a second meeting, and, more than anything, empower and excite the workers to go back to their coworkers and say, 'Hey, we are alive! We didn't just sit there and get told stuff, we sat there and *we* set the agenda.' They were all . . .'"—here he does a an impression of the FCC managers—"'We don't want to set another meeting,' and we were . . . 'NO!,'" slamming his hand into the table to emphasize the point, ". . . if you want this process to continue." He laughs. "So you know, it was just so fucking cool!"

Alejandro, for his part, still voices concerns about worker engagement and is surprisingly circumspect given William's excitement. "I think the most important thing we accomplished was that our leaders continue to be solid. They met last week to prepare, to do the final touches and prepare for the meeting today, and that was crucial for the meeting today, to have in the little time that we've been together in the campaign, to be prepared. But you know it's, still feels fragile." He sighs. "One day they're there and the next day they're turned off by something that someone said. The fact that our leaders showed up today, I think that was the most important thing that we accomplished. They also accepted and understand that they need to meet regularly, and accepted to do that."

William senses his hesitation and tries to bring him back to a higher level of optimism. "Please reach down, just reach down, and try. . . ." He pauses. "Because I think . . ."—here he emphasizes each word—"This . . . is . . . the moment! The company says they won't retaliate in the letter, workers sat face-to-face with the whole entire senior management team and their lawyer . . ."; his tone shifts as he gets excited, emphasizing each word. "And the workers made their voice heard, and were strong, and the company has asked"—again, he emphasizes each word—"'what . . . are . . . your . . . demands to make . . . this . . . campaign . . . not pressure us anymore!' This is the opportunity, this opportunity is here, and it won't be here for long. It's now. It's now. You know? I feel like if we go on with a very amazing opportunity message, we can get people together! We can get people around this table! Here are your coworkers! They're alive! Their heads didn't get chopped off! They're here back at work, look, they're loving it, they're buzzing!" His voice rises. "They're feeling their power. You know?"

Alejandro still has concerns, though. "One thing I feel is, that . . . I of course have, either on the phone or face-to-face, encountered workers to update on the progress of what the campaign has done. And their responses are mixed, the majority are still. . . ." Here he uses a bored tone of voice: ". . . 'Oh that's good. Good to know,' but still I can't engage them and. . . ." He looks up, searching for his words. "I haven't been able to . . . with those workers that are lukewarm, to find the space for them to . . . they're holding back. They want to wet their feet but that's . . . ," he mumbles and leans back in his chair as he leaves his thought unfinished.

My own perspective is that the FCC will do whatever it takes to keep the CLP—or any organized group of workers—from having any kind of power within the company. While their language was about caring for their employees, fairness in treatment, and concerns about affordability, they were clearly not open to any arrangement of worker–employer relations beyond the traditional capitalist model. In their view, workers should take what they're given, and if they don't like it, they can leave. Further, they *should* like it, and be thankful to work at a company like this. The company will make changes that will benefit their bottom line—if this includes raising wages or other benefits to employees, then so be it. But if those items are not what management wants, there is no interest in negotiating or compromise. The challenge for the CLP was that most of the workers didn't seem interested in challenging this structure.

The meeting also made it clear to me that, at this point, workers were not substantive leaders in the campaign. I saw this in the overall arc of the conversation, found in the large gaps in translation efforts, William's facilitation of the conversation, and the simple lack of worker participation in the conversation. In fact, beyond some brief discussion with William about their availability for the next meeting, none of the workers spoke for the final forty-five minutes of the meeting. William later explained to me that some of his approach in the meeting was intentional, geared to try to get "under the skin of the opponent" and to show workers that they could "stand up to the boss and survive." But given his consistent fear that "staff initiative displaces the genuine voice of the worker," he was unreflective as to how staff had driven the process.

As I saw in earlier planning meetings, workers participated in trainings and offered feedback on the demands and agendas that staff members developed. This mirrored many of the earlier examples from the campaign, from the decisions about the public launch to later strategies such as the Bank of America Letter or the retail actions. If worker leadership is supposed to mean some degree of substantive agency over the campaign, the organization, and staff members, it was absent. Much like every other step of the campaign, the support offered by the CLP would be better described as leadership over, and direction of, workers. Of course, this handful of workers helped to legitimate the narrative of worker leadership, actualizing the discourse with limited forms of participation and endorsement. As I have stated before, the staff did not see the campaign in this way, with William going so far as to offer a critique of other groups with thin member participation: "Like how [another local worker center] does it, they send one worker, you know? Not that I'm saying that's good or anything, don't get me wrong! . . . without that one worker in their whole operation things would get really dicey."

One reading of this meeting would be to critique the CLP on its own terms, arguing that in speaking on behalf of workers in a meeting or designing a campaign plan without their substantive input, they are indeed displacing the initiative of workers. But I think any analyses along these lines are misplaced. First, from a purely strategic orientation, we should accept that the attempt to make space for more workers to participate in the campaign via the actions of non-workers, and to attribute those actions and their impacts to the workers, was not successful. At least in this context, the retail actions, phone calls to the company, official letters to the workers, and the experience of training for and holding a meeting with senior management was not enough. Though the discourse of worker leadership tried to frame these activities in worker-centric ways, they nonetheless centered on the power, agency, and perspectives of staff and allies.

Further, we should interrogate the misplaced expectation that any worker new to movement work could exert any real authority over a campaign.

These workers need the training, guidance and leadership development that those with skills, expertise, and vision can offer. In other words, they require the guidance and expertise of individuals such as the CLP staff. However, the narrative of worker leadership combined with the insistence of pushing the campaign forward at all costs fails to acknowledge this reality, thereby disregarding the needs and capabilities of workers in favor of ideological consistency and keeping to a campaign timeline. Consequently, staff members blur the distinctions between their own leadership and the influence of allies with that of the workers. As illustrated earlier, this results in the goals of the organization and the campaign overshadowing the actual development of the workers themselves, where an important campaign milestone can overshadow the lack of substantive worker leadership and reflections on how to achieve it.

A Funder Visit

In one of my last days at the office we have a visit from two foundation staffers who work are considering renewing a large grant for the CLP. For this occasion, William and Alejandro prepped two workers to join, one from the FCC and one from Finn's Distribution.

The meeting gets started with the worker from Finn's, talking through Alejandro as an interpreter, sharing his experience at work and organizing with the CLP. He talks about the problems with job security and safety, lack of respect as workers, and low pay, emphasizing the role of the CLP in training him how to meet with and organize his coworkers. I have heard this speech many times, as we have recently had several meetings with elected officials and we always begin with his speech introduction. And while one of our shared critiques of other worker centers and unions is that they "walk out a worker to share some sweatshop story, and then the rest is just staff and funders talking," this is what we've been doing for a few weeks now with this worker. And when one of our visitors asks about the state of the CLP's campaigns, it is William who answers.

He starts by noting the success and limitations of the worker-center model in similar terms to what was described in Chapter 2. "But the life we imagine for members and supporters, it's not just legal compliance! So the new chapter is, how do we go from the wonderful work the worker-center community has done with lawsuits and codes of conduct to ... what's a decent job that people aspire to? Benefits, retirement, raises, time off . . . so today our campaigns are much more ambitious and require us to muster a lot more power and members. For example, the FCC needs to accept membership forever, not just a retroactive code of conduct. To get that we went out and our members won regular meetings with the company leadership." The FCC worker then shares about their issues with wages and healthcare, but notes that we have a second meeting scheduled with management happening very soon.

William chimes in, sliding two pieces of paper across the table. "I've never seen the power of workers to go from this," here he points to the anti-union letter FCC shown in Chapter 3, "to this," pointing to the letter from the company indicating they are free to join the CLP. "We've never had the ability to move things like this. I just have high respect for what workers have done." After describing the narrative of how the campaign has unfolded, he points to the second letter from the campaign. "And the company started talking to our ally coalition and [the new letter] came out of that, we've had two meetings, and [this worker] has been a lead negotiator."

The program officers both seem very impressed, nodding along with William and looking over the letters. One asks, "Can you say more about the trainings and leadership development?"

"Well, it's A to Z," says William. "We start with the basics. We use role-playing and inoculation, show the campaign strategy, and how to leverage strengths and influences. This training is where the ally press conference idea came out of. We also train in public speaking. Our aspiration is—and not every worker wants this, but those who do become full-fledged organizers. Learning about facilitation, agenda making. We use a combo of classroom work, role-playing, and learning by doing. So, at the FCC they negotiate with the company, and our staff is there in a support role or to answer questions."

Although I nodded along in the meeting, later I would come to recognize that our descriptions of worker leadership to the program officers exaggerated the state of two campaigns that were each struggling to connect with workers. We similarly overstated our leadership development program—what William described is more aspirational than descriptive. At the same time, it is something that all of us in that meeting believed.

This is one example of how the commitment to worker leadership as a source of legitimacy—one shared by staffers, allies, and founders—had grown deep roots into our movement. As staff we made every effort to conceive of our work as worker-led. As allies we had clear preferences about which organizations were most worth our time. And for funders? As James would later explain it to me, "The members have to lead; if it's staff driven the funders don't like that." I would find these roots in my conversations with staff at other worker centers, where these systemic preferences shaped how organizations had to position themselves and the role of members in their work. The conversation recounted above, with its aspirational characterizations of the campaigns, must be understood within this wider movement context. We might reflexively point to these descriptions as a problem. But given the structural demands and ideological expectations of this ecosystem, what else should we expect? The core of the problem is not found in the descriptions of worker leadership used by staff at the CLP, but rather it is in the particular version of worker leadership that defines the structure. The solution is not a higher standard of worker leadership but, as I describe in the final chapter, a different way of approaching what leadership is and where it comes from.

Moving Forward

The next meeting between the workers and the company was scheduled to occur two weeks after the first. As part of this, the company shared their revised driver payment plan with us, which seemed to make a complicated payment system more transparent but did not increase wages. My analysis of the new healthcare plan was that, while it offered new options, it did not offer much to workers who would effectively face the same out-of-pocket costs. From what I could surmise, it was the cheapest that the company could implement within the law.

In turn, we sent our proposal to fully address the workers' requests and institute a framework that combined high standards for workers with high profits for the company. The topline item was the creation of a "Profitable Development Committee" comprised of FCC, the PLJA, the CLP, and the workers' union. The details of what the committee would do are not yet fleshed out, though William imagines that it would involve promoting the company on social media and could be used to help spark campaigns at other companies with lower standards.

Of the remaining demands, some were low-hanging fruit, such as ensuring that paychecks are in full compliance with the law. Others were much larger, including a raise for all employees, substantially increasing the company's healthcare contribution, regular meetings between the campaign and management, and allowing workers to talk about the union during work time. However, we did not send the final letter until the evening before the meeting, leading management to ask for more time to consider the workers' proposal, and the next negotiation was pushed back by a month.

A few weeks after the first meeting, it seems that Alejandro's concerns about worker interest are still valid. Even with the letter from the company encouraging workers to participate, a successful first meeting, and a list of demands that would seemingly help all the workers, he still struggles to keep them interested in the campaign. As he explains in a staff meeting, this includes some of those who attended the first negotiation. "I had long conversations with two different workers, but I have been just chasing the third. I couldn't get him a single day last week, which has been worrisome, he's sliding back. But one of the others sees him at work, has been trying to talk to him, so I've been trying to support them to try to get co-workers to come to the next meeting, to try and get the snowball getting bigger, but we're on a very steep part of the hill right now, and as far as staying with the campaign, they continue to say they're in the fight, that they're not going to let go. However, one of them. . . ." He sighs. "The challenge is keeping them motivated. Today one thing we wanted to do was practice roleplays, and when we got to that he refused to do it. He said, 'Why? We've talked to the other workers so much, but now everybody or most people are not talking to me anymore.' He feels like he talks and talks and talks to them all the time and he isn't able to make any progress. And the new workers that have come here, they say, 'Let Alejandro call me.'" He lets out another sigh. "They need a lot of help, a lot of intervention, a lot of help and a lot of just checking in, I think, because they're not moving other workers forward. You get the sense when someone doesn't respond to multiple texts and voicemails that they're getting very scared."

Again, William tries to coach him through it, but Alejandro remains frustrated at the challenge. "The thing is that a lot of workers still have the misconception that it's just going to happen, that, you know, that this has a start and a finish, as if you're negotiating a contract. Many people are saying that, 'I'll join when you guys are done fighting, I'll join when this is over.'" He continues. "Talking to workers doesn't solve the problem of the deeply engrained loyalty and feelings that the company deserves what they make, which I have personally heard from many workers directly, also from our leaders."

"That's the challenge with working class organizing overall," says William. "I think Marx called that false consciousness." He laughs. "I dunno, I'm not a Marxist! But you think of the boss's interest and not your own interest. Maybe the workers . . . maybe they need to see something bigger, something moving, you know, that's what got this moving in the first place. We showed them some power, we took the lead as a staff and community with David . . . and we did use external help, which is fine! There's nothing wrong with that, as long as it's connected to worker leadership."

We talk about some strategies for how to motivate the base of workers at the FCC, considering some different actions that could illustrate the community's support for the workers. "Let's be real, I think sometimes we're too pure? You know, it's like, you expect workers to lead the way and that everyone follows that, and that's what we're aiming for, but we also have to see the world as it is. We've talked to worker after worker, you know? They want to know when the government's going to come in and help, they want to know what politicians are helping, they want to know where the lawyers are, they want to know what other forces are there for them. And in our ideological minds we reject that, and we say, 'you're the leaders and that's all bullshit.' Maybe we just have to be more flexible, and we do have to pull out the allies and others to show you're not alone, and maybe you're not even leading right now!"

He throws up his hands before quickly walking it back. "No that's too extreme, but, you're . . . co-leading, or something. Just give people what they want! I mean, within the vision, obviously we're not going to be their representatives and take care of their problems, and go fight the boss ourselves every day." He sighs. "I'm just thinking out loud because we have a big opportunity in front of us. Remember, we have the power to engage the company. We have that. That's good. That part is good. Now we just need the other part. Which, granted, is harder, but thank God we've got the first part."

William's comments are the closest thing to an admission of a lack of worker leadership that I will hear the staff offer at my time with the CLP. His gesture to false consciousness is equally provocative, as it implies that workers might *not* inherently know what is best for them. These are treacherous rhetorical snares for those of us ideologically attached to the notion of worker leadership. But it also shows the strength of our convictions as we strove to frame the history, the problems, and the solutions as worker-led.

The Denouement

I continued with the CLP for another two months, during which time we held our second meeting with the company. Management began that meeting by reading a prepared statement discussing the changes that the company had already made for the workers, emphasizing the new healthcare plan and driver payment scheme. For the most part, the company rejected the CLP's demands, only offering to have quarterly meetings to discuss the Profitable Development Committee if the CLP were interested in helping to grow the company. But the company was unwilling to continue meetings nor hold them at the worksite, claiming it already had an "open door policy." The FCC made it clear that workers were free to meet with the CLP, to be members, and to wear whatever organizational insignias they wanted to, but that management did not have anything else to discuss with the campaign.

When we pressed them on all the items—especially pay raises and healthcare—management curtly noted they were unable to offer anything more due to the costs the company was facing, and that there was not anything left to talk about. For the most part, the FCC detailed what it had already offered before the meetings had begun and stonewalled the rest of the demands. The meeting ended with a general agreement to meet again when William pressed for it, but without a clear plan or date.

I remained somewhat in the CLP orbit after my departure, as I spent several months completing supplementary fieldwork, conducting follow-up interviews, and volunteering with the PLJA. This continued participation with the Alliance allowed for some insights into the FCC campaign through the committee we had developed to work with the CLP. At the same time, once I left the CLP there were few updates to be had. A few months after I'd left, the staff was still struggling to organize workers, though the company had agreed to a token raise framed as a response to inflation rather than the campaign (I never did get the details of the proposed amounts). I heard that there had been a few more meetings throughout the next year, and I eventually facilitated a conversation between the CLP and some community activists to discuss a potential letter of support and some leafleting actions.

In the year after my departure, Susan sat in on a few more meetings and reported that the FCC continued to resist any talk of higher wages or increases in healthcare payments, apparently showing the CLP their financial records to prove that they could not afford them. The major boycott campaign that I assumed would be the next step never materialized. Outside of a few social media posts, this seemed to be the end of the CLP campaign at the FCC. All signs indicated that the FCC campaign was over, though perhaps it will live again in the future.

In the immediate aftermath of the FCC campaign, the CLP soon returned to its historic roots—using the supply-chain strategy to campaign on behalf workers dealing with illegal worksite practices, unsafe working conditions, and unlawful terminations with fired workers at the front and center of campaigns. As I noted in the Preface, in the many years since I ended this research, all of the organizations involved have gone through significant strategic changes, all have experienced major turnovers in staff, and some have closed shop. I imagine that those who were involved with the FCC campaign, wherever they are, continue to fight for a vision of radical worker leadership and direct action.

Conclusion

A Courageous Experiment

Introduction

The day of the CLP's yearly fundraiser also marked my final day at CLP after fifteen months with the organization. Amid the pageantry, music, and speeches, the main purpose of the gala was to raise funds for the organization. I spent most of the evening coordinating our team of volunteers who ran the event, but I was able to catch some of William's remarks as I stood in the back of the union hall we had rented for the night:

> The Clara Lemlich Project exists to help workers *lead together*; to create a better world for all of us. . . . When everyday workers—immigrant workers, workers of color, women workers—cultivate their inner strength, develop their leadership voice, and become protagonists of social change; their positive influence extends far beyond the workplace. It's the key to a better world.

On my last day in the field, my own opinion was stuck between the struggles of the campaign and the promise of a worker-led movement. I continued to find the narrative of William's "better world" enticing and important. I saw the value in such a framework, and as I looked around at the assembled group of movement actors, I knew it also resonated for them. When combined with the real, material gains that the CLP has won for workers in its history, who wouldn't want to see more of this vision?

And for all of the struggles that the CLP faced in its campaign at FCC, we should keep in mind the context in which they fought. As discussed in the opening chapters, the workers that the CLP aims to organize routinely face low wages, bad working conditions, and rampant illegal and unethical practices, and they receive limited help from both the regulatory state and the traditional labor movement. Thus, in the end, I still agree with the way that one former staffer put it: "For all of the problems at the CLP and their struggles getting workers on board, what the labor movement really needs is

Worker Centered. Biko Koenig, Oxford University Press. © Oxford University Press (2024).
DOI: 10.1093/oso/9780197784907.003.0008

more CLPs. More people talking to low-wage workers, to immigrant workers, to try to show them how to lead." Such an approach seems crucial to building a powerful, worker-centric movement for a fair and just society. In this final chapter, I aim to distill what I have learned from this case and how we might best put it to use to serve these ends.

Reflecting on the CLP 2.0

What narrative emerges regarding worker leadership in this story, and what accomplishments did it yield? Within this framework, what social realities were constructed, and what sorts of practices were empowered or foreclosed as a result? In the discursive world of the CLP, movement activity was understood to follow from worker leadership. This imbued the FCC campaign with a dual nature—one exemplified by, yet also striving for, worker leadership. We enacted this duality with strategies like the "militant minority," narratives that were understood as the product of worker leadership and simultaneously a pathway to restart a campaign with marginal worker participation. The discourse enabled actors like William, Susan, and me to be true to our political values, while, at the same time, we endeavored to achieve the conditions that would allow those values to be realized.

That the campaign reached significant milestones is a testament to the resolve with which we held onto those values, our belief in the campaign, and the tenacity of the staff to push the work forward. Getting the company to agree to multiple meetings and sending support letters to every worker are incredible achievements in a context where management holds most of the power. But the central goal of the campaign—a worker-led union— was never in sight. After the challenges of the public launch, the gambit was that ally power and staff leadership could make the space that workers would then fill. The more confrontational tactics (and threats of tactics) were successful in convincing the company to change course, but not in encouraging, empowering, or organizing workers to join the campaign. For all of the concerns about staff leadership displacing the initiative of workers, the campaign only went on for as long as it did due to the commitment of allies and staff.

In endeavoring to understand what happened, my reflections circle back to the lack of substantive leadership by workers. Workers participated at crucial moments that enabled the struggle to continue. Without a worker's attendance in the first meeting with Susan, the PLJA press release tactic may have never been developed. David was the only worker to participate in a leafleting action and, for several months, the only worker who was actively involved. The three workers who attended the first meeting with the company provided the information required to make clear demands to the company and acted as representatives in the meetings held with management. But it would be a stretch to find substantive worker leadership in this story. Workers did not consider the trade-offs between the tactics of street actions and ally letters, they did not author the communications sent to fellow workers, and they did not provide direction to staff members. Against all the efforts of the staff, the CLP fell into the trap that Jenkins describes where, in practice, the role of the workers was often reduced to conveying the human impact of the campaign to more important power holders (Jenkins 2002). I believe that had the campaign seen more success in organizing workers, the leadership development opportunities of "classroom-based trainings, one-on-one coaching, and hands-on experience" that the staff alluded to may have become more of a reality. But the notion of leadership development itself indicates the power dynamic at play between workers and staff, something the staff was reluctant to acknowledge. In most instances, workers, like anyone new to movement work, need to develop their skills before they can lead.

This leads to the fundamental contradiction of worker leadership in the FCC campaign. As William put it, "Our theory of change is that workers themselves have the decisive power to change the world." It is, of course, true that workers have a unique type of economic power that stems from their relationship to the means of production—workers, when organized, can exert real pressure on their employers through shop-floor actions. Allies and staff can never reproduce this type of power on their own. But at the campaign's strongest moment, the power of allies was paramount. During its greatest achievement, staff members took the lead in talking with the company. In enacting a model of radical worker leadership, the organization reproduced the dynamics of a top-down advocacy organization. The notion of worker leadership was vital to the rhetoric of the campaign, but the power of staff and activists was central to its achievements.

The CLP 2.0 experiment at the FCC illustrates a model with several formidable aspects, especially the ability of allies to leverage power against the company through direct-action tactics, media campaigns, and moral arguments. When placed alongside the organization's history of success, approaches like the supply-chain strategy excelled when allies partnered with workers who had been fired or who were already agitated. Unlike the efforts at the FCC, those campaigns did not require organizing other workers, nor did they need a majority of workers to be involved. But the prevailing market conditions, lack of worker interest, and the difficulties we faced strategizing within this context made the goal of a rank-and-file union hard to reach. These factors were further complicated by an organizing model that coupled an explicit vision of worker leadership with an implicit requirement of significant ally and staff participation to work—a point illustrated by a campaign plan with few requirements for worker action. As we have seen, the underlying organizing model relied on the interpretation of staff as to what workers wanted and how they would act and with limited reflection about what to do when they didn't fit these assumptions. And our discursive framework made it hard for us to appreciate either of these dynamics in real time. What we see instead, perhaps unsurprisingly, is a model that would work well in a classic worker-center workplace justice campaign where ally power can push a company to a meeting or hold them accountable in the face of illegal practices. But the goal of widespread worker leadership struggled in situations where workers were not already eager to join and offered scant conceptual room for organizing strategies that required significant direction from staff members. Put simply, for all the power the campaign could leverage, it could not make a worker-led union without workers.

While this research has focused on a case of a failed campaign, this should not be interpreted as a condemnation of the organization, nor a denunciation of the individual actors involved in the story. Many high-profile union drives and social justice campaigns suffer defeats and setbacks. But given our inability to capture the interest of workers at the FCC, my aim has been to explore not just the efficacy but also the limits of our worldview. This conclusion should be understood within a wider movement context where labor faces an uphill battle in practically all organizing drives. At this point, we need deeper analyses of organizing strategies if we are to improve the possibilities for workers to exert power at their workplaces and throughout society.

For the remainder of this chapter, I have three aims. The first is to urge that we evolve our expectations about effective worker leadership. When campaigns stem from staff-led and ally-supported organizations that desire to empower the rank and file, worker leadership is an *outcome* rather than an *origin*. The same is likely true with campaigns that start with a small committee of worker-leaders if our goal is to expand that cadre to a majority. Building on this, I then consider not only the roles that allies and staff members can play in the development of worker agency, but how this requires frank, transparent reflections about our own power and privilege. I argue that the question is not about how we can best set aside our authority to let workers authentically lead but, rather, how can we best put our resources and knowledge to work in our collective struggle for liberation? Finally, in light of this research, I end with a consideration of how allies might hold firm to their desire for worker power while actively contributing to movement spaces that seek to build it. Here I advocate for deeper ties between allies and labor organizations, clear definitions of authority within organizations, the development of membership-based ally organizations, and active engagement in policy advocacy to empower workers and advance labor justice.

Ethics, Power, and Outcomes

What would it mean to evolve beyond the limitations of worker leadership that occurred in the FCC campaign while nonetheless trying to center the voice, power, and agency of workers? Among many of the staff and allies I spoke with throughout the labor movement, the feeling was that the choices outside of efforts like the CLP model seemed quite stark, either a return to traditional, staff-led unionism or the "mere advocacy" of professionally led non-profits—worthy of our time but limited in strategy and vision. In such a framework, supporting organizations like the CLP so that they could "hold space" until "workers were ready" to assert leadership and take charge of the movement seems necessary. These polarized choices stem from the ideological purity at the heart of the worker-leader discourse—either workers are leading *right now* (good), or they are not (bad). We need to move past this binary that motivates our allyship and recognize that we can't organize our way out of the dilemmas of authenticity and representation discussed in the first chapter. Instead, we must accept the nuance and messiness that is a part of movement work in a complex social world and embrace the contingent and emergent nature of leadership within organizing contexts.

In environments where movement activity often requires some people to facilitate the processes by which others are changed, processes laden with power and privilege, how can liberatory projects move forward without reproducing the very structures we aim to contest? This is an especially cogent question in contexts that involve actors from outside of the communities of oppressed people. These situations seem to present a political impasse, where the structural conditions of resource generation and political contestation make it difficult, if not impossible, for activists to genuinely speak for and represent oppressed communities in a way that doesn't simply empower those activists and reinforce their privilege. Linda Alcoff refers to this as the "crisis of representation"—regardless of the political content, when we advocate on another's behalf, we cannot escape how representational speech acts center the authority and interpretation of the speaker over that of the represented (1995, p. 100).

One solution might simply be to stop doing any work that could be considered advocacy—if the workers are not ready to lead, then we should not take any steps that might place us in such an authoritative position. While such a position allays the concerns we have about allyship, it emphasizes purity at the cost of both nuance and efficacy. If some speakers are well placed to speak and act against the oppression of some groups, should they not do so? In fact, the ability of the CLP to raise money, launch campaigns, and win substantial gains for workers against illegal and immoral employers is the sort of activity we need more of, even if it cannot be separated from the relative position, privilege, and power of the staff compared to the workers whom they are organizing. Alcoff offers a sharp critique of what can happen if we abandon representational practices altogether:

> But a retreat from speaking for will not result in an increase in receptive listening in all cases; it may result merely in a retreat into a narcissistic yuppie lifestyle in which a privileged person takes no responsibility for her society whatsoever. She may even feel justified in exploiting her privileged capacity for personal happiness at the expense of others on the grounds that she has no alternative. (Alcoff 1995, p. 107)

Rather than a wholesale rejection of speaking for others, we instead need approaches that are grounded in context-dependent power analyses, that are sensitive to the relative positions of both represented and representative, and that held together through a commitment to collective liberation. With this sensitivity comes nuance and, most likely, the discomfort of those who would prefer an egalitarian power dynamic but who must recognize and leverage their own authority in the process of liberation.

As Amy Hinterberger, quoting Sara Ahmed puts it, "ethical representational strategies, which seek to account for power and authority, might require a commitment to collective struggle supplemented by 'the fact that a full ethical engagement with the 'other' is impossible'" (2007, p. 80).[1] In cases like the CLP, ethical or ideological purity may leave no options except retreat or self-deception. We need to move beyond this.

Applied to the world of social movements, this points again to the political nature of emancipatory organizing work. When organizations like the CLP engage with oppressed peoples, their dialogue is a political activity laden with power relationships and grounded in the relative social positions of the participants rather than taking place in an apolitical, power-free vacuum of authentic representation. We are all situated within relationships of power, relationships that create subject positions, produce social truths, and both enable and constrain social action. The aim for those who want to support emancipatory movement work should not be to pretend that there is some relationship we can form with oppressed people or each other that is free from this dynamic. Rather, we should work toward Hayward's "basic democratic norm that people should be, not only the subjects, but also the architects of key boundaries that delimit and circumscribe their fields of action" (2000, p. 166). Such an approach underscores the imperative for those of us engaged in emancipatory movement work to acknowledge and actively navigate the inherent power dynamics within our relationships, emphasizing that our goal is to increase the collective agency of individuals to shape the parameters of their lives.

Outcomes

Given the impossibility of working with the relatively powerless without stumbling into the complications of authority and representation, we should expand our assessments of what makes movement work legitimate to incorporate how "speaking for" can be a powerful, and potentially liberatory, political act. Indeed, there are threads of this in the narrative of worker leadership in the FCC campaign. It enabled staff to declare the "truth" that workers were bound together in common struggle, that they should leverage their position as workers to engage in direct action, and that they should lead their own campaigns, organizations, and worksites. Crucially, staff members asserted that workers were already leading—an important representative speech act whose purpose was to help create the reality it purported to describe, the interpretive "worldmaking power" of the discursive contest (Austin 1975; Bourdieu 1987). The CLP asserted this by using their historic successes as evidence that workers *could* lead and win important gains. But organizers also reframed ongoing campaign work through worker-leader narratives in strategic ways, re-telling successful actions taken by staffers or allies as victories of worker leadership. They used this in their conversations with workers as crucial evidence of worker agency and efficacy—worker leadership not as a possibility, but as something *already* happening. Organizers used this re-telling to persuade workers to reconsider their current understandings of how they fit into capitalist employment relationships. The mythology of worker leadership thus became an important representational speech act in a broader discursive strategy for future worker leadership, regardless of participation. Staff "spoke for" workers as a strategy to inspire the workers' agency and increase the power of the campaign.

But in determining what movement endeavors are worth supporting, our evaluations should not simply gauge the reputation of the organization or the political content of their rhetoric, but also the "where the speech goes and what it does" (Alcoff 1995, p. 113). To put it simply, we should look to outcomes. Within the political tension and power dynamics of representational movement work, we must work toward outcomes that have the aim of empowering oppressed communities to become the architects of their lives. This requires acknowledging the power and authority that movement organizers and organizations possess.

Many on the Left are suspicious of power and authority given longstanding values of egalitarianism. But the assertion of and desire for leaderlessness, horizontality, or bottom-up democracy are no guarantee that power and authority will not operate in movement spaces, and these desires can make it challenging to address problems of accountability and hierarchy (Freeman 1972; Smucker 2017). Rather than working solely from a place of suspicion, we need to combine our ideological desire for frontline leadership and liberatory political values with clear strategies that treat this as a serious goal. What would it mean to truly center the leadership development of oppressed people as a central movement outcome? What would this mean in the context of organizing workers?

Theresa Sharpe takes up these questions in a superb qualitative study of a hotel workers' union campaign (2004). Wrestling with the issue of "union democracy," Sharpe considers what organizers should do if the rank and file are not on the same page as the organizers. Having workers who are new to collective action take on responsibility without any training or support might seem democratic, but is not likely to either win campaigns or increase the ability of workers to lead. She finds that substantive participation requires an understanding of and the ability to judge different strategic and tactical options, skills that are the outcomes of an organizational structure designed to develop the capacity of workers to make decisions. Workers had to experience real growth in their movement skills to exert agency in the campaign; growth that required the authority and leadership of organizers. In this vein, Sharpe argues that it is naïve to expect every worker in a campaign to have the capacity for full democratic agency from the first day they attend a meeting. And, far from the discovery of authentic leadership free from the influence of others, when a worker *does* become a leader, they are likely to speak with the language and think with the sensibility developed in dialogue with organizers and other workers. Sharpe sums up the important role of staff in this dynamic:

> Leadership development implies that there is an authoritative agency with the skills and knowledge lacking in others who need such training. . . . In this context, authority enables, rather than constrains, participatory democracy. (2004, p. 69)

If what we want is a more democratic, participatory, and liberatory labor movement, then we would be well served by putting our power, resources, and knowledge behind these goals in as strategic a manner as possible.

Strategizing Liberation

The concerns that have been levied against top-down advocacy work in the labor movement are relevant in understanding the limitations of the CLP campaign at the FCC. With an organizational vision and campaign strategy designed without the participation of workers and requiring the resources and power of non-workers, staff ended up in the classic dilemma where "advocates almost always end up emphasizing their own power resources rather than those of workers" (Gray 2007, p. 208). Against the efforts, desires, and intentions of the staff, the limited participation of workers made their role largely symbolic as they represented their problems to those actors who ended up taking the most decisive actions in the campaign. As the CLP well knew from its previous campaigns, without workers, labor allies are limited in their power. This glass ceiling was at play in the FCC campaign so long as non-workers provided most of the campaign's power.

Critiques of the advocacy model in this volume only get us so far, in that the CLP did seek to organize workers and enable them to directly hold employers accountable to high standards. In this context, it is useful to add an additional analytical layer, one that Hahrie Han explains as the distinction between transactional mobilizing and transformational organizing (2014). Where organizing invests members with skills, capacities, and political education to become organizers and leaders themselves, mobilization turns out supporters who already agree with the cause. It is the latter that best characterizes what happened at the FCC, where staff mobilized a dedicated base of allies. But we should be careful to not underplay how important this was for the CLP's strategic model or for society in general. In a low-wage economy characterized by illegal practices, immoral behavior, and exploitative conditions, the value of mobilizing allies to enforce better standards is critical.

But, as Alberti argues in her research on union organizing in the United Kingdom, low-wage workers need ally support *and* a strong union campaign to sustain the participation of workers (Alberti 2016). Allies from outside of the workplace are crucial in a labor movement context where unions tend to ignore or deemphasize the myriad ways that low-wage workers are oppressed throughout society, including issues like housing, immigration issues, and healthcare, that can be the specific barriers preventing workers from participating. And while too much focus on allies can divert strategies away from the place and power of workers, ally power can become a tantalizing tool for winning campaigns when it is challenging to bring workers into the organization (Alberti 2016, p. 87). This dynamic is only amplified in situations where non-profit organizations need victories to sell to supporters, creating a structural imperative to win campaigns in one form or another.

A related dynamic concerns the place of workers in wider society and its role in both winning campaigns and empowering workers. CLP staffers possessed sharp critiques of racial injustice, misogyny, and the exploitation of immigrants in modern society. But while workers were seen as complex people facing a variety of oppressions, the campaign did not aim to involve the personal communities of workers outside of the workplace (Alberti 2016). Instead, the campaign primarily understood workers in relation to their jobs and mobilized supporters from preexisting networks of labor activists rather than looking to other aspects of the workers identities and experiences. The CLP incorporated the risk and vulnerability of immigrants into narratives and strategies about their work, but generally did not focus on the issues that workers faced outside of the workplace unless it could be channeled into worksite campaigns. At the end of the day, founding their own unions was understood as the only legitimate way that workers could address the problems they faced, including those outside of the workplace.

In their research on the labor movement in the United Kingdom, Alberti, Holgate, and Tapia conclude that this limited approach can impede efforts to build unions (2013). When unions see immigrants primarily as workers "rather than as migrant workers with particular and overlapping forms of oppression," the opportunities to recruit workers based on the myriad oppressions they face become more limited (Alberti, Holgate, and Tapia 2013, p. 4132). Their research illustrates that successful unions incorporated the problems faced by workers both inside and outside of the workplace into their organizing drives. Jane McAlevey offers a similar analysis in her insistence on "whole worker organizing," which understands workers as "embedded in a range of social relationships in the workplace and the community" (2015, p. 417). McAlevey counsels that labor groups who aim to organize for mass collective struggle should anchor their campaigns in those social networks that are important to workers and in which workers are already embedded. This serves a dual purpose. First, it can broaden the power of a campaign by bringing new allies into the struggle. But it also develops additional places to organize workers by bringing the campaign to their social networks and incorporating non-workplace issues into the vision of change. For McAlevey, the way that outside groups can best "make space" for workers to organize is when those groups are in some way already connected to the workers. This is distinct from the CLP's model of ally organizing, which sought to mobilize supporters based on the organization's distinct vision of unionization and labor justice. The CLP did not go to the community bases of workers, but rather tried to bring workers to the CLP's community of activists.

As we have seen, the approach that we used in the FCC campaign to organize workers was similar to our approach to mobilizing supporters—removing barriers and providing opportunities for workers to participate. But, as opposed to mobilization, Han's discussion of organizing is intended to be transformational (Han 2014). It asks that activists engage with people who *don't* already agree with the campaign and emphasizes the development of collective identities that are then deployed for collective action. Clearly, the CLP staff would have preferred to transform workers in this way, but, as discussed in Chapter 4, we were hamstrung by an ambitious campaign plan with limited organizing power and the unexpected challenges of getting workers to participate in campaign activities.

McAlevey applies this insight about organizing to the challenges faced by labor groups in their efforts to build lasting power. Her most applicable argument concerns the relationship between staff and worker-leaders. Echoing Sharpe's discussion of participatory democracy presented above, McAlevey argues that organizers have an important leadership role, in that "they lead the organizing committee. The rank-and-file organizers lead the workers" (2016, p. 38). While this contradicts the CLP vision that workers would lead their own Leadership Committees, it aligns with the practice of staff leadership in the campaign. Tellingly, McAlevey places this in contrast to strategies that claim the participants are the real leaders, with organizers simply implementing the desires of the membership. Denying that organizers are leaders with real power "leaves the organizer's actions unchecked and not well understood" (McAlevey 2016, p. 45). As we have seen, such an approach obscures the power that staff have in setting agendas, designing strategy, and developing frameworks. Perhaps more importantly, it undercuts the ability of workers to organize and lead.

McAlevey insists further that, in our search for worker leadership, we must understand that "in any strategy for building power, all people are not the same" (2016, p. 48). If any worker who comes to a meeting is labeled a "one" and deemed a member of the Leadership Committee, then there is no way to gauge the relative capacity of members to take on the work of organizing their colleagues. Simply put, an enthusiastic participant may not necessarily be the best rank-and-file leader to reach more workers. In this context, McAlevey argues that the key task of organizers is to identify, recruit, and develop "organic leaders," recognized not through their participation in the campaign but via their credibility with other workers (2016, p. 34). These are the people that co-workers go to for advice, who have standing among the preexisting social networks at the worksite, and who organizers find by talking with workers about who they trust. Crucially, they are often not the workers who are initially interested in joining a union effort, and organizers must spend time and resources to bring them into the fold. Once recruited, their leadership potential is tested via a "structure test" that determines if the worker "can get a majority of her shift or unit to agree to a public, and therefore high-risk, action" (McAlevey 2016, p. 35). This process separates those workers who mobilize from those who organize: "The worker who fails at the test is likely a pro-union activist, not an organic leader, and leaders, not activists, win the campaign and have the capacity to build strong worksite structures" (McAlevey 2016, p. 36). If we apply this concept to moments like the FCC public launch, the leafleting actions, and the meetings with the company, none of the workers involved in our campaign would have passed such a test.

Not only might all workers not be ready for leadership and responsibility from the jump, some workers might not be well suited to substantive leadership regardless of the opportunities. Moving beyond a neoliberal identity politics, one that assumes a person's identity or structural position gives them "intrinsic ideological or strategic legitimacy," forces us to acknowledge three things (Mitchell 2022). First, that the leadership potential, organizing ability, and political orientation of people are qualities that can and must be developed through participation in movements. Second, that movements need to build a diversity of ways that people can participate given differences in interest, resources, and capacities rather than a one-dimensional reading of identity that assumes everyone can and should be a leader. And finally, that we must anchor our accountability not only to particular kinds of people or abstract political values, but also to a "basic strategic imperative to build power" (Mitchell 2022). We must foster the training, motivation, and growth of individuals to actively shape a collective vision for emancipation. We should link our sense of responsibility to this vision rather than to any singular group or identity.

The approach described above is substantially different from the CLP's organizing model. This is a pragmatic framework to build power through the development of workers' leadership and political skills, leadership that is not measured through ideological purity or activist engagement but rather through the ability to reach and persuade fellow workers to join campaigns. It also requires that we recognize that not all workers will start as leaders, and that we must build structures that both provide and find value for those who do not or cannot act effectively in leadership. As we have seen, the CLP diagnosed the organizational structures of traditional unions as a key limitation of the movement, where the intent should be to wrest power away from employers and union bureaucrats alike. In contrast, the critique of unions provided by McAlevey, Alberti, and Holgate aims to rescue the core of traditional unions while pushing them in a more worker-centric direction. And the concrete goals of these scholars are typically to help workers win formal union elections and win collective bargaining agreements, goals that are not necessarily shared by the radical parts of the labor movement.

But the shared vision should be familiar—the mass collective struggle of workers who should be the central actors of union strategy and governance. In doing so, these scholars underline the importance of paid staff and organizers in developing the capacity for workers to become union leaders using carefully planned, top-down organizing strategies. Organizers in this framework do not wait for the spontaneous actions of workers and do not view having a minority of workers on board, no matter how militant, as a victory. Working toward majority support is seen as the best way for workers to express their power in the workplace as well as the clearest process for determining if workers are truly interested in the campaign.

There are plenty of reasons to remain suspicious of this framework and the ability of mainstream unions to become vehicles for widespread radical political action. But while the literature on alternative and radical labor models offers crucial space for strategic innovation and political reflections, there are few cases of concrete movement success.[2] The strategies presented above may offer a way to transcend the paralyzing tension provided by an orientation which can struggle to see workers as anything other than radical leaders and offers only limited political space for the necessity of staff expertise and authority. By focusing on the practical steps by which labor organizers identify organic rank-and-file leaders, build power across the workforce, and supplement that power with that of the wider community, the strategic capacity to reach radical, worker-centric outcomes may increase. Granted, this involves a staff-driven process that some on the left will find overly pragmatic, bureaucratic, or simply ignorant about how the dynamics of leadership and power end up hurting the movement within the institutional structure of traditional unions (Brook 2022). Nick Driedger, in his critique of McAlevey's model, faults McAlevey for ignoring how the conservative orientation of many unions ends up depressing worker leadership and reduces the strength of the labor movement as a source of rank-and-file power: "Talking about union militancy and where it comes from is important; talking about how union militancy disappears is essential" (2019). But given the decades-long decline of the labor movement, compounded by the challenges that the CLP faced with its model, these points need to be considered.

Rethinking Allyship

Throughout this volume, I have illustrated the problems that arise from a strict, ideological commitment to worker leadership as the only form of legitimate action in the labor movement. As I have argued in this chapter, to escape the false binary of good worker leadership against bad staff direction, we must confront the nuance and messiness of how power and authority operate in movement work and in all relationships. At the same time, the world is full of so-called movement organizations that spurn confrontation, avoid liberation, or that would rather collect checks from a distant membership than organize people and build power. There is a radical vision that we must hold to in the story presented in this book, one that aims to empower all kinds of people and embolden them to act against power structures that oppress and marginalize. But we must support this vision in a way that doesn't mythologize, naturalize, or essentialize people. Such orientations might seem to laud people like the workers at FCC as powerful, but can, in practice, take away their agency and describe them only in terms of their hardships rather than the fullness of their humanity. What does this all mean for allyship? What would it look like to evolve our commitments to worker leadership, direct action, and liberatory struggle?

First, the critical approach in this book does not mean that we should abandon organizations like the CLP. If anything, allies should increase their involvement. The arc of the FCC campaign illustrates the immense power that well-placed allies can have in supporting a labor campaign. Grounded in the supply-chain strategy, CLP's earlier campaigns only emphasize this. Non-worker allies can leverage their own power through outside actions and media campaigns and, through tactics like secondary boycotts and street action, amplify the power of the labor organizations. When groups like the CLP have institutional knowledge about how allies can build and leverage power, they are also well placed to incubate and steward new ally organizations, ones that should be more fully integrated into these groups. Further, the CLP would have benefited from boarder conversations about ideas like the Regional Distribution Strategy and the campaign plan at the FCC. Frank discussions about the available resources for campaigns, the practice of worker leadership in the organization, and short- and long-term strategy goals would have encouraged both allies and staff to have a stronger and more realistic analysis about the shared goal of worker-led unions.

Deeper ties between allies and labor organizations would also encourage us to have a more nuanced approach to what leadership looks like and how it is developed. This means taking care with our counting statistics. For example, rather than requiring member representation on the board of directors, as some funders do, we should develop clearer guidelines for how organizations provide training and education for members to serve in effective and powerful ways. It also asks us to fully accept that not all participants—members, allies, and staff—are equally ready for all positions of leadership in organization and campaigns. Making space for workers to fully participate in the life of a movement organization means making space for all kinds of capabilities and capacities. Moving past a "leadership or bust" mindset can create more room for more people to participate and to do so in different ways. And to keep fast to a vision where workers can assert authority and leadership over their own campaigns and organizations, we need a better definition of what that leadership looks like and how it is developed.

These ties might also help us reconcile our concerns about staff leadership with the practical aspects of leadership development. Of course, the resistance and suspicion that many on the left have of power and authority in movement work is not misplaced. Plenty of organizations have preached justice while enacting oppressive power hierarchies, engaging in corrupt practices, and trampling on the agency of the communities they purport to represent. Ally participation in labor groups can help to be an important check to these issues. But power and hierarchy exist in all relationships, and the focus of justice-minded organizations on communities that are relatively under-resourced only amplifies the power differentials. Rather than pretending that organizations do not exercise forms of authority in their work, we need a more transparent accounting about where hierarchies do exist, what decision making within those hierarchies looks like, and how accountability works in the structure of the organization. If members do not lead the organization, why don't they, and who does? Where staff leadership exists, what ends does it serve? If members are in leadership, to what degree? What are the plans to develop member leadership, and how will they be assessed? This would mean replacing our mistrust of staff authority and our empty gestures to bottom-up leadership with clear definitions of how authority works in an organization and what outcomes that authority is structured to produce. This would empower us to attach accountability to outcomes that produce leadership and member power rather than simplified notions of member agency.

Further, allies who find themselves outside of formal organizations need to build their own. One of the clearest findings of this work is the power of the PLJA, a power leveraged by only a handful of activists. Building this capacity required intentional long-term planning to build a membership-based organization drawn from activists across a region. The key point is that the Alliance was able to engage these forms of power so effectively because it already existed at the start of the campaign. This meant it had its own history of movement work, including its own network of relationships across the region, that it could draw on to support the campaign. Whether attached to an existing organization or simply drawn from communities of activists, building these kinds of groups would allow us to be ready to throw our weight behind workplace justice campaigns and union drives when the time is ripe.

And while we all may be exhausted from the slow pace of electoral politics, the place of allies as citizens and the role of policy should not be understated. For example, the recent wave of union elections at Starbucks stores across the country has been checked by the company's refusal to negotiate, an ability that stems in part from the weak labor laws in the U.S. A concerted effort to pass new labor legislation could dramatically empower workers across the country. State and local efforts are also worth our time, such as the Wage Theft Deterrence Package introduced into the New York State legislature in early 2024. This innovative set of three bills would empower state agencies to close businesses that owe as little as $1,000 in back wages (Baram 2024). And on wage theft specifically, only those handful of states that have the strongest penalties have seen significant drops in violations (Galvin 2016). While policy battles can be drawn out affairs that offer little of the fire of street actions, they stand to impact far more workers than any single campaign and could be an important part of any labor ally's scope of work. And, as some have argued, the policy arena is a place where worker centers have had surprising success making life better for their members (Galvin 2024).

The Dream of Leadership

In his provocative book *Dream*, Stephen Duncombe asserts that the failure of the political left is rooted in its fascination with facts, rational argument, and the truth. With such an emphasis, it has been increasingly unable to offer a creative vision of what society could look like: ". . . plagued by their own Enlightenment guilt complex, progressives regularly disown their own, often effective history of mobilizing fantasy, declaring that spectacle is silly and that their sense of superior seriousness will win debates, convince the public, and lead them back into the halls of power" (2007, p. 23). In response to this "superior seriousness," Duncombe calls for a politics of fantasy, a "*dreampolitik*" that offers an alternative vision of what the world could be:

> The truth does not reveal itself by virtue of being the truth: it must be told, and we need to learn how to tell the truth more effectively. It must have stories woven around it, works of art made about it; it must be communicated in new ways and marketed so that it sells. It must be embedded in an experience that connects with people's dreams and desires, that resonates with the symbols and myths they find meaningful. The argument here is not for a progressive movement that lies outright, but rather for a propaganda of the truth. As William James one wrote: "Truth *happens* to an idea." (Duncombe 2007, p. 20; emphasis in original)

While Duncombe offers this critique to the broad left, it is particularly apt for the labor movement. In an examination of the discourses and practices of the movement, Deva Woodly and I conclude that it routinely fails to offer an aspirational vision of what the world could look like, instead focusing on people who are already members and the narrow material benefits that membership offers (Koenig and Woodly 2019). Like earlier calls for social movement unionism, we called on the labor movement to develop the conceptual and ideological tools necessary to organize *all* people—and not simply union members—into a movement built on a dignified working life.

In some sense, the narrative of worker leadership in this book answers the call for a "politics of fantasy." The vision of worker-led movements organically wresting control of society away from the evils of modern capitalism is a seductive antidote to concerns of rising economic inequality and ineffective organizations. By focusing on the values of the Left, narratives of bottom-up leadership offer alternative images of society and an emotional appeal to leftist concerns about democracy, fairness, and power. At the same time, the strategy of a worker-led movement provides a pathway to reach that vision—workers, when organized in their own authentic organizations, will remake the nature of work and society. Allies fit into the story by offering resources and leverage based on their own positionality.

Attempts by political actors to contest meaning and power are nothing new, and the process of collectivizing and politicizing identities is, on some level, the essence of movement activity. Between the structures of modern capitalism that keep workers relatively quiescent and that concentrates movement resources among non-workers, the narratives of worker leadership that defined the FCC campaign can be useful in movement work. Through its framing of historical and present campaigns as worker-led, it created a discursive, prefigurative space for workers to fill by providing stories of success and empowerment—another world is not just possible, it is something that is already happening. For political actors who are driven to change commonsense understandings and power relations, it is not enough to note that the status quo and all potential alternatives are socially constructed. Rather, these actors must advance a compelling and empowering interpretation of reality that works when it is accepted *as* reality. For a workforce that is unlikely to spontaneously organize because of their current interpretive frames, re-articulating those frames is necessary if political realignment is the goal. Asserting worker leadership in this way is intended to make "the future that one utters come into being" (Bourdieu 1991, p. 222).

But for all its value, this vision of worker leadership is primarily one of movement elites. Generated in foundation meetings, among college-educated staffers, in court-houses, and in the conflicts between leaders and employers, non-workers develop and deploy the values that they think workers ought to have and the actions that they ought to take. As I have said, this dynamic may be impossible to avoid, and to hold onto a "truth" of worker leadership that ignores the power and authority that support it does not help make it a reality. If the vision is coupled to real, strategic commitments to build the power of workers, we should find some hope in it. The reality is that most workers, like most people, are not activists waiting for an opportunity. A radical dream for worker action, regardless of where it comes from, must prescribe both radicalism and action. In doing so, it cannot discount the shared growth, conflict, and communication that are integral to the lifeworld of successful movement organizations. Instead, our dream must have the tools and the vision to incorporate everyone—from workers new to movements to experienced organizers—to broaden their political horizons and provide them with strategies to build power.

As any organizer will tell you, you have to meet people where they are at. But the popular education professed by the likes of Miles Horton and Paulo Freire understood that empowering and politicizing people was a different process from winning campaigns and building organizations. Horton expressed this concern when describing the difference between winning a campaign and political education:

> Saul [Alinsky] and I differed because my position was that if I had to make a choice between achieving an objective and utilizing the struggle to develop and radicalize people, my choice would be to let the goal go and develop people. (Horton 1998, p. 180)

This inversion of the CLP's assertion that "it's better to lose the organization than to lose a campaign" reminds us that member empowerment and leadership development are distinct from union drives and workplace justice campaigns. As we have seen, even a worker-centric organization can get a resistant company to sit for a meeting without a corresponding increase in the power or capacity of its members. It will be for others to assess what it would look like to transparently center the development of people over the need to win campaigns. But this seems worth reflecting on for those of us committed to the empowerment of workers in unions, at jobsites, and throughout society.

Given the continued problems of low-wage work and their likely expansion over time, workers will continue to need groups to advocate on their behalf as well as activists who strive to organize them into vehicles for collective power. The reality of building a broad movement of committed rank-and-file leaders will require a different pathway than the one presented in these pages. When I asked about what the labor movement should do next, a worker expressed frustration at the lack of easy answers.

"I've literally been asking myself that question for the last year with my friends, you know? Because it's fucking sad to see people, you know . . . in that state. So how the hell do you do that?"

"That's the question," I replied.

"Right? Yeah, I don't know. I think that . . . overall I think CLP is, is . . . a really courageous experiment. And I hope that . . . well . . . maybe they'll figure it out one day."

Endnotes

Prelims

1. As discussed below, all identifiers have been modified in this book.

Chapter 1

1. As discussed in the Preface, all identifiers have been changed throughout this volume, and all quotes are drawn from field notes or interviews. Worker centers share similarities with labor unions in that both advocate for workers' rights, but they diverge in configuration, focus, and methods. Unions, structured as formal labor organizations with elected leaders, primarily engage in collective bargaining and negotiation with employers to secure better wages, benefits, and working conditions for their members. Conversely, worker centers concentrate on a wider array of issues affecting low-wage and marginalized workers, including workplace rights advocacy, community organizing, service provision, and policy advocacy, and do not aim to formally represent workers through contracts or collective bargaining agreements (Fine 2006; Kim 2015; Fine et al. 2018; Garrick 2021). This is discussed further in Chapter 2.
2. A "campaign" in a social justice context can be broadly defined as a coordinated effort to address systemic injustices and inequities within society, typically with the aim of promoting fairness, equality, and the protection of human rights for all individuals or specific marginalized groups. In a labor context, campaigns are organized efforts aimed at addressing and rectifying issues of fairness, equity, and dignity within a specific workplace or industry. Traditional labor unions often, but not always, run campaigns to establish unions and win collective bargaining agreements (colloquially termed "contracts") among the members of a particular worksite. The workplace justice campaigns of worker centers focus on improving working conditions, ensuring fair wages, advocating for employee rights, combating discrimination and harassment, and promoting overall workplace democracy outside of the contract structure.
3. This approach shares some similarities with secondary boycotts. A secondary boycott occurs when a campaign, in the context of a dispute with one company (the primary employer), calls for a boycott of another company (the secondary employer) that has a business relationship with the primary employer. The aim of a secondary boycott is to exert pressure on the primary employer by disrupting its relationships with other companies, such as suppliers, distributors, or customers. Generally, formal labor unions are limited in the actions they can take against secondary targets. As I will discuss, the supply-chain strategy involved engaging hotel, grocery, restaurant, and wholesale customers to drop their contracts with the target employer until the campaign was settled. In practice this would involve workers and allies standing in front of secondary employers' locations and handing out flyers to customers on the street, informing them that the products they would find inside were "produced under illegal conditions" or similar language.
4. "A *critical case* can be defined as having strategic importance in relation to the general problem. For example, an occupational medicine clinic wanted to investigate whether people working with organic solvents suffered brain damage. Instead of choosing a representative sample among all those enterprises in the clinic's area that used organic solvents, the clinic strategically located a single workplace where all safety regulations on cleanliness, air quality, and the like had been fulfilled. This model enterprise became a critical case: if brain damage related to organic solvents could be found at this particular facility, then it was likely that the same problem would exist at other enterprises which were less careful with safety regulations for organic solvents. . . . [The case selection provides the] possibility to formulate a generalization characteristic of critical cases, a generalization of the sort, 'If it is valid for this case, it is valid for all (or many) cases.' In its negative form, the generalization would be, 'If it is not valid for this case, then it is not valid for any (or only few) cases'" (Flyvbjerg 2006, pp. 229–230).
5. For institutional donors, relationship is evident in funding priorities. As James, the CLP development staffer, explained it, "the members have to lead; if it's staff driven, well, the funders don't like that."

6. On the role of immersion in the study of politics, see (Schatz 2013). On the trade-offs between different methods for a given research question, see Flyvbjerg (2006).

Chapter 2

1. The authors calculate this figure by using a threshold of two-thirds of the median wage, adjusted for local purchasing power (Ross and Bateman 2019).
2. According to an analysis of tax records, the median budget for a worker center was $410,000 in 2012 (Griffith and Gates 2019).
3. Throughout this book I use the term "nonprofit" to indicate an organization structured as a 501(c)3 unless otherwise noted.
4. For instance, if union members engage in a strike action outside of legal and contractual boundaries, the union as an organization and its leadership can be held financially responsible for losses the company sustains. The typical union contract today contains a no-strike clause specifically for this purpose. Thus, under many contracts, union officials have an incentive to keep their members from striking outside of authorized actions (known as "wildcat strikes"); otherwise, they risk penalties and possibly jail time.
5. Here it is worth underlining that between the challenges worker centers have faced under the Trump administration, during COVID, and in the wake of the Department of Labor's probe into the Centro de Trabajadores Unidos en Lucha, many worker centers have adjusted their relationships with unions (Penn 2020). This is partially due to the legal campaigns mounted by business groups such as the U.S. Chamber of Commerce and the ironically named Center for Union Facts to strip worker centers of their nonprofit status and hence their major sources of funding.
6. Activists may also play an outsized role in street actions when there is a language differential. A newspaper article covering a leafleting action at a supermarket noted that while fired workers were handing out flyers to customers, labor activists and CLP staffers took on the public speaking duties due to the discomfort a worker had with spoken English.
7. Some worker centers utilize a dues payment model, though when it involves low-wage workers these dues are often symbolic rather than an important source of money. During my time at the CLP, membership was free.
8. Simply put, there is more funding available for programs such as job training, policy advocacy, or service provision. "[In] the US, the total pool of grant dollars allocated to social change is proportionately small compared to other funding areas, and funds for local community organizing groups are even more limited. Jagpal and Laskowski (2013, p. 1) found that overall, social justice philanthropy accounted for only twelve percent of total grants made by their sample of foundations, while the community foundations in their sample only allocated seven percent of their grant dollars to social change" (Frantz and Fernandes 2016, p. 5).

Chapter 3

1. This is still a possibility even in sectors that require close proximity to local markets. For example, the Laundry Workers Center ran a successful workplace justice campaign at B&H Photo, a New York City photography and film supply store with a warehouse located in Brooklyn. When warehouse workers voted in favor of unionization, the owners shut down the Brooklyn location and re-opened in New Jersey, effectively breaking the momentum of the union drive.
2. Emphasis in original.

Conclusion

1. Ahmed (2002), p. 572.
2. See the following edited volumes for case studies on worker centers, alternative labor, and radical labor organizing: Milkman and Ott (2014); Ness (2014).

Bibliography

Adler, Lee H., Maite Tapia, and Lowell Turner. 2014. *Mobilizing Against Inequality: Unions, Immigrant Workers, and the Crisis of Capitalism*. Ithaca, NY: Cornell Univeristy Press.

Ahmed, Sara. 2002. "This Other and Other Others." *Economy and Soceity* 31 (4): 558–572.

Alberti, Gabriella. 2016. "Moving beyond the Dichotomy of Workplace and Community Unionism: The Challenges of Organising Migrant Workers in London's Hotels." *Economic and Industrial Democracy* 37 (1): 73–94.

Alberti, Gabriella, Jane Holgate, and Maite Tapia. 2013. "Organising Migrants as Workers or as Migrant Workers? Intersectionality, Trade Unions and Precarious Work." *International Journal of Human Resource Management* 24 (22): 4132–4148.

Alcoff, Linda. 1991. "The Problem of Speaking for Others." *Cultural Critique*, (20): 5–32.

Ashar, Sameer M., and Catherine L. Fisk. 2019. "Democratic Norms and Governance Experimentalism in Worker Centers." *Law and Contemporary Problems* 82 (3): 141–191.

Austin, J. L. 1975. *How to Do Things with Words*. Cambridge, MA: Harvard University Press.

Baram, Marcus. 2024. "Proposed Wage Theft Legislation Would Strip Violators of Their Ability to Do Business in New York." *ProPublica*, February 6. Accessed February 8, 2024. https://www.propublica.org/article/wage-theft-law-new-york-violators-doing-business.

Bartels, Larry. 2016. *Unequal Democracy: The Political Economy of the New Gilded Age*. Princeton, NJ: Princeton University Press.

Bernhardt, Annette, Ruth Milkman, Nik Theodore, Douglas Heckathorn, Mirabai Auer, James DeFilippis, Ana Luz Gonzalez, et al. 2009. "Broken Laws, Unprotected Workers: Violations of Employment and Labor Laws in America's Cities." Center for Urban Economic Development, National Employment Law Project, UCLA Institute for Research on Labor and Employment. New York City, NY.

Berube, Alan. 2016. "Job Shifts May Help Explain Why Earnings Are Declining for Black Americans." Brookings Institution, August 29. https://www.brookings.edu/blog/the-avenue/2016/08/29/job-shifts-may-help-explain-why-earnings-are-declining-for-black-americans/.

Boden, Leslie I., Emily A. Spieler, and Gregory R. Wagner. 2015. *The Changing Structure of Work: Implications for Workplace Health and Safety in the US*. Washington, DC: U.S. Department of Labor.

Bourdieu, Pierre. 1987. "What Makes a Social Class? On the Theoretical and Practical Existence of Groups." *Berkeley Journal of Sociology* 32:1–17.

Bourdieu, Pierre. 1991. *Language and Symbolic Power*. Cambridge, MA: Harvard University Press.

Bronfenbrenner, Kate, and Robert Hickey. 2004. "Changing to Organize: A National Assessment of Union Strategies." In *Rebuilding Labor: Organizing and Organizers in the New Union Movement*, edited by Ruth Milkman and Kim Voss. Ithaca, NY: Cornell University Press.

Brook, Paul. 2022. "Jane McAlevey's Organising Model: Is It a Rank and File Strategy?" *International Socialism* 174: 81–114.

Brookes, Marissa. 2013. "Varieties of Power in Transnational Labor Alliances: An Analysis of Workers' Structural, Institutional, and Coalitional Power in the Global Economy." *Labor Studies Journal* 38 (3): 181–200.

Capps, Randolph, Michael E. Fix, Jeffery S. Passel, Jason Ost, and Dan Perez-Lopez. 2003. *A Profile of the Low-Wage Immigrant Workforce*. Washington, DC: Urban Institute.

Capps, Randolph, Karina Fortuny, and Michael E. Fix. 2007. *Trends in the Low-Wage Immigrant Labor Force, 2000–2005*. Washington, DC: The Urban Institute.

Cascio, Wayne F. 2006. "The High Cost of Low Wages." *Harvard Business Review*, December 84 (12): 23.

Cooper, David, and Teresa Kroeger. 2017. *Employers Steal Billions from Workers' Paychecks Each Year*. Washington, DC: Economic Policy Institute.

Dempsey, Sarah E. 2009. "NGOs, Communicative Labor, and the Work of Grassroots Representation." *Communication and Critical/Cultural Studies* 6 (4): 328–345.

Dirnbach, Eric. 2019. "Are Worker Centers Unions?" *Organizing Work*, November 27. Accessed May 2022. https://organizing.work/2019/11/are-worker-centers-unions/.

Driedger, Nick. 2019. "No Shortcuts, but to Where?" *Organizing Work*, December 2. Accessed May 2022. https://organizing.work/2019/12/no-shortcuts-but-to-where/.

Duff, Michael C. 2013. "ALT-Labor, Secondary Boycotts, and toward a Labor Organization Bargain." *Catholic University Law Review* 63:837.

Duncombe, Stephen. 2007. *Dream: Re-imagining Progressive Politics in an Age of Fantasy*. New York: The New Press.

Entmacher, Joan, Lauren Frohlich, Gallagher Katherine Robbins, Emily Martin, and Liz Watson. 2014. *Underpaid and Overloaded: Women in Low-Wage Jobs*. Washington, DC: National Women's Law Center.

Fantasia, Rick. 1988. *Cultures of Solidarity*. Berkeley: University of California Press.

Fine, Janice. 2006. *Worker Centers: Organizing Communities at the Edge of the Dream*. Ithaca, NY: Cornell University Press.

Fine, Janice, Linda Burnham, Kati Griffith, Minsun Ji, Victor Narro, and Steven Pitts. 2018. *No One Size Fits All: Worker Organization, Policy, and Movement in a New Economic Age*. Champaign, IL: Labor and Employment Relations Association, University of Illinois at Urbana-Champaign.

Flyvbjerg, Bent. 2006. "Five Misunderstandings about Case-Study Research." *Qualitative Research Practice* 12 (2): 219–245.

Food Chain Workers Alliance. 2012. *The Hands that Feed Us*. Los Angeles, CA: Food Chain Workers Alliance.

Food Chain Workers Alliance. 2016. *No Piece of the Pie.* Los Angeles, CA: Food Chain Workers Alliance.

Foucault, Michel. 1982. "The Subject and Power." *Critical Inquiry* 8 (4): 777–795.

Frantz, Courtney, and Sujatha Fernandes. 2016. "Whose Movement Is It? Strategic Philanthropy and Worker Centers." *Critical Sociology* 42 (1): 1–16.

Freeman, Jo. 1972. "The Tyranny of Structurelessness." *Berkeley Journal of Sociology* 17:151–164.

Frye, Jocelyn. 2017. "Not Just the Rich and Famous." *The Center for American Progress,* November 20. https://www.americanprogress.org/article/not-just-rich-famous/

Galvin, Daniel J. 2016. "Deterring Wage Theft: Alt-Labor, State Politics, and the Policy Determinants of Minimum Wage Compliance." *Perspectives on Politics* 14 (2): 324–350.

Galvin, Daniel J. 2024. *Alt-Labor and the New Politics of Workers' Rights.* New York, NY: Russell Sage Foundation.

Garcia, Ruben J. 2009. "Toward Fundamental Change for the Protection of Low-Wage Workers: The Workers' Rights are Human Rights' Debate in the Obama Era." *University of Chicago Legal Forum* 2009 (1): 421–457.

Garrick, Jessica. 2021. "How Worker Centers Organize Low-Wage Workers: An Exploration of Targets and Strategies." *Labor Studies Journal* 46 (2): 134–157.

Gray, Margaret. 2007. "The Mechanics of Empowerment: Migrant Farmworker Advocacy." In *Global Migration, Social Change, and Cultural Transformation,* edited by Emory Elliott, Jasmine Payne, and Patricia Ploesch, 207–233. New York, NY: Palgrave Macmillan.

Greenhouse, Steven. 2021. "Embracing and Resisting: The Variable Relationships between Worker Centers and Unions." *The American Prospect,* April 22. https://prospect.org/labor/the-alt-labor-chronicles-america-s-worker-centers/embracing-resisting-variable-relationships-between-worker-centers-unions/

Griffith, Kati L. 2015. "Worker Centers and Labor Law Protections: Why Aren't They Having Their Cake?" *Berkeley Journal of Employment and Labor Law* 36 (331): 331–349.

Griffith, Kati L., and Leslie C. Gates. 2019. "Worker Centers: Labor Policy as a Carrot, Not a Stick." *Harvard Law & Policy Review* 14 (1): 601–627.

Han, Hahrie. 2014. *How Organizations Develop Activists.* Oxford: Oxford University Press.

Hayward, Clarissa Rile. 2000. *De-Facing Power.* Cambridge: Cambridge University Press.

Hinterberger, Amy. 2007. "Feminism and the Politics of Representation: Towards a Critical and Ethical Encounter with 'Others.'" *Journal of International Women's Studies* 8 (2): 74–83.

Holgate, Jane. 2021. *Arise: Power, Strategy and Union Resurgence.* London: Pluto Press.

Horton, Myles. 1998. *The Long Haul.* New York, NY: Teachers College Press.

INCITE!, Women of Color against Violence, ed. 2007. *The Revolution Will Not Be Funded.* Cambridge, MA: South End Press.

Jagpal, Niki, and Kevin Laskowski. 2013. *The State of Social Justice Philanthropy 2011.* Washington, DC: National Committee for Responsive Philanthropy.

Jenkins, Steve. 2002. "Organizing, Advocacy, and Member Power: A Critical Reflection." *Working USA* 6 (2): 56–89.

Katz, Lawrence F., and Alan B. Krueger. 2016. *The Rise and Nature of Alternative Work Arrangements in the United States, 1995–2015.* NBER Working Paper No. 22667. Cambridge, MA: National Bureau of Economic Research.

Kim, E. Tammy. 2015. "Organizing the Unorganizable." *Dissent* (Spring). Accessed March 2022. https://www.dissentmagazine.org/article/worker-centers-immigrant-organizing/.

Kohl-Arenas, Erica. 2016. *The Self-Help Myth: How Philanthropy Fails to Alleviate Poverty.* Oakland: University of California Press.

Koenig, Biko, and Deva Woodly, 2019. "Building Justice in the American Labor Movement." *Alternate Routes: A Journal of Critical Social Research* 30 (2): 107–134.

Leigh, J. Paul. 2011. "Economic Burden of Occupational Injury and Illness in the United States." *The Milibank Quarterly* 89 (4): 724–772.

Lessa, Iara. 2006. "Discursive Struggles within Social Welfare: Restaging Teen Motherhood." *British Journal of Social Work* 36:283–298.

Levi, Margaret. 2003. "Organizing Power: The Prospects for an American Labor Movement." *Perspectives on Politics* 1 (1): 45–68.

Liu, Yvonne Yen, and Dominique Apollon. 2012. *The Color of Food.* Washington, DC: Applied Research Center.

Logan, John. 2006. "The Union Avoidance Industry in the United States." *British Journal of Industrial Relations* 44 (4): 651–675.

Majic, Samantha. 2014. *Sex Work Politics.* Philadelphia: University of Pennsylvania Press.

Martin, Lori Latrice. 2015. "Low-Wage Workers and the Myth of Post-Racialism." *Loyola Journal of Public Interest Law* 16:47–62.

Massey, Douglas S., and Kerstin Gentsch. 2014. "Undocumented Migration to the United States and the Wages of Mexican Immigrants." *International Migration Review* 48 (2): 482–499.

McAlevey, Jane. 2015. "The Crisis of New Labor and Alinsky's Legacy: Revisiting the Role of the Organic Grassroots Leaders in Building Powerful Organizations and Movements." *Politics and Society* 43 (3): 415–441.

McAlevey, Jane. 2016. *No Shortcuts: Organizing for Power.* New York, NY: Oxford University Press.

McNicholas, Celine, Margaret Poydock, Julia Wolfe, Ben Zipperer, Gordon Lafer, and Lola Loustaunau. 2019. *Unlawful.* Washington, DC: Economic Policy Institute.

McQuade, Susan. 2014. "Creating 'Open Space' to Promote Social Justice." In *New Labor in New York,* edited by Ruth Milkman and Ed Ott, 208–226. Ithaca, NY: Cornell University Press.

Meixell, Brady, and Ross Eisenbrey. 2014. *An Epidemic of Wage Theft Is Costing Workers Hundreds of Millions of Dollars a Year.* Washington, DC: Economic Policy Institute.

Milkman, Ruth. 2014. "Introduction: Toward a New Labor Movement? Organizing New York City's Precariat." In *New Labor in New York*, edited by Ruth Milkman and Ed Ott, 1–22. Ithaca, NY: Cornell University Press.

Milkman Ruth, and Ed Ott, eds. 2014. *New Labor in New York*. Ithaca, NY: Cornell University Press.

Mitchell, Maurice. 2022. *Building Resilient Organizations*, November 29. Accessed December 3, 2022. https://forgeorganizing.org/article/building-resilient-organizations.

Monforton, Celeste, and Jane M. Von Bergen. 2021. *On the Job: The Untold Story of Worker Centers and the New Fight for Wages, Dignity, and Health*. New York, NY: The New Press.

Mouffe, Chantal. 2013. *Agonistics: Thinking the World Politically*. London: Verso Books.

Naduris-Weissman, Eli. 2010. "Worker Centers and Traditional Labor Law: How to Stay on the Good Side of the Law!" *National Lawyers Guild*. January. Accessed February 18, 2018. http://nlg-laboremploy-comm.org/media/ProjWkrCtr_2010_Naduris-W_WkrCtrStratGuideLbrLaw.pdf.

Narro, Victor, Saba Waheed, and Jassmin Poyaoan. 2015. *Building a Movement Together: Worker Centers and Labor Union Affiliations*. Washington, DC: Labor Innovations for the 21st Century (LIFT) Fund.

Ness, Immanuel, ed. 2014. *New Forms of Worker Organization*. Oakland, CA: PM Press.

Oswalt, Michael M. 2016. "Improvisational Unionism." *California Law Review* 104 (3): 597–670.

Passel, Jeffery S., D'Vara Cohn, and Molly Rohal. 2015. *Share of Unauthorized Immigrant Workers in Production, Construction Jobs Falls Since 2007*. Washington, DC: Pew Research Center.

Penn, Ben. 2020. "Worker Centers Primed to Test We're-Not-Unions Stance in Court." *Bloomberg Law*, January 17. Accessed February 2021. https://news.bloomberglaw.com/daily-labor-report/worker-centers-primed-to-test-were-not-unions-stance-in-court.

The Philadelphia Inquirer. 2022. "A New Kind of Union Emerges for Lower Paid Workers across the U.S." *The Philadelphia Inquirer*, February 8. https://www.inquirer.com/business/worker-center-jobs-labor-union-rights-poultry-farm-poor-20210529.html.

Piven, Frances Fox, and Richard A. Cloward. 1979. *Poor People's Movements*. New York, NY: Vintage Books.

Rosenfeld, David. 2006. "Rosenfeld, David. "Worker Centers: Emerging Labor Organizations—Until They Confront the National Labor Relations Act." *Berkeley Journal of Employment & Labor Law* 27 (2): 469.

Ross, Martha, and Nicole Bateman. 2019. *Meet the Low Wage Workforce*. Washington, DC: Brookings Institution.

Schatz, Edward, ed. 2013. *Political Ethnography What Immersion Contributes to the Study of Power*. Chicago: University of Chicago Press.

Schiffer, Nancy. 2005. "Whither vs. Wither: How the NLRA Has Failed Contingent Workers." Paper presented at the annual meeting of the American Bar Association, Chicago, IL.

Searle, John R. 1975. "A Taxonomy of Illocutionary Acts." In *Language, Mind and Knowledge*. Edited by Keith Gunderson, 344–369. Minneapolis: University of Minnesota Press.

Sharpe, Teresa. 2004. "Union Democracy and Successful Campaigns." In *Rebuilding Labor: Organizing and Organizers in the New Union Movement*, edited by Ruth Milkman and Kim Voss, 62–87. Ithaca, NY: Cornell University Press.

Simmons, Erica S., and Nicholas R. Smith. 2017. "Comparison with an Ethnographic Sensibility." *PS: Political Science & Politics* 50 (1): 126–130.

Smucker, Jonathan Matthew. 2017. *Hegemony How-To: A Roadmap for Radicals*. Chico, CA: AK Press.

Standing, Guy. 2014. *The Precariat: The New Dangerous Class*. London: Bloomsbury Publishing.

Strolovitch, Dara Z. 2006. "Do Interest Groups Represent the Disadvantaged? Advocacy at the Intersections of Race, Class, and Gender." *Journal of Politics* 68 (4): 894–910.

U.S. Bureau of Labor Statistics. 2024. "News Release: UNION MEMBERS—2023." *U.S. Department of Labor*, January 23. https://www.bls.gov/news.release/pdf/union2.pdf.

U.S. Department of Labor. 2017. "Foreign-Born Workers: Labor Force Characteristics Summary." *U.S. Bureau of Labor Statistics*, https://www.bls.gov/news.release/forbrn. nr0.htm.

Van Doorn, Marjoka, Jacomijne Prins, and Saskia Welschen. 2013. "'Protest against Whom?': The Role of Collective Meaning Making in Politicization." In *The Future of Social Movement Research: Dynamics, Mechanisms, and Processes*, edited by Jacquelien van Stekelenburg, Conny Roggeband, and Bert Klandermas, 59–78. Minneapolis: University of Minnesota Press.

Voss, Kim, and Rachel Sherman. 2000. "Breaking the Iron Law of Oligarchy: Union Revitalization in the American Labor Movement." *American Journal of Sociology* 106 (2): 303–349.

Weil, Davil. 2011. "Enforcing Labour Standards in Fissured Workplaces: The US Experience." *Economic and Labour Relations Review* 22 (2): 33–54.

Woodly, Deva. 2015. *The Politics of Common Sense*. Oxford, UK: Oxford University Press.

Index

For the benefit of digital users, indexed terms that span two pages (e.g., 52–53) may, on occasion, appear on only one of those pages.

accountability and structure, of CLP, 19–22
  radical rank-and-file-led union vision, 22, 37, 41–42, 130, 152–153, 161
  resources and power, representation, 20
  staff and allies values in, 19–20
  staff leadership and representation, 22
  staff leadership roles, 19–20
  worker-led presentation of, 19, 21–22
advocacy organizations, 12, 21–22, 154
  Alcoff on crisis of representation of, 154–155
  ethics in oppressed community representation by, 154–156
  top-down, 152, 158–159
affordable healthcare, FCC union-organizing campaign demand for, 1–2, 110–111, 114, 122, 132, 136, 145
Ahmed, Sara, 155–156
Alcoff, Linda, 154–155
Alinsky, Saul, 168–169
allies
  domination fear and, 7–10
  labor organizations deep ties to, 165
  power in workplace justice campaigns, 152–153, 166
  staff leadership commitments and, 151
  values in CLP accountability and structure, 19–20
  worker leadership narratives to support, 21–22
allies, in CLP, 4–7, 9–10, 151
  CLP 2.0 power leverage against FCC, 152–153
  in CLP-PLJA relationship, 112–113
  courageous experiment and rethinking of, 164–166
  cultivation of, 47
  FCC campaign outreach and petition from, 56, 60, 70
  impact on FCC meeting, 132

  mobilization importance in low-wage economy, 159
  money, time, and effort support by, 18
  PLJA and, 27, 95, 112–113
  potential and limits of pressure by, 18–19
  power of, 152, 164
  union-related goals lack of clarity, 43
  worker leadership and, 109–112, 152
  worker support by, 18–19, 26
alt-labor organizations, 39–40
asymmetrical power, of militant minority, 3–4, 117
authenticity myth, of CLP, 22–26
  future oriented authenticity of worker, 24
  leadership of marginalized people, 23
  outcomes of successful movement activity, 24–25
  predetermined political orientation, 25
  process of movements and, 24
authority and representation complications
  in emancipatory organizing work, 156–157
  in worker leadership narrative, 156–157

Bank of America letter, FCC campaign planned action, 100–102, 142
  CLP authorship and signing of, 101–103
  CLP mission for worker training for union, 102
  FCC Small Business Association loan from, 100–101
  focus on workers authorship and signing of, 101–102
  staff failures *versus* worker leadership, 102–105
  on supply-chain strategy credit risk, 100–101
  worker and staff leadership tension of, 102
Bank of America rally, 114–115
Black Lives Matter, 7–8
bottom-up labor movement, 25–26, 97, 165
  ethics of, 7–8

vision of, 93–94
for worker leadership, 10
boycott, 103–104
Delori Food Supply campaign CLP, 95, 128
in Garrity Foods Campaign, 32
high-profile customers of FCC, 118
Montgomery Bus, 7–8
secondary, 40, 170 n.3, 171 n.4
strategy of CLP, 126
business unionism
CLP 2.0 staff criticism of, 42–43
of traditional labor unions, 39

Campaign Associate, of CLP, 98
campaigns, 170 n.2, *See also specific campaign*
Horton and Freire on political education
and, 168–169
Centro de Trabajadores Unidos en la Lucha
(CTUL), 41, 171 n.5
Chinese Staff and Workers Association
(CSWA), 41
Clara Lemlich Project (CLP). *See also*
accountability and structure, of CLP;
strategy and power, of CLP; *specific topics*
allies cultivation, 47
annual fundraiser for, 150
authenticity myth, 22–25
author departure from, 148–149
author promotion to Campaign
Associate, 98
author role in, 27–28
immigrant workforce lack of issues outside
workforce, 159–160
as nonprofit worker center, 4–5, 11–13,
19–20
PLIA ally and partner of, 27, 96–97,
112–113
PLJA and, 93–94
power and, 4–7, 9–10
previous supply-chain strategy of, 4–5, 12
representation in, 4–7, 9–10
as social movement organization, 6
social networks and non-workplace issues
not addressed, 160
staff members withdrawal from, 117–118
union militancy commitment, 6–7
WFIO and campaign narrative reframing
of, 123–125
Clara Lemlich Project (CLP), history and
organizing model of. *See also* membership
metrics rating

Finn's Distributors workplace justice
campaign victory, 35–36, 54, 76
Garrity Foods Campaign, 31–34
inspiration sources diversity, 45
labor movement for low-wage and
immigrant workers, 32–33
nonprofits in labor movement, 29, 39–40,
49, 50–51, 171 n.3
organizational growth, 35–38
rank-and-file led unions approach of, 37
relationship navigation, 42–44
roots of, 30–38
structure and operating areas, 45–46, 52
successful campaigns against illegal labor
practices, 29
unions, worker centers and evolution
of, 38–44
working model of, 44–48
workplace organizing campaigns of, 36
Clara Lemlich Project (CLP) courageous
experiment
allies rethinking, 164–166
CLP 2.0 reflection, 151–154
ethics, power of, 154–158
introduction to, 150–151
leadership dream, 166–169
liberation strategizing, 158–163
outcomes in oppressed community
empowerment, 156–158
CLP 1.0 model
FCC move toward workplace union
organizing and, 80–81
litigation plus settlements in, 41
membership challenges, 41
workplace justice campaign in, 43
CLP 2.0 model, 2
allies power leverage against company
in, 152–153
business unions criticism by staff, 42–43
rank-and-file power with direct
management demands, 41–42
reflection on, 151–154
union-worker center pairings, 41–44, 171
n.5
vision of worker-led independent unions, 44
worker collective power and leadership
in, 42
CLP-PLJA relationship, for FCC campaign
allies in, 27, 95, 112–113
CLP ask for PLJA involvement for, 96–97
CLP shift to staff driven, top-down,
ally-centric approach, 109

CLP-PLJA relationship, for FCC campaign
  (*Continued*)
  coalitional power in, 112
  committee formation for, 110–112
  history and work of PLJA, 108
  meeting for, 97, 105
  member-based organizations, 108
  PLJA public outreach and education
    offer, 108–109
  PLJA public support letter, 96–97
  PLJA social media campaign, 96–97
  press conference action plan, 109–110, 112,
    114, 121
  public arena focus, 112
  supply-chain strategy coalitional power
    and, 123
  support and trust in, 110–112
  two member-led organization
    meeting, 107–109
  worker leadership and ally support
    in, 109–112, 123
coalitional power of consumers, activists,
    workers, of CLP, 11–12
  supply-chain strategy and CLP-PLJA, 123
  worker centered model with moral power
    and, 12
collective bargaining, 41–42
  worker centered model inability for, 40
collective identity work, of social
    movements, 25
committee formation, for CLP-PLJA
    relationship for FCC campaign, 110–112
community unions, 39–40
core organization, for worker-led street
    actions, 119–120
crisis of representation, of Alcoff, 154–155
critical case commitment, to worker
    leadership, 9, 170 n.4
critical targets
  of CLP, 46
  of CLP membership goals, 46–47
  for Finn's Distributors workplace justice
    campaign, 46–47
CSWA. *See* Chinese Staff and Workers
    Association
CTUL. *See* Centro de Trabajadores Unidos en
    la Lucha

Delori Food Supply campaign
  CLP boycott in, 95, 128
  supply-chain strategy at, 35

Development department, under CLP
    Program department, 45
direct-action tactics, in worker centered
    model, 11–12, 134
  of CLP and militant minority strategy, 116,
    122, 152–153
  FCC public campaign launch failure and
    options of, 74
domination, allies and fear of, 7–10
donors and foundations, 50–51, 171 n.8
  CLP role of, 49
  institutional, 171 n.5
  as nonprofit resource, 35, 49–50
  self-help myth of, 50
Dream (Duncombe), 166–167
Driedger, Nick, 163
dues payment structure, in worker centered
    model, 49, 171 n.7
Duncombe, Stephen, 166–167

economic structure, of food industry, 13
emancipatory organizing work
  authority and representation complications
    in, 156–157
  goal of individual collective agency
    increase, 156
  political nature of, 156
  of social movements, 150
ethics
  in advocacy organizations representation of
    oppressed communities, 154–156
  of bottom-up labor movement, 7–8
  Hinterberger and Ahmed on ethical
    representational strategies, 155–156
  power in CLP courageous
    experiment, 154–158
  of representational strategies, 155–156
ethnographic method, for worker leadership
    exploration, 26–28

FCC. *See* Fishtown Condiment Company
Finn's Distributors workplace justice
    campaign, 35–36, 54, 76
  critical target for, 46–47
  funder meeting and, 143
  membership metrics for, 48
  worker-led union lack of success, 43
Fishtown Condiment Company (FCC)
    campaign. *See also* meeting with FCC
  allies outreach and petition, 56, 60, 70
  Bank of America Small Business Association
    loan to, 100–101

CLP proactive approach, 54–55
critical target for, 46–47
job retention concerns and worker lack of
    participation in, 14–16
lack of union victory, 5
LC meetings launch preparation, 62–65
LC of workers, 53
low-wage workers and, 78–79
low worker involvement in, 98–99
membership and, 55–59
membership metrics for, 48
move toward workplace union organizing
    and CLP 1.0 model, 80–81
options presented to workers by staff
    leadership, 85–86
practice and strategy of, 76–83
press release, 55–56
process of bringing worker into LC, 60–62
public launch of, 53, 55–56
RDS of CLP and, 54, 79, 81
Regional Distribution Strategy for, 54
representative meeting, 56–59
soft campaign launch, 55–56, 66–67
staff failures *versus* worker
    leadership, 102–105, 119–121, 123
staff leadership development of demands
    and agendas for, 142
union breaking, 68–70
union-organizing public phase, 1–2
worker-led street actions and agreement to
    meet by, 126–129, 131
worker-led union lack of success at, 43, 114
Fishtown Condiment Company (FCC) public
    campaign launch failure, 71–72, 151
Bank of America letter, 100–102
campaign narrative reframing, 123–126
CLP ask for PLJA involvement, 96–97
company letter to workers, 81–83
direct action options, 74
elected official campaign
    intervention, 73–74
exploration of, 75–76
ideological needs and internal
    contradictions, 84–89
institutional factors of, 81
LC active members absence, 76–79
LCP ambition, 79–80
loss of momentum and membership, 116
membership metrics place, 89–92
Organizing and Campaigning
    supervision, 74–75
planned actions cancellations, 100

positive steps forward for, 73–74
pressure and performance of worker
    leadership, 83–92
pressures to launch, 80–83
RDS and, 79
Sprint Plan and, 76–78
unrealistic timeline and, 80
worker campaigning for LC build, 74
food and labor movement, worker leadership
    and action in, 2
food industry
    economic structure of, 13
    low-wage economy in, 13, 29
foundations. *See* donors and foundations
Freire, Paulo, 168–169
frontline actors, challenge of leadership of, 24
funding. *See also* donors and foundations
    Finn's Distributors workplace justice
        campaign meeting for, 143
    funder visit to CLP, 143–145
    nonprofits procurement of, 49
    for nonprofit worker center, 49
    worker leadership narrative for, 144–145

Galvin, Daniel, 33–34
Garrity Foods Campaign, 31–34
    boycott use in, 32
    counter campaign by, 32
    dire conditions at, 31–32
    illegal worker termination, 31–32, 35, 43
    organizational revenue of, 35, 171 n.2
    supply-chain strategy of, 32, 35
    undocumented and immigrant workforce
        at, 31–32
    worker class action lawsuit against, 32
governmental advocacy. nonprofit worker
    centers and, 40–41
grassroots politics, 25–26
    CLP 2.0 model commonalities, 44
grocery leaflets distribution, in worker-led
    street actions, 103–104, 119–121, 123

Han, Hahrie, 159–161
higher wages, FCC union-organizing campaign
    demand for, 1–2, 110–111, 122, 132, 136,
        145
Hinterberger, Amy, 155–156
Horton, Miles, 168–169
hot-shops, 54–55
    illegal employment practices of, 40–41
    workplace justice campaigns involvement
        of, 40–41

identification, for worker leadership, 162–163
identity work, of movements, 25
ideological needs and internal contradictions,
    FCC public campaign launch failure
    and, 84–89
illegal labor practices
    CLP campaign at FCC against, 150–151
    CLP successful campaigns against, 29
    Garrity Foods worker termination, 31–32,
        35, 43
    of hot-shops, 40–41
    without penalty, 38
immigrant workforce. See undocumented and
    immigrant workforce
individual collective agency, emancipatory
    organizing work goal of, 156
institutional donors, 170 n.5
institutional power of regulatory state, of
    CLP, 11–12

job retention, FCC worker concerns for, 14–16

labor activism, national news piece on, 126
labor movement. See also nonprofits, in labor
    movement
    top-down advocacy work in, 158–159
    worker leadership priority in, 84
labor organizations
    allies deep ties to, 165
    alt-, 39–40
Laundry Workers Center, 41
law enforcement, worker centered model
    and, 40–41
Leadership Committee (LC), of CLP, 1. See
    also membership metrics rating
    campaign secrecy and, 88
    at FCC, 53, 60–65
    FCC campaign meetings and launch
        preparation, 62–65
    McAlevey on identification of organic
        leaders for, 161–162
    meeting on FCC campaign phases, 64–65
    press conference presence, 64–65, 67,
        70–72, 81
    re-investment step for, 73
    staff conception of, 16–17
leadership development program, of
    CLP, 144, 163
    Sharpe and, 157–158
    staff leadership and, 165
leadership dream, 166–169
    aspirational vision of world, 167

Duncombe on politics of fantasy, 166–167
liberation, strategizing for, 158–163
    CLP campaign at FCC and top-down
        advocacy limitations, 158–159
    worker limited participation and, 158–159
litigation plus settlements, in CLP 1.0
    model, 41
low-wage economy, 169
    allies mobilization for improvement of, 159
    FCC campaign and low-wage
        workers, 78–79
    in food industry, 13, 29
    qualities of, 32–33, 171 n.1
    for undocumented and immigrant
        workers, 34, 159–160

marginalized people, leadership of, 23
mass mobilization, worker centered model
        limitations of, 42
McAlevey, Jane
    on organic leaders for LC, 161–162
    on organizers leadership role, 161
    on whole worker organizing, 160
meetings
    allies in CLP impact on FCC, 132
    for CLP-PLJA relationship for FCC
        campaign, 97, 105
    CLP-PLJA two member-led
        organization, 107–109
    of FCC campaign launch
        preparation, 62–65
    FCC campaign representative, 56–59
    FCC forced meetings with workers, 69, 72
    Finn's Distributors workplace justice
        campaign funder, 143
    of LC before FCC campaign soft launch, 60
    of LC on FCC campaign phases, 64–65
    of RDS of CLP, 98–99
meeting with FCC, 135–139, 151
    allies impact on, 132
    CLP goal of worker-led union, 130
    company letter for workers participation in
        CLP tactic, 131–133, 151
    FCC contact on agreement for, 126–129
    FCC refusal for firm
        commitments, 136–138
    funder visit to CLP, 143–145
    initial opening remarks at, 135–136
    lack of worker participation, 146–147
    on members delegate model, 138–139
    next meeting scheduling,
        138–140, 145

preparation for, 132–135
processing of, 140–143
Profitable Development Committee
    creation, 145, 148
results of second meeting, 145–147
social media and customer attacks
    suspension request, 126–127, 131
three workers in attendance at, 135,
    151–152
worker agenda drafting tactic, 131
worker motivation strategies, 147
membership
    churn of, 89–90
    CLP 1.0 model challenges, 41
    in FCC campaign, 55–59
membership metrics rating, of CLP, 46–48
    for FCC and Finn's Distributors
        campaigns, 48
    FCC and LC membership, 60–62
    FCC public launch failure and, 89–92
    for Finn's Distributors workplace justice
        campaign, 48
    McAlevey on, 161–162
    membership churn and, 89–90
    method for worker conversation about
        campaign, 60–61
    RDS meeting on, 99–100, 105
    reporting of numbers, 99–100
    staff leadership challenge in use of, 48
    vanity, 58
    worker rating, 47–48, 51, 99–100, 114
militant minority strategy, 115, 130–131, 151.
    See also worker-led street actions
    asymmetrical power of, 3–4, 117
    CLP direct-action model and, 116, 122,
        152–153
    Phase II and Phase III and, 3–4, 115
    reaching out to FCC, 114
    staff goals for, 14
    supply-chain strategy and, 116
    worker leadership narrative in, 117
minimum legal standard, worker centered
    model and limits of, 1–2
Montgomery Bus Boycott, 7–8
moral power of public, of CLP, 11–12
    worker centered model with coalitional
        power and, 12
movements. See also social movements
    identities collectivizing and politicizing
        in, 168
    worker leadership and elites of, 168

National Domestic Workers
    Alliance, 40–41
National Labor Relations Act, 38
nationwide organizations
    National Domestic Workers
        Alliance, 40–41
    Restaurant Opportunities Centers, 40–41
nonprofits, in labor movement, 48–52, 154
    funding procurement, 49
    officers of labor unions, 39–40, 171 n.3
    social movements confrontational
        function, 50–51
    strategic flexibility of, 29
nonprofit worker center, 39–40
    campaign strategies and resource
        mobilizations of, 40
    CLP as, 4–5, 11–13, 19–20
    CLP resources and, 20
    CLP use of funds for collective worker
        power, 12–13
    foundations as resource for, 35, 49–50
    funding for, 49
    long-term membership and organizational
        effectiveness challenges, 29
    one-time campaign success, 40–41
    political lobbying of, 40
non-traditional employment relationships
    illegal practices in, 33–34
    for workers in CLP campaigns, 33

OAs. See Operating Areas
one-time campaign, nonprofit worker centers
    success in, 40–41
Operating Areas (OAs), under CLP Program
    and Development departments, 45
    critical targets of, 47
oppressed communities, advocacy
    organizations ethics in representation
    of, 154–156
organic leaders, McAlevey on, 161–162
organizational growth, of CLP, 35–38
organizing
    Han on transformational, 159
    lack of capacity for, 13–14, 152–153
    of PLJA, 105–109
organizing process model, staff leadership
    and, 61–62
outcomes, in oppressed community
    empowerment, 156–158
    power and authority suspicion in, 157
    Sharpe on leadership
        development, 157–158

outcomes, in oppressed community
    empowerment (*Continued*)
    staff leadership speaking for
        workers, 156–157
    worker organization and, 157
outcomes, of successful movement
    activity, 24–25
outreach blitz, in FCC campaign soft
    launch, 67, 81, 90–91

participatory government, Sharpe on, 161
Phase II and Phase II, militant minority
    strategy and, 3–4, 115
phases
    FCC campaign union-organizing
        public, 1–2
    LC meeting on FCC campaign
        phases, 64–65
    militant minority strategy Phase II and
        Phase III, 3–4, 115
Philadelphia Labor Justice Alliance (PLJA), 27,
    95–96. *See also* CLP-PLJA relationship,
    for FCC campaign
    CLP and, 93–94, 96–97
    CLP ask for involvement from, 96–97
    CLP support from, 95
    grassroots organization of union members
        and labor activists, 95
    labor allies of, 27, 95, 112–113
    local politicians lobbying, 95
    organization of, 105–109
    power from small group of activists, 166
    press release of, 151–152
    promotion of, 97–105
    protests attendance, 95
    strike support, workplace justice campaigns
        of, 95
    support and trust, 110–112
    worker leadership and ally
        support, 109–112
    worker-led campaign support, 94
policy
    weak enforcement for undocumented and
        immigrant workforce, 34
    worker centered model influence on, 40–41
political discourse, 7
political lobbying, of nonprofit worker
    center, 40
political nature, of emancipatory organizing
    work, 156
politicization, social movements and
    intentional work for, 7–8

politics of fantasy
    Duncombe on leadership dream
        and, 166–167
    for worker leadership, 167
power
    of allies in CLP, 152, 164
    of allies in workplace justice
        campaigns, 152–153, 166
    CLP and, 4–7, 9–10
    of ethics, in CLP courageous
        experiment, 154–158
    in movement work and relationships, 164
    of PLJA small group of activists, 166
    regulatory state of CLP and
        institutional, 11–12
    relationships of, 156
    social movements authority and, 164
    staff-driven campaign emphasis of allies
        external, 117, 153–154
    of supply-chain strategy, 36
    in worker-led street actions, 114
predetermined political orientation,
    authenticity and, 25
press conference, 96
    of CLP-PLJA members, 109–110, 112,
        118–119, 121, 123
    LC presence at, 64–65, 67, 70–72, 81
press release
    in FCC campaign, 55–56
    in FCC campaign public launch, 55, 60, 65
    of PLJA, 151–152
Program department in CLP, OA's under, 45
public arena focus, in CLP-PLJA
    relationship, 112
public launch, in FCC campaign, 53, 55–56
    press release document, 55, 60, 65
    scheduling after proposed letter to
        management, 64–65

radical political action, traditional unions as
    vehicle for, 163
rank-and-file unions vision, of CLP, 22, 130
    advice and strategy, training and resources
        for, 37
    challenges for, 152–153
    McAlevey on organizers leadership
        role, 161
Regional Distribution Strategy (RDS), of
    CLP, 54, 164, 171 n.1
    contentious meeting of, 105–107
    FCC and, 54, 79, 81
    meetings of, 98–99

staff organizer deficit in, 13–14
worker numbers reporting at, 99–100, 105
on worker participation problems, 100,
    105–107
representation, in CLP, 4–7
representational strategies, ethical, 155–156
resources
    challenge of giving workers, 23
    of CLP after Garrity Foods campaign, 35
    of foundation grants and donations, 35,
        49–50
    institutional donors, 170 n.5
    nonprofit worker center mobilizations of, 40
    power, representation, accountability
        and, 20
    worker centered model, 37
    worker leadership narratives and, 20–24
Restaurant Opportunities Centers, 40–41
retaliation by FCC, worker participation and
        fear of, 17, 64, 121–122, 124, 125, 131,
        132–133

secondary boycott, 40, 170 n.3, 171 n.4
SEIU. See Service Employees Industrial Union
self-help myth, of foundations, 50
Service Employees Industrial Union
        (SEIU), 41
setbacks and defeats, of social movements, 153
Sharpe, Theresa, 157–158
    on participatory government, 161
social movements
    CLP as organization of, 6
    collective identity work of, 25
    emancipatory organizing work of, 150
    examples of, 7–8
    intentional politicization work in, 7–8
    nonprofits function as
        confrontational, 50–51
    political nature of emancipatory organizing
        work, 156
    power and authority in, 164
    setbacks and defeats of, 153
soft launch, of FCC campaign, 55–56, 66–67
    company forced meetings with workers, 69,
        72
    demands letter delivery, 66–67
    LC meeting before, 60
    management offer to meet without
        CLP, 68–69
    outreach blitz for, 67, 81, 90–91
Sprint Plan, FCC public campaign launch
        failure and, 76–78

staff-driven campaign
    external power of allies emphasis, 117,
        153–154
    worker leadership as outcome
        from, 153–154
staff failures versus worker leadership, in FCC
        campaign, 102–105
    FCC campaign plan grocery leaflets
        distribution, 103–104, 119–121, 123
    staff direction practices, 104–105
staff leadership
    ally and staff commitments, 151
    Bank of America letter and worker tension
        with, 102
    CLP representation and, 22
    development of demands and
        agendas, 142
    FCC campaign development
        by, 62, 85–86
    FCC campaign options presented to
        workers, 85–86
    leadership development and, 165
    membership metric use challenge for, 48
    organizing process model, 61–62
    reframing of worker-led street
        actions, 123–125
    role in CLP accountability and
        structure, 19–20
    speaking for workers strategy, 156–157
    traditional union campaign with, 15–16
    worker leadership absence and initiative
        of, 88–89, 151
Starbucks union elections, 166
state regulatory practices, workplace justice
        campaigns and deterioration of, 40–41
strategic flexibility, of nonprofits in labor
        movement, 29
strategic limits, of worker centered
        model, 40–41
strategy and power, of CLP, 11–19
    coalitional and moral power
        combination, 12
    coalitional power of consumers, activists,
        workers, 11–12
    economic structure challenges, 13
    institutional power of regulatory
        state, 11–12
    lack of organizing capacity, 13–14
    lack of worker participation
        challenge, 14–15, 29
    militant minority strategy, 14
    moral power of public, 11–12

strikes
    PLJA support of, 95
    United Auto Workers, 7–8
    worker centered model and, 40, 171 n.4
structure and operating areas, of CLP, 45–46,
        52
    Program and Development departments
        in, 45–46
supply-chain strategy, 125
    allies partnering with workers
        and, 152–153, 164
    Bank of America letter on FCC credit risk
        and, 100–101
    CLP-PLJA coalitional power and, 123
    CLP previous, 4–5, 12
    at Delori Food Supply Company
        campaign, 35
    FCC and, 54, 64
    Garrity Foods and, 32, 35
    historic success of, 87–88
    militant minority strategy and, 116
    power of, 36

tactical flexibility, of worker centered
        model, 40
top-down advocacy organizations, 152
    CLP campaign at FCC limitations
        from, 158–159
    in labor movement, 158–159
top-down organizing strategies, for worker
        development, 163
traditional labor unions, 154
    business unionism of, 39
    campaign with staff leadership, 15–16
    downhill trend for, 38
    Driedger on conservative orientation of, 163
    Trumka on failure of, 39
    as vehicle for radical political action, 163
    worker-centric direction for, 162–163
    workplace violations and, 38
transactional mobilizing, Han on
        transformational organizing
        and, 159–161
transformational organizing, Han on
        transactional mobilizing and, 159–161
Trumka, Richard, 39

UE. See United Electrical Workers
undocumented and immigrant workforce
    CLP lack of focus on issues
        outside, 159–160
    at Garrity Foods, 31–32

low-wage economy for, 34, 159–160
    successful unions on oppressions inside and
        outside workplace, 160
    weak policy enforcement for, 34
union militancy, CLP commitment to, 6–7
union-organizing campaign, at FCC
    affordable healthcare demand, 1–2,
        110–111, 114, 122, 132, 136, 145
    failure of, 5
    higher wages demand, 1–2, 110–111, 122,
        132, 136, 145
    lack of leadership definition in, 17
    lack of worker participation in, 2–7, 17, 29,
        105–107, 116–117
    Phase II media and customers hit on
        consequential relationship, 3–4, 115
    Phase III hit on wholesale buyers, 3–4, 115
    public phase of, 1–2
    respectful work treatment demand, 1–2,
        110–111, 122, 132, 136
    worker misunderstood expectations for
        union, 15–16
    worker resistance to, 3
union-worker center pairings, in CLP 2.0
        model, 41–42, 44
    legal distinctions in, 42–43, 171 n.5
    relationship navigation, 42–44
    staff support for, 42–43
United Auto Workers strikes, 7–8
United Electrical Workers (UE), 41

values, of staff and allies in CLP, 19–20
vanity membership metrics, FCC and, 58
vision
    of bottom-up labor movement, 93–94
    of CLP 2.0 model worker-led independent
        unions, 44
    leadership dream aspiration of world, 167
    of movement elites on worker
        leadership, 168
    for radical rank-and-file-led union, 22, 37,
        41–42, 130, 152–153, 161

wage theft, 35
    Galvin on, 33–34
Wage Theft Deterrence Package, New
        York, 166
We're Fucked: It's Over (WFIO), 1–2, 5–6,
        114, 115
    CLP campaign narrative
        reframing, 123–125
    lack of worker participation and, 118

movement to strategy validation, 129
turning point with conversation of, 115–116
whole worker organizing, McAlevey on, 160
Woodly, Deva, 167
worker centered model, 170 n.1, *See also*
    nonprofit worker center
  CLP training, litigation and resources
    for, 37
  coalitional and moral power combined
    in, 12
  collective bargaining inability in, 40
  direct-action tactics in, 11–12, 74, 116, 122,
    134, 152–153
  dues payment structure in, 49, 171 n.7
  law enforcement and policy influence
    from, 40–41
  limitations of, 4–5, 40–41
  mass mobilization limitations of, 42
  minimum legal standards limits in, 1–2
  one-time campaign success and government
    advocacy of, 40–41
  strategic limits of, 40–41
  strikes, secondary boycotts, community
    campaigns and, 40, 171 n.4
  success and limitations of, 143–144
  tactical flexibility of, 40
  traditional unions and movement
    toward, 162–163
  workplace justice campaigns and, 39–40
worker leadership
  allies and, 109–112, 152
  assertion of, 168
  bottom-up labor movement for, 10
  CLP 2.0 model and collective power of, 42
  CLP commitment to, 2, 6, 7, 13
  critical case commitment to, 9, 170 n.4
  development opportunities
    absence, 151–152
  ethnographic method for, 26–28
  FCC campaign pressure and performance
    of, 83–92
  food and labor movement and, 2
  increased staff need for training of, 13–14
  movement elites vision of, 168
  performative practice of, 117
  politics of fantasy for, 167
  potential identification for, 162
  practical steps for identification of, 163
  staff-driven campaign and outcome
    of, 153–154
  staff failures *versus*, 102–105, 119–121, 123
  union militancy in, 9–10

worker support low numbers contradiction
    with, 93
worker leadership narrative, 22, 26, 123
  authority and representation complications
    in, 156–157
  CLP educational role emphasis in, 50–51
  CLP resources and, 20–24
  for funding, 144–145
  meeting with FCC and, 142
  in militant minority strategy, 117
  staff and allies power, agency, perspectives
    and, 142, 156–157
  to support allies, 21–22
  worker-led street actions and, 114
  workers lack of participation
    and, 142–143
worker-led presentation, of CLP accountability
    and structure, 19, 21–22
worker-led street actions, of militant minority
    strategy, 44, 116, 118, 171 n.5
  CLP staff reframing of, 123–125
  core organization for, 119–120
  FCC contact on agreement to
    meet, 126–129, 131
  grocery leaflets distribution, 103–104,
    119–121, 123
  worker leadership narrative, 114
  worker power in, 114
  workers lack of participation, 119
worker-led union
  failure to achieve, 151–153
  Finn's Distributors workplace justice
    campaign failure, 43
  LCP goal of, 130
worker participation and engagement
    absence
  barriers for, 125
  challenge to CLP strategy and
    power, 14–15, 29
  in FCC meeting, 146–147
  in FCC union-organizing campaign, 2–7,
    17, 29, 105–107, 116–117
  from fear of FCC retaliation, 17, 64,
    121–122, 124, 125, 131, 132–133
  job retention concerns in FCC
    campaign, 14–16
  liberation strategizing and, 158–159
  RDS on problems with, 100, 105–107
  staff leadership initiative and, 88–89, 151
  WFIO and, 118
  worker leadership narrative and, 142–143
  in worker-led street actions, 119

workers, in CLP campaign. *See also* worker-led
  street actions
  allies support of, 18–19, 26
  challenge of giving resources to, 23
  collective power and leadership of, 42, 46,
    156–157
  future oriented authenticity of, 24
  leadership development and, 144, 151–152,
    163, 165
  non-traditional employment
    relationships, 33
  organization and oppressed community
    empowerment outcomes, 157
  resistance to FCC union-organizing
    campaign, 3
workplace
  CLP organizing campaigns for, 36
  organizing campaigns, workplace justice
    campaigns shift to, 36

  successful unions on immigrant workforce
    oppressions inside and outside of, 160
  traditional labor unions and violations
    in, 38
workplace justice campaigns, 12
  allies power in, 152–153, 166
  in CLP 1.0 model, 43
  hot-shops involvement, 40–41
  of PLJA, 95
  state regulatory practice deterioration
    and, 40–41
  worker centered model and, 39–40
  worker-led public campaign, 41
  workplace organizing campaigns shift
    from, 36
work treatment respect, FCC union-organizing
  campaign demand for, 1–2, 110–111,
    122, 132, 136